TO
Paul
ENJOY!

Mike Moore

Victory WWII Publishing Ltd. books are also available at discounts in bulk quantity for industrial or sales promotional use. For details write to Victory WWII Publishing Ltd, P.O. Box 670, Rogers, MN 55374-0670 USA.

Library of Congress Cataloging in Publication Data
Victory WW2 Publishing Inc. International Standard Book Number 0-9700567-4-5.

Author: Looney, George Micheal 1949-

Title: The Battle of The Bulge:The Untold Story of Höfen

Publisher: Tom Berndt
Design & Layout: Colleen K. Meyer
Proofing: D. Wicht
US Army Signal Corp Photographs supplied by author, historian and publisher, Tom Berndt

ISBN# 0-9700567-4-5

Distributed Exclusively Worldwide by: Victory WWII Publishing Ltd, P.O. Box 670, Rogers, MN 55374-0670 USA.

To order write to:
    Victory WWII Publishing Ltd
    P.O. Box 670
    Rogers, MN 55374-0670
    USA

FORWARD

The Trail of Captain George W. Looney

World War II was not only a chaotic affair, but truly a "World War" with fighting going on around the globe, on land, on sea and in the air with participants from virtually every country. Details of the war stretch to infinity and are impossible to grasp in total. To be understood at all, one must approach it in piecemeal fragments. One way is to study the history of an individual soldier and relate his actions to the whole.

George Washington Looney served as an artillery forward observer for the 196th Field Artillery Battallion, a vital, but relatively unfamiliar military assignment. George was a modest man who rarely spoke of his many accomplishments in the Army; Mike Looney has researched his Father's service history and wrote this book in an effort to properly recognize not only George's contributions to the Allied success during the war, but also the efforts of his fellow members of the 196th. Thor Ronningen, an infantryman at the battle of Höfen states the following;

"I was an infantry rifleman in the little village of Höfen, Germany, when the German army attacked in overwhelming numbers on 16 December 1944—the start of The Battle of The Bulge. The American front line was lightly manned and our artillery literally saved our lives as well as allowing us to hold our positions. At times, American artillery rounds would land within a few feet of our positions, decimating the attacking enemy, but not touching us. This was a textbook example of how artillery should defend against attack. George Looney was the forward observer directing these guns and assigning targets up and down our lines. He played it like a concert organist. I am here today because of his expertise.

On a summer day in 1990, I had the distinct and unforgettable pleasure of taking George W. Looney's photo in front of "OP 6", his location on that December day that he saved my life. I feel fortunate to have shared that moment with him and to thank him for what he had done in '44. Men like him won WW II."

Thor Ronningen

We need a UN Resolution or something that says all combat soldiers in the future will be over forty-five years of age. No exceptions. Let the teenager's stay home and get rich making munitions. I don't know much, but I do know that would be the end of war for all time on this planet.
Robert Wyatt Thrasher,
395th Infantry Company, World War II

A fine photo of Mike Looney's father George and his mother Mary, standing in front of Mike's home in the early 1990's.

Table of Contents

The Battle of The Bulge:

The Untold Story of Höfen

By Mike Looney

Victory
WWII
PUBLISHING, LTD.

Chapter One

GWL
George Washington Looney

George Washington Looney, I suppose, started to seriously strip off the layers of time during a Battle of the Bulge reunion trip in the fall of 1990. Seeing that three story building in Höfen, Germany for the first time since December of 1944, triggered an exchange of the bleacher seat in the back of his mind for a front row box seat.

Born February 22, 1918 in the hills of Charleston, Arkansas, George was fittingly named after our first president. A Texas Ranger baseball game in Arlington, Texas one hot summer night in 1996 served notice that more than one George Washington never told a lie. A six-car fender bender leaving the parking lot, kick started by me, rapidly brought two young petite, though tough talking, policewomen to the scene. While filing a report, one of the policewomen asked in a deathly tone if we were wearing seatbelts.

"Yes," I heard myself reply with more respect than honesty.

My lying eyes immediately latched onto George's and I read his look easier than a weekly reader. George, who wore a seatbelt as often as he fibbed, offered a hint of a grin that had nothing to do with smiling. "I suppose I should say yes, but I can't truthfully say that I was wearing my seatbelt," he said, staring at little miss toughie through big brown eyes that had seen so much. Worry bled into the seriousness of his expression.

What did the policewoman see? A seventy-eight year old mellow grandfather, shoulders slightly stooped, his gray retreating hairline swept straight back and bushy white eyebrows annexing part of his high forehead? Or did she somehow know that she was looking at a potential poster boy for one of Brokaw's books on the last great generation?

The more she struggled to hide her warm expression, the harder it fought for freedom. She lowered her pad without writing the ticket and simply said, "You can go now."

George worried the entire trip home that the cop would send him a ticket. I should have known then that the world was slightly off its axis inside my father's head.

I caught a glimpse that night of how blood coagulates thicker than reason. Though the accident was clearly the result of my rear-ending the car that continued the chain reaction, George decided a big trucker, about twenty vehicles ahead, caused it all by slamming on his brakes before leaving the access road for the interstate.

Later that summer, I visited my parents' home, located less than two miles from my own residence. George had retired as head of the juvenile system of Dallas in 1980, previously serving as Dean of Men at a small college in Monticello, Arkansas after the war. In retirement, my old bedroom had become his hangout which was now a cross between a library and museum with mounds and stacks of pictures, books, mementos and handwritten notes on an old card table by his bed. Cardboard boxes filled with more of the same claimed most of the available floor space. Though the room was hardly an advertisement for tidy housekeeping, the sight did not strike me as overtly peculiar at the time.

After randomly selecting an off white worn paper from one stack, my eyes scanned the page. It was a citation for a Bronze Star awarded to George for his actions in World War II on the night of December 3rd, 1944, in the Hürtgen Forest, a 50 square mile area of dense trees and hilly topography located in southern Germany along the Belgium border. While dealing with one of the most

A vehicle hides in the gloom of the Hurtgen Forest, as if aware danger lurks everywhere. Pine needles blanketed the forest floor and disguised trip wires and mines.

miserable winters in Europe's history, the Hürtgen fight raged from mid-September to mid-December, devouring its dead with a torrid vengeance as the Americans suffered over 33,000 casualties! With George's infantry company encircled by the Germans, George, an artillery observer for the 196th Field Artillery Battalion, directed artillery fire for three days and nights under heavy enemy fire. After finally being relieved, he started for the rear to join his

Battalion Command Post. It seems George soon found himself lost behind enemy lines and stumbled across ten wounded GIs who were also lost, including one in no condition to walk. Another lieutenant asked if Lt. Looney would assume command and lead them from harm's way. I'm sure George shrugged and said he would try his best and off they went with my dad carrying the wounded GI on his back. Somehow my old man—he was 26 and older than many GIs—navigated them through darkness, sniper fire and land mines to safety. I learned 55 years later from his radio operator that he never saw the Lt. lost during the war.

"A recon plane stashed under tree in Germany." GWL. Also probably the Hürtgen Forest.

No small feat to stay on track in the Hürtgen, a forest so dark and dense, it was perpetually covered in a moist fog. "Anybody that says he wasn't lost in that forest is a damn liar," a GI was quoted as saying in the Ken Burn's TV special, "The War"—the GI was dead within days. How ironic or perhaps fitting that later in George's life, his own neighborhood would present him more of a navigational problem than a hostile forest in Europe. After I finished reading the citation, a thick silence smothered the air while father and son formed an island of inactivity in a room crammed with mementos of a life time. Finally, I looked up at my father and said with more admiration than surprise, "Dad, you were sort of a hero."

Fitting the text book profile of an artillery observer, George shunned attention or recognition, so it should come as no surprise that George tossed words around like heavy artillery shells and offered only a sheepish raise of his shoulders in reply. It was, I believe, the gesture of a man that saw his most productive years in the rearview mirror. Oh what a perfect opportunity to express my love and appreciation for him, but self absorbed with the complexities of raising my own family, I blew the chance. I was bright enough to decipher that his brain stored a wealth of history concerning the war so I said, "Dad you need to start writing down everything you can remember about the war. It's important history." George simply shrugged again but that is what he started to do.

We held the family Thanksgiving feast at my house that year. It was a beautiful day with a clear blue sky and temperatures probably in the seventies. The ensemble surrounding the dining room table included my wife Sandra, our three daughters ages 14, 12 and 7 at the time, George, my mother Mary. Sandra's mother Miss Marion, her oldest brother Roger and his son Troy, is the real life version of the movie "Top Gun," a bona fide Navy fighter pilot, his wings recently acquired.

After the blessing and amid clanging silverware and the smoky aroma of turkey filling the air, Troy said innocently enough,

Charleston Man Gets Oak Leaf Cluster

Charleston, Ark.–(Special)–First Lieutenant George Looney, with the First army in Germany, has been awarded an Oak Leaf cluster for heroism the night of Dec. 3.

After having directed artillery fire for three days and nights, during which time he was in a most exposed position and under extremely heavy enemy fire, Lieutenant Looney was relieved by friendly forces, and started toward the rear to reach his battalion command post. He was joined by a group of ten walking wounded who asked him to lead them from the area. Without knowing an exact route. Looney safely led the group through dense sniper-infested forests. Although fired upon by enemy snipers and although he had to support one of the wounded who had become too ill to walk alone, Looney led the men to the command post.

He is the son of Mr. and Mrs. M. W. Looney of Charleston, and a brother of Andrew Looney of Fort Smith. He has also been awarded the Bronze Star medal for meritorious service in France.

The original hometown newspaper clipping for George's second Bronze Star or Oak Leaf Cluster from the autumn of 1944 for his actions in the dreaded Hürtgen Forest.

"I didn't know your dad was in a plane crash in the war."

This bit of news caught me by surprise and my immediate glance found the familiar boyish look of my father. "I don't know about that," I heard the fool in me say. "I think we would have heard that story before," the fool continued.

An awkward silence accompanied a pained distant expression that played about my father's face; there was a brief defeated sag in his shoulders and he offered no rebuttal or reply. Thankfully, the festive mood soon returned. I now believe that for most of my father's life, he kept the darker side of the war to himself because he knew the gap between family life and combat was wider than the Atlantic Ocean, too difficult and lengthy a journey for his children to undertake. Months later, I discovered a picture of that

George with the Cub plane. "Knocked out German gun battery by observing from one of these." GWL.

airplane buried in the rubble on the card table by the bed. On the back of the picture, his scribbled handwriting stared back at me, practically speaking in his voice, *knocked out German post observing from this plane. Felt the wings ripple from ground fire. Later crashed into the side of a mountain. Walked away without a scratch. Chose not to observe any more from the air. George*

I heard his chuckle. George had a sense of humor.

It's not to say George never talked about the war. On the contrary, he told the same stories over and over. World War II ended only four years before my birth or roughly the same amount of time needed to complete high school—a blink of an eye really; but when George told his young sons of World War II, he may as well have been telling about the days of Sir Lancelot or Ivanhoe. Vivid, exciting swashbuckling tales filled with bravery and heroics and, as if cut from a movie script, all with a happy ending.

One favorite involved encountering several Germans in the bitter cold of what I now believe was the previously mentioned Hürtgen Forest—so the event probably occurred in late November or early December 1944. For reasons I can only guess, George was walking alone in a wooded area thick enough for animals to move from tree to tree without the risk of taking flight. A few yards off the worn snow covered trail, George saw human steam clouds rising within the forest.

"Come out with your hands up!" George barked, surely hoping his eyes were playing tricks on him.

No such luck. Lt. Looney promptly heard ice and fresh snow cracking in sheets under the weight of combat boots. Three German soldiers, shivering from the cold and wearing expressions of defeat, stepped out of the white forest into the plain view of George. A tad concerned with the odds, Lt. Looney decided to retrieve his officer's pistol that lay in hibernation inside his topcoat. The Germans, understanding his actions but not his intent, took off in a mad dash down the trail.

"Comrade!" George yelled.

The Germans stopped and turned to see George, arms spread wide as if welcoming long lost relatives. I imagine he offered a hint of a smile or some similar inviting expression. Now the Germans got it, marching back to him and surrendering.

"They were just cold and hungry and didn't want to fight anymore. Anyone could see that," George would say, cocking his head sideways and waving his index finger in the air, his big brown eyes dancing with satisfaction. Oh, to have seen the youthful smirk on his face as he marched those prisoners into camp. I wonder if he ever pulled out that pistol.

We repeatedly heard of the time he lay face down in the meadows of the French countryside and felt the grass sway above his head from machine gun fire or when his jeep driver, Frank Williams, delivered food and a bedroll to George behind enemy lines at great risk.

Another favorite: George entered Paris with the French 2nd Armored Division about noon on August 25th, 1944. With Paris now rid of the Nazi regime, George was soon participating in a giant celebration at the Arc de Triumphe when a German sniper's bullet whizzed by one of his ears, ricocheted off an armored vehicle and then buzzed his other ear! "I heard it loud and clear. A French officer pulled me down by my arm, hollering don't be afraid. Of course, he meant be afraid and get down which I did," George explained with as much emotion as his family ever heard while describing his war experiences.

But the war's dark side was always there and like a fishing cork hiding under water, ready for a return to the surface. We caught a glimpse of this dark side only after his reunion trip to Belgium and Germany in 1990; I believe this was no coincidence since his children had, by then, entered the sometimes sobering

world of adulthood. Almost three years would pass before I would understand the significance of a conversation with my father on the night of June 6th, 1994, the 50th Anniversary of the Normandy invasion—a day more commonly referred to as D-Day. While we watched a flurry of television shows concerning the historic day at my home, I asked George if he had landed at Normandy, a string of five beaches running along the coast line of France.

George and men discover the horror of the concentration camp near Leipzig in deep East Germany. "Set a fire with the bodies." GWL.

At this point in time, my understanding of World War II proved dismal. When viewing archived footage on television of the Allies' celebrating the liberation of Paris or old movies of the same, I thought the war was over. For those equally inept in American History, the Allies actually had eight more months of hard fighting in Europe before Germany would surrender.

George tolerated my ignorance of World War II and politely replied, "Yes" but added that his arrival at Utah Beach came days after the Allies had driven the Germans inland. "I drove off our boat in a jeep. There was no fighting at all," he said in a tone up beat with admiration for a job well done.

His manner soon turned dark when describing a battle of an unspecified later date. Something about deafening bombs exploding all around him. His hands darted to cover his ears; his eyes traveled to a far away place. Hearing his words made the battle come alive—the artillery guns firing with blinding flashes, their massive barrels recoiling, and after the explosions, mud and frozen snow showering down from a sky painted orange from war. I heard the high pitched cries of battle and drew in the warm scent of artillery smoke. I don't remember his exact words, only the vulnerability on his face during all this explaining. Unknown to me at the time, George was describing the surprise German winter offensive known as The Battle of The Bulge. How much of a surprise? Consider this: during The Bulge's opening hours, General Eisenhower was attending a wedding at Allied headquarters in Versailles, fellow American Generals Bradley and Hodges were visiting a Belgian gun maker for a custom made hand gun and British General Montgomery was playing golf in Holland! The attack referred to secretly as Operation Autumn Mist by Hitler, occurred over 6 months after D-Day and over 3 months after the liberation of Paris.

Another day, with absolutely zero foreshadow, George announced that he once saw frozen dead bodies stacked like firewood to the top of a three story building. As with many men of his era, my father possessed an unfailing ability to conceal his emotions, so the revelation stunned me more than his customary matter of fact demeanor. Unable to comprehend the magnitude of his feelings, I said nothing and we sat in silence for a minute, but it seemed longer than that before our conversation finally moved to another topic. I now expect horrific visions of war had accompanied his words—frozen faces twisted in torment, missing limbs, blood streaked dunes of snow. Obviously, this image could never be forgotten—these brave "boys" lying there, but I still knew

"Followed the dirt road to where the bodies were found." GWL.

nothing of his experience at that building nor how much the war was replaying in his mind.

At approximately this same time period, the movie Schindler's List was released. I mentioned the movie to my dad, also informing him of the film's plot. "Do you believe there was a Holocaust?" he immediately asked in a serious tone.

"Sure," I said. After all, I just saw the movie. Still, I wondered if he knew something that I didn't.

"Some people don't believe the Holocaust ever happened," he said, turning serious up a notch.

I let his thought hang a bit before asking, "What do you think?"

"I know it happened because I saw it," he quickly replied, his brown eyes conveying disgust.

I riveted to attention. This was not the hundredth rendition of capturing the Germans in the snow. According to George, and we now know that's the gospel, his battalion moved toward the sound of gun fire followed by black plumes of smoke climbing high into the sky. I later learned the event occurred around March of 1945 near Leipzig which is in eastern Germany. Soon they discovered a concentration camp. The Germans, evidently aware of the American's proximity, had rounded up all the prisoners, shot them and then ignited a human bonfire.

No Germans remained, but cigarettes still smoldered in ash trays and music played from outdoor speakers. George and friends had missed the enemy by only a few minutes. Recounting that story, George sounded downright pissed. I never doubted him on this one and sure enough, I later found pictures of the camp, taken immediately after the Americans arrived.

Another incident occurred in the summer of 1995 that would

"The remains of the concentration camp in Leipzig. Germans riddled it with bullets before leaving, killing many." GWL.

seem to reiterate that George was privately fighting the war over again. I had written a fictional short story about a GI's landing at Omaha Beach. In my story, set in June of 1994, an American veteran was a passenger on a commercial airliner filled with other veterans traveling to Normandy for a D-Day Reunion. The old GI, reliving his experience, informs his new acquaintances of his role in the disastrous landing at Omaha.

While driving to one of my daughter's softball games, I hatched the brilliant plan for my dad to read the story. After all, we were held hostage in the car and my briefcase lay in the back seat, containing the masterpiece. The story was 13 pages long and graphic in detail taken from a Dallas newspaper article of a veteran's actual experience. Loaded with pride and anticipation, I handed the manuscript to my Dad.

George never made it to the happy ending. After reading only a few pages, he returned the story, saying only through a terribly troubled expression: "I get the picture."

I expect the graphic details got the best of him. Maybe the part when the veteran said, "it was a day of death, killing or being killed. When I finally got to that beach, there must have been a row of dead Americans seven yards wide." Or maybe the part when the veteran said, "the brain wounds were the worst. I never knew brain tissue was so pink and fluffy."

I also felt pain but only because of his lack of interest in my story. How could it fail to attract his attention? In retrospect, it's clear that his mind was transmitting in high definition clarity a scene powerful enough to burst open the flood gates to a deluge of unpleasant memories—disturbing images that virgins to combat could never fully comprehend by mere discussion.

Reprinted from Ken Burns book "The War," correspondent Eric Sevareid said it best in the spring of 1945 when the tunnel scars of World War II were still as visible as fresh paint. *War happens inside a man and that is why, in a certain sense, you and your sons from the war will be forever strangers. If, by the miracle of art and genius, in later years two or three of them can open up their hearts, then perhaps we shall know a little of what it was like.*

I'm now convinced the longer George would have lived, the more his family would have learned the true extent of his role in World War II; but on this day, a commercial strength vise could not have fully pried open his heart to reveal what the war was truly like. Like I said, he understood our inability to give the subject its proper respect, also accepting his own inability to rid himself of the lingering horrors of war.

Chapter Two

He Plowed Real Deep

Cheating death of its chance to inflict misery, George passed away unexpectedly in his sleep at approximately 3 am on December 9th, 1996. People often remember their location, actions or even thoughts at the news of prominent deaths. People like JFK, or Bobby Kennedy, Martin Luther King, Elvis, John Lennon, Mickey Mantle or Princess Di. I was in the dental chair when the call came from my assistant, Adrienne, at about 9 a m, only minutes after my mother discovered her husband of almost 50 years in my former bed.

George fought a war without suffering a scratch and had lived near 79 years practically illness free. He left this earth without causing anyone trouble or inconvenience which was precisely the way he inhabited it. Opening its gates wide to welcome George, heaven sent an absolutely gorgeous morning. The weather remained perfect the entire week with a Caribbean blue sky, no winds and balmy temperatures. It turned cold and rainy the next week.

My brothers and I rushed home at the news. During my ten minute drive, anxiety manifested itself in a clammy deluge from forehead to armpits. I arrived first and while drawing upon the memory of my youth, visualized squirrels scrambling on the roof, heard birds singing sonnets in the front yard trees, maybe even an occasional bark from the dog, Sam, in the backyard. A scene consistent with previous countless trips home, now lurked in the unknown. After entering the house, I immediately encountered my Mother, Mary, in the den; with fear controlling her eyes, her face resembled white ash. Creeping down the long hallway leading to my old room, the taste of vomit crept up my throat. My heart pounded fierce enough to escape. Butterflies collided inside my gut. I inhaled enough to swell my chest and dreaded entering that bedroom more than I'd dreaded anything in my life. The image remains forever stamped in my mind. Sunlight from the brilliant morning slashed through the adjacent window directly on my Father who lay on his back, eyes closed, his mouth slightly ajar; gasping for one last breath, I wondered? One hand was raised in the symbolic gesture of waving goodbye and I was reminded that from birth, life streaks toward this moment no matter how deep we try to bury that harsh reality or wish otherwise. I'll never have to worry about him again was my next conscious thought.

The fragrance of both musk and old paper soon filled my nostrils. Time froze and the room became an oversized photograph of itself. My eyes, welling with mist, took note of all that clutter in the room. And then I got it, the way the Germans got it that day in the forest. Offering a hint of his travel plans, my father had insulated himself with a lifetime of memories. He knew the time of departure had been rapidly approaching for his final destination. (Dr. Ted French, a dentist, later told me George had shunned recommended dental repair shortly before his death, citing with a grin, "I don't have that much time left.")

I again randomly selected a piece of paper from the table by his bed. It was his army discharge papers which disclosed five Bronze Service Stars indicating that George served in five major battles. Also, a Bronze Star, and an Oak Leaf Cluster which meant another Bronze Star. Besides the Bronze Star for leading the ten walking wounded to safety on December 3, 1944, George was awarded a Bronze Star for placing artillery fire upon an enemy fifty yards from Allied troops while exposed to heavy enemy fire. This action took place in Charleville, France between July 9th and September 7th of 1944.

Reading of my Father's excellence in combat stirred a notion, sometimes haunting and never distant in thought: could I muster the courage to serve my country in a similar manner? Or would I buckle at the knees at the moment of truth, like the coward in the movie "Private Ryan?" For those of us who never served in the military, it's a riddle likely to remain unsolved. Now knowing the extent of George's war record provided little support in bolstering the concept of father passing on these remarkable genes of combat to number one son. One consolation discovered later: Neither of George's brothers saw action during the war and at least one brother reached deep into his soul and found no disgrace in missing the experience. "There's no doubt your Dad's the only one of us that could have done it," said middle brother, Zolon, who served in the Army in the Pacific and, only by the luck of the draw, avoided combat. Zolon, cut from the same cloth as George, was surely selling himself short. Oldest brother, Andy, was 4-F.

Attendance at the Gaston Oaks Baptist Church was the largest anyone could remember. "George kept a pretty low profile but he plowed real deep," commented one of his church deacon buddies, Noble Hurley.

"Truth is, I love George Looney," Dr. Brian Anderson, the fair haired Baptist preacher, announced from the pulpit, the flag–draped casket located directly below. "If I were to share with you everything that needs to be said about George, we'd be here for days. Then it would be your turn." Through wire rimmed glasses, the preacher's stare took in everyone in the room. "George Looney was more than what's printed in your program. More than what we will say about him today. He was friend, father, husband, grandfather. A decorated war hero—the kind of hero who saved

That's George in uniform standing in front of his parent's home in Charleston, Arkansas. His oldest brother Andy, who was 4-F, stands center; middle brother, Zolon, who also served in the army but was stationed in the Pacific and the Philippines, flanks Andy.

this country," continued the preacher who was closer to George's sons in age.

"But there's one more medal for George. It is not a medal for his uniform but a crown for his head." His hands gripped the sides of the pulpit. His voice rose to a crescendo. "It is the greatest reward of all: eternal life in the presence of a God pleased with this man's life. It's fitting that one of George's own family said it best." The preacher paused but when the sound of silence faded, it was replaced by gentle sobs and gasps until that sound was overridden by Dr. Anderson's voice who began to read a note my 12-year old

daughter left on my pillow the night before. 'Dad, I hope you feel better soon. I miss him a lot too! But now he's in heaven with God. I think it's a better place for him. Heaven is twice as great as earth is! He will always be in your heart deep inside. I will pray for our family and for you every night. Love, Kate.'

Pictures of Kate crying at approximately two years old had accompanied the note. As soon as I could stop crying inside, I would return to my father's room and take a journey back into time.

6

Chapter Three

Spooky Holy

It's my belief that mortals often speak with forked tongues. We deceive; we deceive family, friends and ourselves, making bold statements and then change our minds faster than the Texas weather. "I'll never marry again." Or, "Lord, let me get away with it this one time and I'll never do it again." Yeah, right.

Humans backslide over and over when life forces difficult choices—especially concerning the issue of death. But when my father laid eyes on his brother-in-law practically chained to a respirator while suffering from a nasty case of emphysema, he announced in a no nonsense tone: "that ain't livin and I don't want any part of it."

George, a deacon in the Baptist Church since the days of petticoats and black and white tv, made it his practice to weigh the consequence of his words before sending them out into the world. Like his namesake, he avoided speaking with a forked tongue with no less commitment than he would avoid tripping a land mine. Considering the way George departed, maybe "the Man" above took under consideration George's views on "livin." And maybe the following will rock the foundation of faith, or more fittingly the lack of faith, of even the staunchest of non-believers.

After my Dad's passing, my family received a sympathy card from dear friend, Ann Dannis, featuring the words of the writer, Charles Alexander. *The night my Father died there came to me, as never before, the worth of a human soul. He could not take any of us with him: he must go alone. And I saw how the thing that mattered was to be sure that the soul was safe in God's keeping.*

I cried to God: "If there is any way that Thou revealest Thyself to people, give me the certainty that my Father is with Thee, and safe." And I promised Him that I would serve Him all my life.

As clearly as anything I ever experienced, the impression came to me: "Your Father is up here, safe with Me." There and then, looking up at the stars, I promised to serve Him all my life, and the load lifted right off me.

But where was my sign?—the impression that Alexander spoke of. Soon thereafter, I discovered a notebook from a writing class that I had taken a few months earlier at SMU. A quick search of its contents revealed a handwritten page that leapt out at me the way Alan Arkin went for Audrey Hepburn in the movie, "Wait Until Dark."

It read: *My Father supported his family never thinking of himself always putting his family ahead of his own needs. I never*

knew he fought at D-Day until the 50th anniversary, but then I've never heard him talk about the day. (I'm wrong here. George landed at Utah Beach on July 8th, almost one month after D-Day.) I think he saw much death and has only recently shown a desire to discuss it. It peeked my interest and he seemed most proud to show me his war medals. It appears my dad was a hero carrying a wounded man across mine fields in the dark across enemy lines to safety thus avoiding death, but of course only temporarily as Jim Morrison says: "No one gets out of here alive." I guess every child wants to think of his father as a hero so I feel lucky every time I hear the phone ring in the middle of the night. I figure it is the call saying my father is dead. I've chosen to believe he will die painlessly unexpectedly in his sleep. He deserves that.

After a thoughtful pause, I recognized my handwriting, remembering the teacher had provided the class with a word, instructing us to write whatever came to mind without censorship of thoughts. Oh, the power generated from unforeseen irony. Through the conduit of my own words, words written months prior to my Father's death, I'd received the certainty that my Father is with thee and safe. Spooky holy huh?

A youthful George ponders his future in wartime. I expect this picture was taken during basic training in Ft. Leonardwood, Missouri, 1941-1942.

7

The C-47 dispersal area at Saltby Field, England, prior to the Normandy jump.

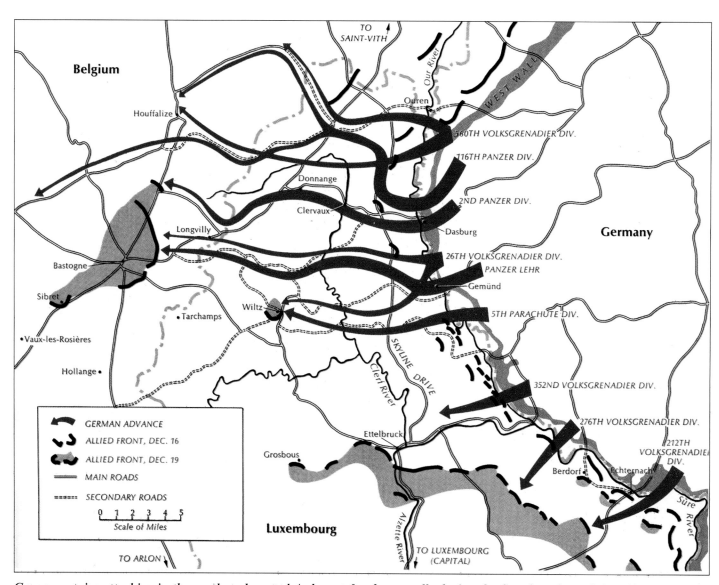

German armies attacking in the south and central Ardennes fared unequally during the first four days of the offensive. At the southern end, one division on the Seventh Army broke through to Wiltz, but three others were stopped by the Americans on a line (shaded area) between Echternach and Grosbous. In the center, the Fifth Oanzer Army wrung out sizable gains; in the main attack, four divisions broke through and drove toward Bastogne. Farther north, a panzer division and a Volksenadier division launched a two-pronged assault on Houffalize. U.S. Army Signal Corp

Chapter Four

Entering A Time Capsule

I found it both sobering and comforting to learn so much about my father's life as a child and young man. Looking at pictures he took, holding items he held, smelling his paternal smell, all left me flooded with a longing sense of separation. But it was also like he didn't die all at once, as if a part of him still remained in that room, waiting for the appropriate time to move completely upstairs. My exploration efforts usually took place on Sunday afternoons and lasted for several months.

My childhood room contained a stunning collection of memorabilia spanning George's lifetime, many touched by a sentimentality it's now clear my dad always possessed. He threw away nothing. I found valentines given to him as a small boy, also his Boy Scouts of America membership card from 1930. Report cards dating back to grade school revealed consistent grades—barely passing which may explain his lack of grave concern when his sons brought home mediocre marks. Irregular school attendance due to duties on his parent's farm, contributed to his less than stellar academic career, my mother theorized. Since one decade in age difference and a few hundred miles in geography separated my mother and father during this period, it sounds more like my mother, the school teacher, rationalizing a

A sign of things to come. One of George's agriculture students at Monette High School in Arkansas, before George entered military service, 1939-1941.

palatable reason. If a son is to judge, apathy, induced by an overdose of fishing and hunting, was more likely the culprit.

His high school and college graduation announcements, still tucked away in the original envelopes, managed to simultaneously reek of musk and that fresh ink smell. Nostalgia dripped from the photocopy of a dark beige handwritten invitation to the high school football banquet of the Charleston Tigers. George played center on the football team, an unglamorous position that would not call attention to himself—the ideal personality trait of a future field artillery observer. Scheduled at the American Legion Hut on January 24th, 1935, the night's agenda included topics such as Harmony of Love Crooners and Recovery of Athletics. The menu was a meager depression influenced offering of fruit cocktail, chicken salad, potato chips, pickles, butter rolls and thankfully cherry pie. I held the announcement to my nose pretending to check for the aroma of homemade pie but truthfully longing for the scent of a teenaged George Looney.

A 1948 letter from the President of Arkansas A&M in Monticello, Arkansas recommended George for employment to International Harvester stating that; *Mr. Looney has an inordinate capacity for getting things done, a splendid war record but his military experience is an asset rather than a liability.* Sounded like a period piece. At the time, George served as Dean of Men at Arkansas A&M; he never worked for International Harvester.

He kept tickets and programs from sporting events, some of which we had attended together. Hundreds of golf balls from his municipal course days during retirement cluttered his closet, also fishing rods, his Rotary badge, black and white pictures of his youth and medicine for athletes foot, a condition that tormented him all of his adult life. Like a well timed handoff, I acquired the fungus but only after his passing. We found precious little cash in his last wallet, but it contained pictures of his three grown sons as small children.

The depression left an indelible mark on George and he believed in saving for a rainy day. His chest of drawers contained at least a dozen shirts, all birthday or Christmas gifts and never worn.

Soon I rode a time capsule into World War II, blasting off with a Stars and Stripes newspaper from June 7th, 1944, displaying the headlines *Sea-Air-Ground Opposition Less Than Expected.* Try telling that to the GIs that landed at Omaha Beach with some reports claiming over ninety percent losses on the initial assault.

The War and Navy department provided Lt. Looney and his fellow GIs a post card size, 37 page guide to educate the Americans on Great Britain and its customs. As distant as it sounds today, the book immediately attempted to bridge any resentment or hangover from the American Revolution by stating, *We don't worry about which side our grandfather fought in the Civil War because it doesn't matter anymore.*

Similarities were stressed: language, democracy, freedom of speech and religion and love of sports, the most obvious, but differences were stressed too. *The British are often more reserved.* Not so in my recent trip to London, maybe an example of our shrinking world. George and friends learned that England is only about the size of North Carolina; also London has no sky scrapers because London's built on swampy ground. The Brits would not take to bragging advised the War Department, especially, concerning money since the American soldier made

No more pharmacy as of December 3rd, 1942. George is now training for life as an artillery observer at Fort Sill, Oklahoma. Oh, what those eyes would see! "We fired for classes every day. Because of this, we became very proficient and skilled which helped us later in combat." GWL Excellent photo of Geroge with his hand on the panoramic telescope on one of the battery's 105mm Howitzers.

higher wages. Especially any mention of the US bailing out Great Britain in World War I. American lost 60,000 men in that war—Great Britain a whopping one million!

Other differences: Driving on the left side. Lousy coffee (but good tea.) Warm beer. Small cars (no gas). Word meanings. For example the word "bloody"—not a good word in mixed company. The monetary system: pounds instead of dollars. Don't call it funny money, warned the guide.

But mainly the War Department reminded the GI that Great Britain was not just a country at war but a war zone—something totally foreign to the American soldier. *Every light in England is blacked out every night. Grazing land is now plowed for wheat and flower beds turned into vegetable gardens.* Since all factories were totally occupied for turning out goods for the war, Great Britain suffered from all type of shortages—gas, income, clothes, food, soap, paint and so on.

The all consuming war effort led to neglect in other areas. *Britain may look a little shop worn and grimy to you,* informed the guide. *The British people are anxious to have you know that you are not seeing their country at its best.* My guess is that Great Britain with its mass transit, castles, cathedrals, domes, channels, cliffs and more, looked eye-popping fine to the lieutenant from Arkansas.

Prior to George's arrival, over 60,000 British civilians—men, women, and children—had already died under German bombs! Great Britain was a country determined to destroy Hitler; this included many women in the military who had seen intense action during air raids, decades before it became an accepted practice for American Women to see combat.

Prior to the Normandy invasion, the war department also provided each GI a similar thirty-six page pamphlet entitled the Pocket Guide to France. On the very first page, *we learn you will probably get a big welcome from the French. Americans are popular in France* therefore proving some things do change. The book defended France's early collapse in the war by drawing a parallel to a dark chapter in American history, declaring that *our Sunday morning defeat at Pearl Harbor still galls us.* The literature disputed the claim of Dr. Goebbel, the Nazi propaganda minister, that France was a push over, informing GIs that in the previous World War, France held out for four years as the Allied battlefield.

Lt. Looney read that Frenchmen were proud, family people, religious and an agrarian culture. Forty percent of France lived off the soil at the time. The economies of French life was based on the parent's rule of working and saving for the children's future therefore proving some things never change. Sound familiar?

There was the inevitable warning of the French prostitutes, claiming the Nazi's planted undercover agents in the world's oldest profession. *Almost anybody in France can get chummy with a special sort of hard boiled dame sitting alone at a coffee table,* warned the pocket guide. With a crooked smile and between drags on a cigarette that produced rising smoke clouds, I envisioned Bogart cautioning GIs in a black and white film made by the war department. Before the war, the French government made an attempt to examine and license prostitutes but the guide advised GIs that the health card means absolutely nothing. Danger extended beyond enemy bullets and hooker spys. Our war department's literature cautioned the GIs of polluted water in rural areas and further advised them to drink milk only if boiled.

The US Government discouraged marriage to the French, refusing to pay for the transportation of wives back home if soldiers married while in France. *You can't marry without the permission of your commanding officer,* further advised the hand out.

The guide described *a war ravaged country beyond imagination. The Germans have stripped her bare bit by bit. They moved to Germany everything not required by them in France to carry on the war. The Nazi's have eaten the food, drunk the wine and shipped almost everything else back to Germany.*

The French underground worked courageously to sabotage the Nazi occupation plans but paid the price; the book states one Frenchman was shot every two hours on the average, year in and year out. In France's six week battle with Germany, the French lost 108,000 men with 260,000 more wounded.

Allied bombing left many citizens homeless but most French understood the necessity for this or so claimed the War Department literature. In a further effort to educate our soldiers on the merit of liberating France, the US Government peeled back the layers of American history, reminding US Soldiers of the French assistance to Lt. Looney's name sake in the War for Independence. The tiny book also attempted to dispel the notion of the French as insatiable partygoers, citing that the French spent far less on entertainment than Americans.

The exotic French Riveria suffered more than most of France. Few babies were born alive in this district because of the dire food conditions. *Live strictly on your rations,* the guide states, *or you may deprive others whose need is greater than yours.* Adults living in this area lost an average of forty pounds under the Nazi regime. My Dad's writings did make note of his discomfort when eating in front of the French.

Like the American and British women of World War II, the French women performed most admirably. *French women plowed and planted on the farm or ran shops in the city. They have fed their children horse meat when other food failed. They educated them at home when the schools broke down. French women deserve appreciation.*

In a startling reminder of the world's evolution in communication and technology, the pocket guide stated, *we don't know just what the war has done to Paris. These notes will assume that there still will be lots to see.* The author wondered if Field Marshall Goring, the art lover, had wrapped his Nazi paws around the Mona Lisa or the Venus di Milo.

I internally smiled when reading that the GI should not expect French plumbing in hotels or homes to equal the modern American plumbing. *After all, maybe your granddad wasn't brought up in one either (modern plumbing) and he managed to survive.* My thoughts retreated to the deep water well on the back porch of my father's childhood home and also the outhouse located across the dirt road. Both remained functional in visits to my grandparents in the 1950's. The author closed with *let us remember our likenesses not our differences,* leading me to question the writer's disappointment if he could see the world today.

George came out firing with a Valentine's Day letter in 1966, to Larry Collins and Dominque Lapierre, authors of "Is Paris Burning?"

I went into Paris with the French 2nd Armored Division on the morning of August 25th. 1944. The thing that disturbs me most is that no mention of our unit, the 196th Field Artillery Battalion, was ever made in your book.

On August 23rd, we started moving toward Paris. We fired from positions near Cherreuse, Chateaufort and Small-Woods. On 24th we were in Toussus le Noble, Villacoublay, Vanves, Claremont and Issey les Moulineaux. On the morning of August 25th, we moved directly into Paris. We arrived at the Arc de Triumphe under heavy machine gun and rifle fire. Our 196th FAB

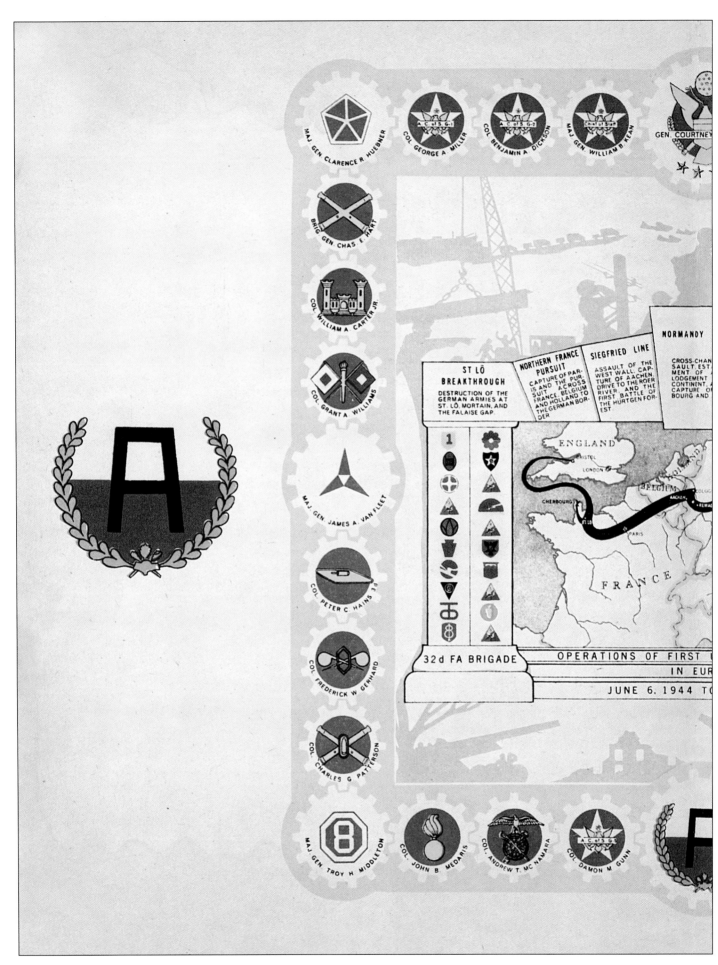

MAJ. GEN. CLARENCE R. HUEBNER

COL. GEORGE A. MILLER

COL. BENJAMIN A. DICKSON

MAJ. GEN. WILLIAM B. KEAN

GEN. COURTNEY

BRIG. GEN. CHAS. E. HART

COL. WILLIAM A. CARTER JR.

COL. GRANT A. WILLIAMS

MAJ. GEN. JAMES A. VAN FLEET

COL. PETER C. HAINS 3d

COL. FREDERICK W. GERHARD

COL. CHARLES G. PATTERSON

MAJ. GEN. TROY H. MIDDLETON

COL. JOHN B. MEDARIS

COL. ANDREW T. MC NAMARA

COL. DAMON M. GUNN

ST LÔ BREAKTHROUGH

DESTRUCTION OF THE GERMAN ARMIES AT ST. LÔ, MORTAIN, AND THE FALAISE GAP.

NORTHERN FRANCE PURSUIT

CAPTURE OF PARIS AND THE PURSUIT ACROSS FRANCE, BELGIUM AND HOLLAND TO THE GERMAN BORDER

SIEGFRIED LINE

ASSAULT OF THE WEST WALL. CAPTURE OF AACHEN. DRIVE TO THE ROER RIVER. AND THE FIRST BATTLE OF THE HÜRTGEN FOREST

NORMANDY

CROSS-CHANNEL ASSAULT. ESTABLISHMENT OF A LODGEMENT CONTINENT. CAPTURE OF BOURG AND

32d FA BRIGADE

ENGLAND
BRISTOL
LONDON
CHERBOURG
BELGIUM
AACHEN
PARIS
FRANCE

OPERATIONS OF FIRST

IN EUR

JUNE 6, 1944 TO

12

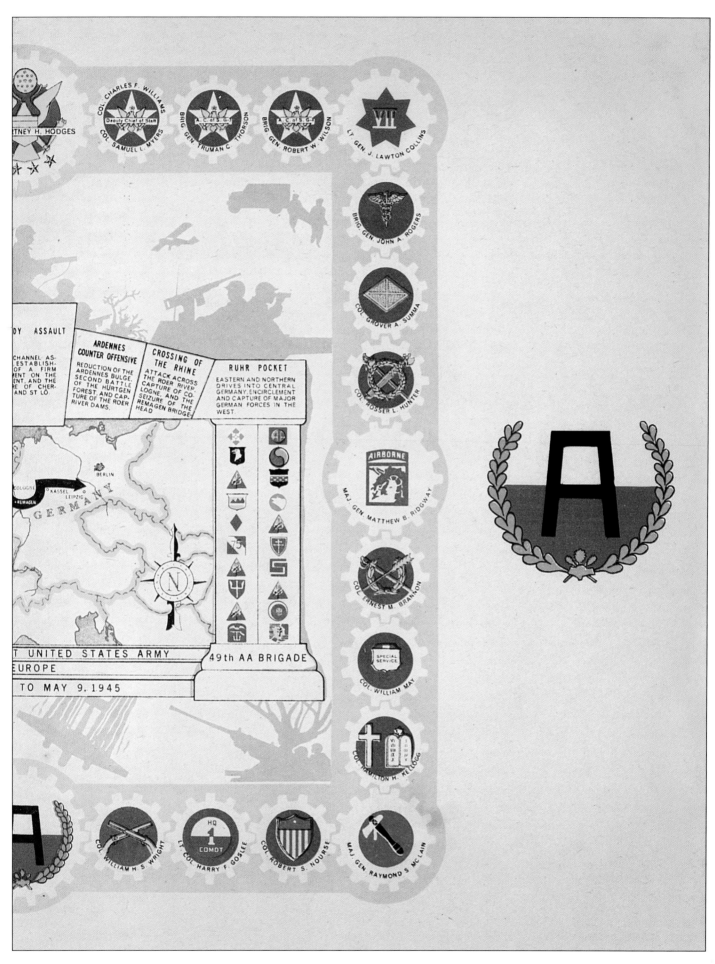

liaison planes landed on the Avenue De La Grand Armee at 1840 hours and flew out the first press release from Paris.

George closes with, *Did I make my point?*
Sincerely yours,
George W. Looney, Capt.
196 FA Bn. 01174356

Staring at the letter's closing, in particular his rank and serial number, I felt the same warmth and comfort I would feel from an old reliable winter blanket.

A week later, Larry Collins responded, apologizing for neglecting to mention The 196th. Collins added, *one of these days we may revise some passages of our book and I shall enjoy very much having a chance to discuss the 196th role in the liberation of Paris.*

Good for George.

A French newspaper dated August 27th, 1944 confirmed George's presence in Paris on Liberation Day. Sporting the headline, *Liberation,* the front page contained pictures of the French celebrating with wild abandon in the streets. Lt. Looney, his sense for recording history never more evident, had written in one margin *I bought this paper in street this day.* On another margin, he recorded *I saw this. GW Looney.* At the bottom of the paper, he scribbled *I went in with French 2nd Armored Division lead troops. Was at Arc De Triumph about 1 pm.*

A war map of Normandy, the size of the French art coveted by the Germans and stained with European soil, contained his scribbling in blood red ink along the map's coast line: *Saw first dead body here*, the sight certainly bursting his illusion of an all expenses paid European vacation.

Without preamble, remorse tugged hard at my emotions. Perhaps it was because my Father had chosen to bury these startling pieces of history in the paper jungle of my former room as deep as he had buried his innermost feelings on the war.

A George letter to my Mother from Belgium in 1990 during his Battle of The Bulge Reunion trip forced an audible laugh. *We attended a ceremony at cemetery where most of boys killed in Bulge was buried. Even looked for my stone. Just lucky I guess.*

I discovered a written history of George's unit, a manual of legal size sporting a bright red cover; gold letters across the front spelled *196th Field Artillery Battalion.* Presented to George at war's end, he had scribbled in pencil along the margin of page one *Battalion Commander told us it was an easy war on everybody except field observer and infantry.*

Indeed, I soon learned field artillery battalions remain mobile, constantly attached to divisions in combat. Another cheery bit of news: the enemy knew the field artillery observer would typically direct artillery from the highest point near the battle site and often in front of the infantry he was supporting, making the observer a

The picture of a young French woman most likely taken by a German officer. George took the camera from a deserted German vehicle after calling for air support that strafed and destroyed a German platoon. I found the camera in George's room.

Another picture from the German camera that George confiscated from the abandoned German vehicle. Did these young ladies soon receive a free burr haircut courtesy of the French Resistance for befriending the Germans?

visible target for hostile fire. The casualty rate for field artillery observers was very high. I now understood why George never seemed young to me—even from my earliest memory.

An inspection of a portable wooden cabinet, practically hidden in one corner of the bedroom, revealed a vintage German camera with a handwritten note from George tucked inside the camera's leather case. Before reading one word, I expected this would be a good one. My hunch was instantly rewarded.

To Whom It May Concern:

After we broke out of Normandy beachhead and the Germans started their run back to Germany it was our unit chasing a German unit in retreat. They had no supply units and we had trouble getting supplies also, especially fuel for vehicles.

My artillery BN was attached to a 5th Armed Command for artillery support when needed. For two or three days we chased a German unit across France. They would bivouac in an area at night and we would stay there the next night. Neither one could get enough fuel to attack the other side. On about the third day we topped a hill and caught them strung out moving thru a small town. It was too far for me to reach them with artillery but we did have an air corps observer along with me in a jeep. He called in fighter planes and then really worked the

column over. When we moved on down on them we found vehicles of all kinds, horse drawn artillery all shot up. Apparently they took their dead and wounded with them and ran. I found this small camera in one vehicle. I took rest of film and had it developed. I have three or four pictures that came out of it. If I can find them I will put them with the camera.
George W. Looney

Written on the margin of the paper: *Natives had stripped all the meat off of horses in a very short time, 30 mi to 1 hour.*

Sure enough, four small black and white pictures tumbled from the unraveled note. A young handsome German, presumably an officer, wore a white bathing suit while standing by a railing at a large swimming pool. Maybe part of a villa, certainly part of a comfortable setting. The German enjoyed the company of two young women, presumably French and also attractive. Brief swimsuits, at least for the times, clung to the women like spandex. The German, along with the French women, wore bright expressions. Life appeared good, at least until George and friends entered the picture.

My deductive reasoning calculated the picture was taken shortly before June 6th, 1944, the day of the Allies invasion of France. George confiscated the camera sometime in September, after the Allies liberated Paris in August. Life can change on a man

I expect this is the German officer who took the pictures of the young women also found in the camera.

George took this picture somewhere in France with the German camera.

15

in a hurry, I thought. A barrage of questions flooded my mind. Did the German survive the air attack? Only a major wound or death would cause him to leave his camera, the pessimist or possibly the realist in me reasoned. Did the French resistance later label the women as Nazi sympathizers by shaving their heads and branding the Swastika onto their foreheads?

Every picture tells a story, the photographs reiterating the pocket guide's assertion of the Nazi's lust for the spoils of France—the young women and the fine art, the villas, and castles, the exquisite wines and the rest. Thou shall not covet or something like that.

George described a haunting event in the margin of a subsequent page in his battalion's manual that probably occurred at approximately the same time as the camera incident. *I was with lead troops. As we moved up, I was crawling up ditch by side of road. We had a tank coming up road with us. It was hit close to me. I could hear a boy screaming and tank burst into flames. I don't think anybody got out. We moved on.*

The sobering echoes of war continued on the book's last page entitled *Lest We Forget*. It contained a list of eight fallen soldiers of the 196th. Beside the name of Corporal Joe Ostroski, 11 November 1944 Tennessee, George had written, *Very good soldier. It was late at night. We were on road trying to get guns up and in position. Very deep mud and ice. I went back down line and told all personnel to come up and help with first gun and by all means get off crossroad. A few minutes later they shelled crossroad. Joe had not left. A piece of shrapnel went thru front of helmet into brain.*

With experiences like that, no wonder George remained stoic and bravely resisted overwhelming concern when as a panic stricken twelve year old, I had frantically reminded him that after draining and cleaning the pool for my upcoming birthday party, he overlooked a minor detail of refilling it with water. (The pool, on the grounds of the Hutchins County Boys Home, contained no filter or cleaning system) The party went off as planned but the half empty pool more resembled a concrete pond. Not all was lost as Glenda Gladney announced the birthday bash a rousing success, her giddy opinion a result of her inability to swim. Reinforcing the theory of different strokes for different folks, she could, however, ride a horse with the skill of Annie from the Wild West Show. Regardless, George lost little sleep over the matter though I reminded him of the oversight at timely intervals over the next three decades or so.

After the defeat of Germany, my Father and his fellow GIs received a four page pamphlet from General Bradley, providing special orders on German-American relations. Though conquered, General Bradley still viewed Germany as dangerous, warning his troops of an underground organization for the continuation of the Nazi program for world domination already in existence.

Bradley theorized that Germany, including its people, were unregretful and would view the defeat as only an interlude to prepare for the next war. Germany would attempt to convince the Allies that the gentle and cultured German people never wanted Nazism, the General further warned. Understandably, Bradley ordered all American personnel to avoid violence if at all possible and to conduct one self as an American Soldier, not a Nazi.

Bradley's handout demanded Americans never associate with Germans. It was not permissible to shake hands with them, visit their homes or attend any German social events. *Give the Germans no chance to trick you into relaxing your guard*, concluded Bradley.

On this issue, Lt. Looney evidently violated orders and proved Bradley's point at the same time. Toward the end of my Father's

life, he spent a lot of time in his garage with my youngest brother, Dean, who was in his early thirties at the time. Dean, a motorcycle junkie, would come over to work on his motorcycles and our father inevitably made his way to the garage to keep Dean company.

During these sessions, the hangover of war started to seep through George's interior, as if overloaded with the burden of it all. According to our father, a German column, aware of the vastly superior approaching Allies, fled from a German town in motorcars, horseback and on foot. After traveling a few miles, Allied planes strafed the column into oblivion leaving few if any survivors. Shortly thereafter, The 196th Field Artillery Battalion entered the town, but not before passing the remains of a battle more one-sided than Little Big Horn. While the specifics of the encounter will remain as cloudy as bomb smoke, several German females invited Lt. Looney into their home for dinner. The farm boy from Charleston, Arkansas, longing for a home cooked meal, accepted. George soon learned of his host's true interest. The departed German army of a few days before contained family members of his dinner companions.

"Did the Lieutenant know any information concerning their relatives, whereabouts or safety?" the women practically pleaded, evidently unaware of the massive Allied air strike. "Could he possibly use his considerable influence to find out any details?"

"No," replied the American lieutenant, his eyes surely less convincing than his tone.

The warnings of General Bradley's four page briefing undoubtedly sounded internally with the volume of the air strike itself. Since my Father eventually claimed no ill will toward the German people, I expect contempt, bred by the weariness of war, battled the sympathy generated from his kind brave soul.

I believe that's George is inspecting what's left of an airplane or glider after crashing. His notes say in Normandy.

Chapter Five

Buried Treasure

While rummaging around under the bed, I came upon a lost treasure—a small but weighty wooden box containing over eighty letters written by George during the war, primarily to his parents and his younger sister, Carmen. Never knew of their existence.

George's handwritten letters, I believe, connect to his soul, an extension of the man himself—and importantly, provide a conduit from the past to the present, allowing us to see the world as it was. Is letter writing a lost art? Certainly a craft on the decline in subsequent generations. These letters breathe enough of his personality to fog windows. The constant references to not only food but the topography of each country present a true picture of the times—an agricultural society in the US and Europe. His constant references to the climate even reflect the

During basic training, fun in Ft. Leonardwood, Missouri after flooding. The man loved his cars.

spirit and culture of a farm boy—dependent on the weather for survival. I've condensed much of the letters and presented them in chronological order, thus allowing readers to follow the path of George's words across the Atlantic and then thru Europe in the most violent time in the history of mankind...and also to remind us of how much the world has changed.

George grew up just outside a small town in a frame house on a dirt road with no indoor toilet and a fresh water well located inside a screened back porch. Other than a brief stop in the Big Apple on his way to England, he had previously only seen the dim lights of his college town, Fayetteville, Arkansas. Not surprisingly, especially George's early letters stitch the image of a man enjoying his first trip away from home more than a man touring thru hell. I found strong traces of the man I knew as a father—generous to a fault, optimistic and certainly forgiving as his hard anger with the Germans gradually softened as he began to interface with the German people. Regardless of all he was enduring and would endure, his sense of humor, and concern for family back home never wavered, as if the real danger was in the

Lt. Colonel McClernand Butler in 1945. Lt. Colonel Butler's 395th Infantry Regiment was the outfit that George was giving fire support to during the Höfen Battle.

This was taken at Ft. Leonardwood, Missouri in 1941-42 while George was still a pharmacist, or before the powers to be decided that the unassuming country boy from Arkansas, had the perfect makeup for an artillery observer.

United States and not on the battlefields of Europe—and only after hostilities ended, would his words reveal the true danger of his role in the war. My father had survived a depression and planned on surviving the war so the overriding theme of his letters should come as no revelation to those that knew him: *I'm getting enough to eat and I will be alright.* Every letter ended with *Love, George.*

February 1, 1944 Camp Gordon Augusta, Georgia
Dear Carmen, (his youngest sister)
I got the box of candy from Lois yesterday. It was very good. I had a letter from Zolon (his middle brother) the other day. He needed the price of a car payment. Well it won't be long now. I expect to be leaving before long.

While the women of Europe would soon catch his eye, George, like many GIs, was already juggling his love life in absenteeism. During World War II, the GI's infatuation—no make that obsession with the opposite sex seemed to serve as some type of emotional shield to help deflect the notion of not returning home.

February 1, 1944 Camp Gordon Augusta, Georgia
Dear Mother,
I'm sending my sweaters home with some things I don't need. Give Papa all he can use and then let Fletcher (his older sister's husband) have anything he

can use. I never did give Andy(oldest brother) anything so the tablecloth is for them. I hope to be able to send you something later on. I also got a big box of candy from Lois yesterday. Mother the way I figured it, I owed PaPa about $75, that is leaving off the $72 I let Andy have. I told Zolon I would pay for the license for his car so I'm going to add that on and send a $90 check. I sent a check for a $500 bond yesterday. That leaves a little money there in the bank but not much. I think I'm supposed to have $2125 worth of bonds now. Oh yes, I will get my first lieutenant soon. That will give me a $16 raise.

Well I know a lot of things can happen but I never was much to worry about the future. I'm ready and anxious if we should move out and expect to have a good time. If I don't, well that will be determined in the future. I just hope the rest of you stay well and happy as I expect to. So Fletcher is 1A now. He may well be called but I don't think he will ever have to go anywhere. I believe that most of this will be over this year.

On the next day, George and the 196th Field Artillery Battalion boarded a train for Camp Kilmer, New Jersey, the

Fletcher Wilson, who was married to George's sister, Jessie, served in the infantry. Though GWL's optimistic letters home indicated otherwise, George privately worried for Fletcher: "A man in the infantry where I was a few times didn't hang around long." GWL 5/14/45. The infantry suffered seven out of ten casualties but Fletcher beat the odds, returning home to Charleston, Arkansas and was the local mailman for many years. I remember going on his mail route with him as a youngster.

staging area for the New York Port of Embarkation.

Fellow officers Himmelman and Scholze along with George at the Paramount Hotel in New York, the night before sailing to England in February 1944. "Served a pitiful shrimp dinner which we walked away from." GWL.

Between February 2-10, 1944 East Coast, U.S.
Dear Mother and Dad,
    Well it's about to happen. I am now somewhere on the east coast and expect to go over in the not too distant future. So far I'm having a good time so don't worry. Two other officers (Sinkler Schloze and Geroge Himmelman) and myself went to New York last night and I guess it was just three country boys going to town. You'll hear of my safe arrival from the government.

I bet the lights of the Big Apple were blinding.

February, 1944 England
Dear Mother,
    Probably you have heard by this time I am in England. Like it fine and having a big time. Went to a large dance last night. Haven't been out much yet but expect to visit some of the larger cities if possible. We have a good place to stay and getting plenty to eat. Hope everybody is okay.

February 28, 1944 England
Dear Carmen,
    It seems you can find out things I can't. Confidentially, I haven't asked anybody anything nor made no promises. So far as I'm concerned, I am a free man. Does that answer your question?

No doubt referring to his love life. It's hard to imagine a man later known to wear stripes with plaids was ever a playboy. The night before, George and the 196th arrived at Albrighton, Shropshire, England in a blinding snowstorm.

February 28th, 1944 England
Dear Mother and all,
    I'm having a wonderful time and seeing plenty of sights. I wish I could tell you about them and I guess I'll have to wait until I get back. There really isn't a lot of difference in the country but the people are a little

hard to understand at times. Let me tell you one thing, if I ever saw a determined people they are here. Everybody works.

George always told his family Hitler would have had to kill every last person in England to defeat Great Britain. England literally became a floating dock, jammed with nearly a million and half Americans and 15 million tons of American supplies.

March 1, 1944 England
Dear Mother,
    Airmail and vmail travels much faster than regular mail. I received your letter of the 19th on the 28th and was proud to get it. Well mother, most of the fences here are shrub or stone and every foot of space has been utilized. There's quite a bit of timber but they don't seem to cut it up like we do. Most of the crops seem to be small grains. Almost all of their homes are marble, stone or brick and of fair quality. You see nothing to compare with our shacks. We have been getting good eats. Of course we probably won't get much fresh fruits but plenty of canned fruits and juices. We do get some fresh vegetables. Well mother there isn't a thing to be

George and his sister, Carmen. For every letter he would write to his parents during the war, primarily discussing the weather and agriculture of his current location, he would write one to Carmen evaluating the local women.

Officers of the 196th Field Artillery Battalion. From reader's view, top row left to right. According to GWL, first two unlisted then: J. P. Morgan, Lynn Corcelius, George Looney. Bottom row: Sinkler Schloze, George Himmelman, and Vance Boren. Captain Morgan died of a heart attack July 19, 1944 in France. Due to the winter coats, stands to reason this picture was taken around February/March while still in England.

worried about. As long as I can stay on the left side of the road I'll make it alright. Well this leaves me in the best of health and spirit and hope it finds you in same.

PS. These pounds and shillings are killing me. I just hold out my hand and tell them to take what they want.

"Mail was indispensable. It motivated us. We couldn't have won the war without it." One GI from Ken Burns': "The War."

March, 1944 England
Dear Mother,
Just a few lines to let you know I'm getting along fine. If I keep the appetite I have had lately, I'm afraid all my clothes are going to get too small for me. Everybody is very friendly and wants to do everything they can for us. The women have offered to do any sewing we have to be done. Having a wonderful time.

March 7, 1944 England

Dear Mother,
It seems that it takes about 12 to14 days for airmail going that way. We got in on part of the winter when we first got here but the last two days have been beautiful. I don't believe they have as many pretty days as we do. We have a little ground so I bought some radishes and lettuce seeds and planted them last week. They are coming up.

You can send a farm boy to Europe to fight but he's still a farm boy.

March 20, 1944 England
Dear Mother and Dad,
I hope you are both feeling okay. As for myself, I couldn't feel better. Getting plenty to eat.
I'm invited out to tea in several homes already. The people are nice as they can be. One of them was a farmer. He seemed to be one of the most influential in the whole of England. He farms about eight or nine

20

hundred acres which is a big farm in anybody's country. Mostly for papa's interest, I will tell a little about what he had. The main crop seems to be small grains. However, he does grow a lot of potatoes. Around four or five hundred (?) per acre.

Most of the work is done by draft horses. He does have a tractor and some American equipment such as drills and feed grinders but liked their disc the best. Heavier than ours. They just don't use mules over here. Don't believe they have ever had the good quality we have though.

They fertilize very heavy and use a lot from Tennessees. (T. V. A.) I believe they take much better care of their manure than we do. He was feeding out a big bunch of cattle. They were in very good shape.

Of course this is an old country and if they didn't handle their land right it would have been worn out long ago. They are not bothered with erosion as we are because the rainfall is very slow. They do rotate their crops.

They (the British) seem to get along okay and evidently like it. But frankly speaking, everywhere you look, I think it is USA all the way. Guess Fletcher is answering the bugle call by now is he not?(Fletcher was married to his oldest sister, Jessie.) He will probably get a little home sick but that will soon wear off. Don't guess I'm supposed to think, but I don't get this paralyzing the schools and other civic organizations as they are doing with millions of soldiers in the US doing nothing, let alone the ones that are not even in the Army that should be.

Officers Boren, Himmelman, Looney and Scholze enjoy one of those ball games in England. "I'm a little sore and beat up. About all I have done the last few days is play ball." GWL 3/44. Though frequently hampered by light rains in England, (2/44 –7/44) GIs still managed to enjoy America's national pastime. A British captain helped them find some athletic equipment.

"They certainly go to a lot of trouble to make the ground look well. Every field is as smooth as can be." GWL 1944. As George stood at this unknown spot in Europe, peering down below thru eyes that by now had seen much and would see so much more, he surely thought of his family and farm back home.

March 20th, 1944 England
Dear Carmen,
As far as I'm concerned, I don't care who goes with who. I'm doing alright myself so that is all that matters. A British captain and his wife ate dinner with us yesterday. They live close by. He is going to get us some athletic equipment and radios if possible. Well I met a girl from Canada at a dance the other night. Feels okay to find somebody like that to talk to. You can compare things with them.

Clearly, Carmen was her brother's confidant concerning the women in his life.

March 24th, 1944 England
Dear Mother,
I spent the afternoon in a RAF officer's home. We had a very nice time and of course I should say we had tea, coffee and sandwiches. Everything has begun to turn green and it makes me want to go fishing.
We have softball and baseball equipment now so we have some big games as well as big arguments. I think everybody is having a good time.

My father dining in the home of a British officer is something I would pay the price of a Super Bowl ticket to see. By now, Allied planes, including the Royal Air Force, had destroyed over 4500 German planes in the last 3 months.

April 1st, 1944 England
Dear Mother,
Got my first big issue of mail today and it sure makes you feel good to get a bunch like that. There is no need of worry, at present anyway. This has been a dismal day. Fairly cold and trying to rain. Sometimes we are able to pick up stations in the US over shortwave. Too bad Fletcher had to be called. Don't guess Andy (who was 4F) ever will be called now. Jesse seems to think the Flannigans (neighbors) are doing a good job of evading the issue.
Andy might be better satisfied if he was out on the farm but trying to farm is alright if you are in the right spot and set up but it is just like the old saying—you can't fertilize a forty acre farm with a fart. Andy has

been used to a little money too long to go out there. (farm) Crops are just being planted here and they certainly go to a lot of trouble to make the ground look well. Every field is just as smooth as it can be. No rocks or stumps. Mother, we get plenty to eat but I would really like to have some cornbread and sweet milk. If you ever get ahold of an extra fruitcake you might send it to me.

Oldest brother, Andy, never went back to farming but eventually became a successful owner of an automotive parts store in Durant, Oklahoma. George's concern for Jesse's husband, Fletcher, followed him throughout the war while his reference to cornbread and milk rekindled childhood memories of my father at our family's kitchen table. With food scarce during the depression on the Looney home place, George would eat cornbread crumpled in a glass of milk like soup. He ate cornbread in this manner for the rest of his life.

April 2, 1944 England
Dear Carmen,
    We got some ball equipment the other day so now we have a big ballgame every afternoon. I had a letter from one of the boys in my old outfit and they are down on the South Pacific. I wouldn't mind being with them but I can imagine the skin looks a little better over here. Has Fletcher had to go yet? I guess John Ike and Gary (his sons) are going to take it pretty hard.
    Guess you have that picture by now. (George, Himmelman, and Scholze in New York). This isn't the classiest joint in New York but it was classy enough for me. It seems we three stags spent about $20 before we got out. The show was good but I didn't think the girls were any too good looking.
    I hear from Wanda quite often. She would like to go to California but couldn't get off from her job. For a dollar an hour, I don't think I would want off. Remember a girl from Denver, Suzanne Miller? She sings over NBC every morning at nine. She is to sing the lead in the opera just out of Denver in May. It will be carried by many stations.

A buck an hour!

GIs call timeout from preparing for war and enjoy a boat ride on the River Avon at Stratford-on-Avon in England. "The water was clear and everything was as green as could be." GWL 4/26/44

April 2, 1944 England
Well Carmen,
    I'm always glad to get a letter or package. That is one call they don't have to make twice. Don't get much candy. I hope everybody is okay. I hope Fletcher gets stationed close to home. If mother and dad every need anything be sure and let me know. I have a little money in the bank there. You can use if necessary. We'll get the scores of opening day over the radio. (Baseball)

Peaceful shot of a rowboat on the River Avon at Stratford-on-Avon. "It was the most beautiful place I have seen in the British Isle." GWL 4/26/44.

George always loved baseball. As a small boy, he would check the newspaper in the front yard mail box each day to see if Babe Ruth hit a homerun.

April 14th, 1944 England
Dear Mother and Dad,
    Was really glad to get the pile of mail and package Carmen sent today. I just spent a few days down in Wales but the weather is much better here and that's not saying too much. It rains nearly every day and even several times a day down there it seems. Just wonder what they would do if they ever really got a good rain. You really see some old buildings over here. There's nothing to see one constructed in the 14th or 15th century. They are made of stone as most all buildings are.
    You asked me how much I weighed. Well I'll tell you, about eleven stones and six pounds. Now do you know anymore than you did? I don't think I ever told you about their money. A five pound note equals twenty dollars. One pound note equals four dollars. (Today it takes about two Yankee bucks for a pound.) How did Fletcher take it when he had to leave? Don't guess John Ike and Gary realize what it meant until Fletcher was gone a few days.
    Yes, I can imagine that PaPa will have a good team of mules by next year. If I were him, I wouldn't sell any of the horse stock for the next year or two. Once this is over, there will be a lot of people trying to buy a good team. If he wants to turn most of the farm out there into pasture and buy some cattle, I'll furnish part of the money. All he has to do is let me know. I'm putting all my savings into bonds anyway. If he wants to, tell him to draw two or three hundred there at the bank and I'll pay it off in the next few months and be glad to. Well

mother, I guess I better answer a few of these letters from the fair sex. This leaves me fine.

On this day, the 196th received alert orders. Translation: be ready for combat.

George's notes here provide further evidence of his short, but distinguished time in the air. "Made in spring of 44' while stationed in Brighton England. Sent to Wales for two week training to observe from Cub plane. Guess it paid off. Got credit for knocking out gun battery late one evening from our Cub in France."

April 14th, 1944 England
Dear Carmen,
I received the box today and looks like it should be enough gum to last for a long time but if I gave it to every kid that asked me for it, I would have given it all away yesterday. While I was in Wales, I went to an American USO show and the British equivalent. The British show put on a little skit around Pistol Packin Mama and Texas Dan was there too.
You don't mean Lois would do anything rash? Had two letters from Wanda yesterday. Also had a letter from Suzanne and a girl from Missouri. (The man actually manages to mention four girls in one paragraph!) *I was listening to the news tonight and heard where Maurice Brit had been awarded the Distinguished Service Cross for actions in Italy. I knew him very well while at the University of Arkansas. He played football. It also stated that he lost one arm. Well a boy came up to me today and wanted me to get a five dollar bill changed to English money for him so I gave it to him and am sending you the $5.00. I think I have a little money there in the bank if you ever need it. Be sure and not check too*

much though. Well I guess Fletcher really had to go. Maybe he won't have to go anywhere out of the US.

April 26th, 1944 England
Dear Carmen,
By the time I take care of my social engagements as well as do the rest of my work, I don't have much time to write. I got to take a little trip last week to Stratford-on-Avon. Of course, that is where Shakespeare was born. Was in the room where he was born and the house's still standing but some parts of it have been rebuilt. The Avon is a river but not very big. The water was clear and everything was as green as could be. It was really a beautiful place, I believe the most beautiful I have seen in the British isle. The river was full of boats and canoes. Naturally I would notice but there seemed to be an awful lot of girls there and some very good looking ones. To top it all off I had tea and cookies in Shakespeare's daughter's tea room. Carmen, I met a girl from Canada and she said she was going to write you. It is okay but don't ever ask her to come to see you cause I'm afraid she might do it if she ever gets back to Canada. She is a nice looking girl but the woods are full of them. Please send me a box of candy and maybe fruitcakes if possible. I don't get too many sweets at present. So Fletcher is a cook. Well at least he'll get all he wants to eat.

Unfortunately Fletcher soon went to the infantry.

April 30, 1944 England
Dear Mother and all,
I just wanted to let you know I am okay. The weather here the last week has been much like the pretty spring days at home. Maybe they really have a summer here after all. Everything is a dark green color just like our garden. Their type of farming is more like taking care of a garden. Have received several letters the last few days so it makes everything seem better.

May 4th, 1944 England
Dear Carmen,
Wanda writes fairly often. She's okay but she just made up her mind a little too fast. Carmen, I'm sure you'd be much better satisfied if you'd get a job close to home. I wouldn't go to California. They say it isn't anything but a rat hole out there. It rained again today as usual so we came in early. Carmen if you ever need anything you can write a check for it.

May 12th, 1944 England
Dear Mother and Dad,
I'm having a good time. It sure does get cold sometimes when it rains. I take my overcoat to the field with me every day and usually use it. A girl from Missouri wrote and asked me to write and request something so I did. Had a letter from her yesterday saying she was sending a box of candy.

May 18th, 1944 England
Dear Mother and Dad,
I think I've told you before about how it rains in Wales. Well to top it off, we were out in the field the other day and it hailed for about ten minutes. Some days

the sun would shine down, the next day would be as cold as the dickens. Just came in from hoeing the garden. I've had a few radishes and the lettuce plants are beginning to head. We have some apple trees which are full of little apples. I received Carmen's candy so I'm not doing so badly.

June 1, 1944 England
Dear Mother and Dad,
I am okay. I'm a little sore and beat up. About all I have done the last two days is play ball. We didn't quit until after 12 pm. (still daylight) so we have plenty of time. Well don't worry about me because I will be alright.

Of course, his parents were already worried but the Allied invasion at Normandy on June 6 increased worry to the max level for countless families back in the states. Written three days after D-Day, George's next letter home shattered once and for all the illusion of a government paid vacation for the Looney's youngest son.

June 9th, 1944 England
Dear Mother,
I would like very much to send you something but it is hard to find anything that doesn't cost an outrageous amount. I'm going to try to send a few things one of these days.
As you can see, I wasn't in on the big show. I have no idea when I'll go but I can give them (Hell). May not be so healthy but I'm anxious to see what it is all about. Mother when and if I do go over just remember 3/4ths of the casualties are the men's own fault and that is the part I think I have enough sense to avoid. There is no need to get alarmed for a long time yet because it might be over before I get there. Of course somebody may get hurt and just in case it might be me, I have a few things to go somewhere. I have the $10,000 insurance in your or Papa's name I don't remember which. The only other thing is the little money in the bank there and the bonds.

George's beloved vegetable garden in Albrighton, England near Wolverhampton. The Arkansas farm boy received orders to ship out to France before the pleasure of eating one bite.

I have around $2700 worth of bonds. I may get more and at any rate there will be enough to finish out the equivalent to $500 of bonds to each Andy, Jesse, Zolon, Carmen, John Ike and Gary. Just in case anything should happen that is the way I would like for you to divide it. You and Papa would have to cash the bonds. You would have what money is left and the insurance. Well it may not be as long as it might seem before I am back home. Don't think it will take long to finish up that part of it after Europe is settled down.

Imagine the terror George's mother felt while digesting her son's words—his will. His parents now knew the battlefields of France would sooner than later replace the sightseeing trips, ball games and tea parties of England. It's a good thing George's mother could not possibly have read the following words from a man who would fight at Hofen, Germany within yards of her son before year's end. *But now and then someone died, who tried harder than you did and was smarter than you and didn't deserve to die. Was everything fate? If so, what was the use of trying so hard.* Robert Wyatt Thrasher from his World War II memoirs: "Popcorn Road to Paris...And Back."

June 12th, 1944 England
Dear Mother and Dad,
We had a good ballgame this afternoon even if my team did get beaten. It has been kinda dry but the crops—potatoes, small grain and sugar beets are looking good. That is the main crops. We just don't have any nights here. There's less than five hours of darkness. I'm sleeping under two and three blankets. It gets fairly warm in the day if it isn't raining but sometimes it is colder than heck even during the day.

Later that day, George's battalion received word to be ready for movement by June 20.

June 12th, 1944 England
Dear Carmen,
Say, Lois is doing okay? I haven't heard from her in several days now.
Saw Marjorie the other night. Need not tell her, but I haven't lost anything there.

We don't know Marjorie, only that she must have at least visited England. We do know George kept his sister, Carmen, a beautiful young woman in her own right, considerably more abreast of his love life than his parents.

June 17th, 1944 England
Dear Mother and Dad,
Played ball all afternoon and came in with a headache. Today was a beautiful day. It may stay clear most of the days but it is odd for it to be clear all day. Our garden is okay. We have turnips almost big enough to eat and the lettuce is beginning to head. Everything is much later over here than at home.
Had a couple of letters from Wanda today. I wish Papa would stop by the bank someday to see if my $100 allotment came in. I bought a $50 money order and am sending it to Papa. If he needs it for anything tell him to use it. If not, just put it in the bank. Someday I might want to buy a boat to ride back home in.

This is George or a buddy at Utah Beach on the Normandy Coast, the location of the 196th Field Artillery Battalion's landing on July 8th, 1944. George has joined the war in probably only the last few minutes, or certainly the last few hours.

Officers Vance Boren, Sinkler Scholze, George Himmelman and George Looney—all tight as brothers during wartime. Visits were infrequent after the war. I believe this caused George regret toward the end of his life.

A bridge outside Carentan on George's first day in France so close to the Normandy coast on July 8. He would see his first dead body by nightfall. "Fired first round about 22:15 (or 10:15 p.m.) on July 9th." GWL

Meanwhile, Hitler, hoping to force the evacuation of London, ordered the launching of more than 9,000 two-ton V-1 rockets across the English Channel that summer, killing almost 6,000 Londoners and destroying some 20,000 homes. George was in nearby Wolverhampton and presumably missed the bombings, but because of censorship of letters home, his parents could not know of his exact location.

June 18th, 1944 England
Dear Mother,

I'm still healthy and eating three good meals a day. About buying Zolon's car, I wouldn't want to give $1300 but I certainly don't blame Papa for getting it if he could. I bought three one hundred dollar bonds which will come to Papa I guess. I told you about buying two before. I also made an allotment of $100 to the bank beginning this month. Don't worry because I am okay.

A Red Cross volunteer in the combat zone, inland of the Normandy coast, shortly after the Allied breakout from the beaches. Many American POWs in Europe received food and aid from the Red Cross.

June 20th, 1944 England
Dear Carmen,

Had a letter from Wanda the other day that said she was getting a better job. She was getting over a dollar an hour where she was. It's about the same old thing here—go to a dance once in a while and a show. Am sorry to hear Reuben is missing. There's a good chance that he may be alright. That gal got too personal so I had to back off.

George stays positive in spite of a potential casualty from home. Reuben was never mentioned in letters again. The next day, the 196th would inch closer to combat, relocating to a camp near Oxford, England.

June 25th, 1944 England
Dear Mother and Dad,

This is one more day raining right now and not too warm. Thank goodness I have a good place to sleep and that is more than some of the boys have. I might add that

this is the first real rain I have seen since coming to England. I was able to buy ten bars of candy yesterday and received a box from Carmen so I have enough to do me for awhile.

The man obviously loved his candy as much as he loved family.

At Normandy, France, a GI rides the mule belonging to the lady with the Red Cross.

June 30, 1944 England
Dear Carmen,

What do you mean writing Wanda about Marjorie? No, I was just kidding, she will be alright. Believe it or not, the mail came in with a letter from Marjorie. Guess I'll have to answer it but don't think I'll kill myself trying to go back to see her. Well I guess you have asked about Himmelman three times. He is a first lieutenant in my battery. The four officers in it (Looney, Himmelman, Scholze, and Boren) have been together for over a year.

The youth of France prepare for war if needed.

That's George perched on an German tank in the Normandy coast area, so combat was still new to him at the time of this picture. Though a quiet and reserved man, he was not camera shy while on his first big "vacation" from the hills of Arkansas.

Glad to hear that mother and dad are doing okay. Don't worry about me. It's the Germans you had better worry about.

For the next week George wrote several letters about mainly the weather, amazed at the incessant rain and lack of a real summer, also referencing his money orders home and reminding all of his insatiable desire for candy. He even assured his mother of his attendance in church. Across the English Channel on the day of the previous letter, the Allies captured Cherbourg, the French port city but in the three weeks since D-Day, the Americans had suffered 22,000 casualties. On July 3, the battalion moved, near South Hampton, England, to Camp Holmes, a marshalling area where last minute preparations, like waterproofing of vehicles, were made prior to crossing The Channel. His next letter of July 8th came without foreshadow and, no doubt, caused his mother's breath to arrive with the rapid and irregular bursts of gunfire.

July 8th, 1944 England
Dear Mother and all,
Well here I am aboard a transport awaiting for the rest of our men so we can sail. We were very fortunate in that we drew a special made transport ship. The facilities are very good. There are four triple deck beds

in my room thus holding 12 men. Each of us have a locker. Just outside the door in the hall there is a drinking fountain. Just across the hall is the latrine with 4 showers in it. Down the hall is the officer's mess hall. Of course we have much better facilities than the enlisted men. At least though they are fixed up better than I thought. They are a little crowded in the sleeping quarters but have showers.
So far the meals have been very good. I have had an appetite that just won't stop. Well mother by the time you get this I will probably be across. It will be held for a while (the mail). Tell everybody hello.

Could there ever have been a more anxiously anticipated and hoped for letter than George's first one after sailing a mere 70 miles across The Channel to join the fight? I can see his mother, loaded with worry, hurrying to that front yard mail box with the frequency George once checked it for news of a Babe Ruth homer! The following letter was written two days after his landing at Utah Beach and by this time, he'd already seen combat.

July 10th, 1944 France
Dear Mother and Dad,
I am somewhere in France but don't be alarmed

because I am alright. I've tried to talk to a few of the French people but can't do much good. Most of the people seem very friendly. The sidewalks are lined with them laughing and waving when we go through towns. The farmland is just about the same as England except I believe the fields are a little smaller. Everything is as green as it can be as far as you can see. Well mother there is very little I can tell you except that things look very good for us.

In two days, and on my birthday no less, my father would direct artillery fire from a cub plane and knock out a German gun

Two bicyclers ride in front a chateau somewhere in Europe. It's hard to believe the world is about to explode from this picture.

battery. If only I could swallow back the words.

July ? 1944 France
Dear Mother and Dad,
Just a few lines to let you know I am okay. The sun doesn't shine too much but not much rain. It seems to be a little warmer than in England. Should have seen me taking a bath in a big pond under an apple tree. Have a suit of wools dirty so I think I'll wash them in gas tomorrow. My job may be a little dangerous but I'm enjoying it to say the least. So Wanda and her mother came to see you, huh? Guess Wanda had a lot to talk about, did she not?

Wanda seemed as resilient as the Allied advance.

July 23rd, 1944 France
Dear Mother and Dad,
It has been raining the last few days which makes it very uncomfortable. I have my tent up and have managed to keep my bed roll dry. You know what I came over here for so I guess you can imagine what I am doing. Pretty tough on the unlucky ones but not so bad otherwise. All a person can do is just do what he can

Location unknown. "You don't have to go far to be thankful that the war is being fought over here instead of home." GWL 7/19/44.

George records more of the never ending destruction of W.W. II in an unknown location.

"Not much left of two houses along the RR tracks." Location unknown. GWL

and hope for the best. We have a radio and get reports. Sounds good but looks like the first break failed. There is no doubt what is going to happen but a lot of things can happen between now and then.

Well mother, I think of all of you a lot and hope to see you again before too long. Don't worry because that won't help. I just hope for the best which I feel like will happen.

That night, a truck driver, too close to the front line, smelled gun powder and caused a brief panic by spreading a false gas attack alarm. At the time of this letter, the Allies were still bogged down in the thick hedgerows inland of the Normandy coast and advancing at the rate of less than a football field a day. Things were about to change.

July 29th, 1944 Apple Orchard France
Dear Mother and Dad,
    Looks like there is going to be a good apple crop

Okay, so it's not Marilyn Monroe with Bob Hope, but this show, somewhere in France, was surely a welcome break in the fighting.

this year. They are about as big as eggs now and beginning to have a taste to them. Nearly every French home has one or two kegs of cider at about two or three thousand gallons each. Just like England, it doesn't rain

The country barber shop. Haircut or a dog license?

Somewhere on the battle ground in Europe, a smiling George wraps his arms around his loyal radio operator, James Everett Allen and a local. Frank Williams, George's equally devoted jeep driver, stands left of the unidentified lady.

A grape vineyard along the Rhine river of France escapes the wrath of war.

George Himmelman, George Looney and Sinkler Scholze. "Along the French and German border." GWL

a lot but keeps trying. If I had not come over here I would have been disappointed. Just have to let nature take its course. Took a good hot shower yesterday and traded my dirty clothes for clean ones. I'll have a lot to tell you. You don't have to go far to be thankful that the war is being fought over here instead of home. Tell everybody I said hello.

This apple orchard was 600 yards from the German front line! The references to the apples of France became as common as his weather reports. Remember the scene in Private Ryan with the soldier eating an apple from the ground during battle? Very believable after reading George's letters. George wrote the 7/29 letter only four days after American bombs barely missed him at St. Lo, France. (More on this later) Though George would never have shared this info and cause worry to his family, censors would have edited it out anyway. The American advance

Everett Allen by the radio, Sinkler Schloze with the pipe and George.

The incomparable beauty of French architecture along the Seine River in Paris as seen from the eyes of George in August of 1944. "Paris is truly a beautiful place and in my opinion it is France. Without it there would be nothing." GWL 10/25/44

That's George sitting and Sinkler Schloze standing.

escalated rapidly after the bombing of St. Lo.

July 30, 1944 France
Dear Aunt and Uncle,

All I can say is that every time a shell goes over my head I just dig a little deeper. The less of France I see of it the less I think of it. Sanitary conditions are terrible. Some homes even keep the stock in the same house with them.

These French people really like their cider. Every home has two or three big barrels of it. Most of them have plenty of cognac too. Of course our boys wouldn't drink any of it. The situation looks very good though some of the things you see don't look so good to you. Just hope I'll be seeing you before too long.

George at Siegfried line near Cologne, Germany in 9/44. "We and Germans both ran out of supplies here." GWL.

July 30th, 1944 France
Dear Carmen,

Mother said this girl from England was writing pretty heavy. Just as soon as I found out she had the bright lights of New York in her eyes, I quit writing to her. You can do the same as far as I'm concerned. My social affairs in France, just aren't. You know what I came over here for so there isn't any use to take the time to explain. I have seen a lot and will probably see more. I hear they are going to have church today close by at 3 pm. If possible, think I'll go.

August 7th, 1944 France
Dear Mother and Dad,

How do you like my stationary? It is German special and a good find because I was beginning to need some. You can find just about anything you want but the trouble is carrying it. Spent one night with Germans all

George travels the Autobahn in Germany, possibly during his time with the Red Ball Express during the fall of '44 or shortly before his entry into the gloom of the Hürtgen Forest. "I was in command of a truck platoon. We delivered 2372 tons of urgently needed supplies, traveling over 4,000 miles." GWL

around me and came out alright. Didn't have much to eat for a couple of days though. You know as much if not more than we do. We have a radio and found five German batteries for it the other day so we should keep up with the news for a while.

Every field has an apple orchard so there should be plenty of them. Found a good cherry tree the other day and filled up. I guess I saw the happiest Frenchmen yesterday morning I have seen yet. We are in position close to his home and I was standing in front of it when he walked up. When he saw it was still standing, he just about jumped up and down. He later offered us a calf if we wanted to butcher it but we got all we need to eat. I did have fried chicken the other morning.

It seems that the Germans took most of the horses they came across because they need them to transportation and a lot of the cattle get killed but in most cases, they get their livestock back. Some of our boys doctored a cat the other day that had a big gash on his head and leg.

August 13th, 1944 France
Dear Mother and Dad,

As long as you don't hear from me you will know that everything is okay. The weather has been perfect and the Air Force is really doing a job. Maybe it won't be long till Hitler and his bunch get the works. I am positive that the war over here will be over before Christmas (wrong) but naturally we will have paid a price. Maybe I'll get a little trip to the Pacific then.
I have three men operating with me (Everett Allen, Frank Williams and ?) So we carry everything on the jeep. We have a small burner and prepare most of our meals. Getting to be a good cook. Can fry good bacon. Have been finding a few ripe apples, pears and plums

Oh, the deception of tranquility thrown off from the breath taking views of this unknown European village during wartime. Has this village retained its beauty and link to the past or fallen prey to the progress scars of today's modern world?

Not exactly the Hilton but GWL and associates made concessions with respect to accommodations during the war. "We are getting to where we can build a log hut in nothing flat." GWL wrote on 1/3/45 but this hut was built earlier, before the onslaught of winter.

"Just wish I could tell you where I've been and what I have seen." GWL in a letter home dated 8/44. George, a seasoned combat veteran, stands by a bunker along the Siegfried line near Aachen, Germany. Aachen was the first German city taken by the Allies in October 1944.

George ponders at Siegfried line. Hitler ordered this 630 kilometer defense system built along the German western frontier in a vain attempt to thwart an Allied invasion. The dragon's teeth were intended as tank traps. The tankers simply used a bulldozer to cover the teeth, and then drove over them.

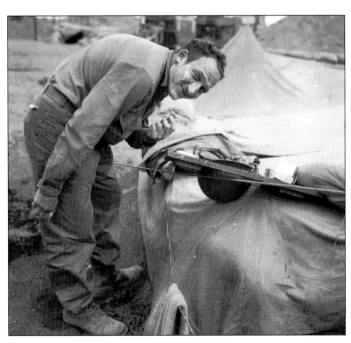

A little moring shave, at the ammo dump. GI's were required to shave, and it was often with cold water out of a helmut.

George's jeep follows a truck moving toward the tranquility of the famous Notre Dame church at the Meuse river crossing at Dinant, Belgium. The German's ultimate defeat at the Bulge prevented them from reaching the river.

lately so I will make it alright.

To be sure, since D-Day, the American Air Force had controlled the air and the German Luftwaffe proved as effective as the French Air Force which is to say none at all. Repeated Allied bombing of Germany's oil plants had reduced the Luftwaffe's fuel supply to considerably less than 50,000 tons, down from 180,000 tons in April. Germany's noose around southern France was slipping rapidly and port cities such as Marseilles were receiving Allied supplies. On August 16, Hitler reluctantly ordered all remaining German troops evacuated from the Normandy area.

August 28th, 1944 France
Dear Mother,

Just wish I could tell you where I've been and what I have seen lately. Talk about the beautiful women, there are plenty of them in France. As you get deeper into France you see the real French people. In Normandy, I really wondered how the French people felt. Now I know. I've never seen people so happy in my life to really be hungry which a lot of them are. The war looks very good but there may be a lot of fighting yet.

It rained last night and the day but I was fortunate enough to be in a German barrack so I made it alright. And on top of that, they had a small garden so we had plenty of tomatoes and onions. By the way we are finding plenty of ripe apples now. As long as you don't hear from me, I'm okay so don't worry.

George's 8/28 letter provided no hint of his participation three days prior in one of the most joyous celebrations in modern history—the liberation of Paris. Obviously, there's no mention of his near miss by the German sniper at the Arch de Triumph either. And what about the German barrack? Like those guys peacefully surrendered their food and shelter to George and his pals.

August 30th, 1944 France
Dear Carmen,

It's unlikely George knew he was photographing such a historic location as the Notre Dame church, nestled in the incomparable beauty of Dinant, Belgium.

I always heard that the French girls were beautiful but now I know. The English girls can't hold them a light to run by. Kind of hard to talk with them but that doesn't matter much. Don't worry about what we have to eat cause we have plenty. I even shot a duck the other day and had fried duck for breakfast. Shot him through the neck at about 40 yards. My radio operator received a box of candy yesterday so we will do alright for a few days.

It has been raining the last couple of days. Sent $350 home in the last two months. Wish I had saved a little of it lately but we'll make out. The people try to give you everything nearly.

Fresh from the triumph of Paris, the Allies were now moving

"I helped build this in Hürtgen Forest but did not get to sleep in it. Ordered up with infantry late that afternoon." GWL. Hürtgen was a casualty disaster for the Americans. For example, of the 50,000 Americans who entered the forest with the 28th Infantry Division, only 7,000 left under their own power. Worse, the Battle of Hürtgen served no significant military purpose.

across France at near warp speed, pushing the Germans toward their Fatherland.

September 12th, 1944 France
Dear Mother & Dad,

The sun is shining though it did rain for two or three days and it was fairly cold but has turned a little warm. About the main crop through France is wheat and there's a good crop in the field. It was not harvested so the Germans could not take it. Looks kind of funny to see the farmers hauling it on carts with two or three horses hooked in a single line pulling them. Many of them use teams. We parked by a large garden the other night and I got me a sack full of carrots, onions and cucumbers, then an old woman gave us a pound of butter so we are doing okay.

A few days ago the Air Corps shot up a column of German vehicles on the road and we moved in to capture the men. Some of the vehicles were burning but I got a good camera off of one that wasn't. (The incident George referred to in his note that he left with the camera by his bed.)

I'm now able to tell you I visited Paris. Believe me it is a beautiful place. I saw more pretty girls there in fifteen minutes than I ever saw in England. It was more like a modern city in the US than anything I have been in yet. People are really glad to see an American. One man gave me 10 quarts of champagne. You hear about as much news as I do but everything looks very good now.

By the time of his 9/12 letter, George had already earned his first Bronze Star. Also by now, George's jeep driver, Frank Williams, had in all probability, personally consumed 10 quarts of champagne—but that's a story further down the trail.

September 23, 1944 France

A GI hunkers down in his foxhole either in late 1944 or early 1945. It was one of the coldest winters in the last quarter of a century and 15,000 GIs suffered from frostbite and trench-foot during The Bulge. George spoke of sleeping nights in the snow during this time.

Dear Mother and all,

I've really been on the move but hope to get a few days rest now. It has been raining quite a lot the last few days and is fairly cold at night. The sun is warm when it shines but it doesn't shine much. Have been in Belgium and it is a very pretty country. The homes and buildings are far ahead of France. The people seem to be cleaner in their living conditions.

To say George was on the move is to say Hitler had riled up

George hunts for deer not Germans, in the Ardennes, probably after the explosion of The Bulge. Raised as a hunter in the hills of Arkansas, George was a good shot and won a pair of boots from Lt. Coyne in a shooting contest. I never saw or knew of George to hunt after the war.

The Americans destroyed a german tank. The Nazi 88's also out performed our tanks and dealt misery to the Allies throughout the war.

The good guys capture a still functional 88, mounted on a tank chassis for better mobility. This gun was incredibly accurate.

Europe a bit. During this time and into October, George commanded a twenty truck unit on the famous Redball Highway, hauling over 2300 tons of supplies while traveling over 4,000 miles.

September 28th, 1944 France
Dear Mother and Dad,

There should have been a $100 check come to the bank sometime in August for July and each month thereafter. Separate from that I sent $75 at the end of July and August but am keeping that this month. The people are bringing out some things that they have hid from the Germans so I might want to buy something and send it home.

October 13th, 1944 Germany
Dear Mother and Dad,

Guess you noticed where I am. Everything looks good. I saw a good looking herd of cattle this morning. What few people I have seen seem to be friendly. Of course we don't have much to do with them. Some of them speak but others don't even look at you. I passed one house this morning and a little girl waved so I spoke to her. Another came running out and gave me an apple but I didn't eat it. It has been pretty today but usually rains at night if only a little. It has begun to turn fairly cold now too.

You know I spoke of the apples. Well we have been having plenty for a long time. Most everybody gives us all we want so we usually walk out and get them. They have so many they don't miss them anyway.

Apples, snapples. Give me a beer and a burger! George

probably wrote this letter from or near Aachen, the first major German city captured by the Allies and virtually destroyed in the process. For the first time, the civilians of Germany were joining the ever increasing population of European refugees.

October 18th, 1944 Belgium
Dear Mother and Dad:,

Well it is still raining and don't look like it is going to quit. I washed some clothes today but don't know when they will get dry. These people over here don't know what cotton and corn are. It looks like they depend on their cattle and apples for a living.

There's very little plowing going on. The Germans took most of the horses as they left. It seems the Germans took just about everything that they wanted and paid for nothing. They would go around every day and pick up milk. One man said they took fourteen of his cows. Just in case you wonder about it we are getting plenty to eat. Most all of the rations have some sort of candy in them. There's a hospital close by so the officers from our battalion and the nurses had a dance. Wasn't bad at all.

October 25th, 1944 Belgium
Dear Aunt and Uncle,

It was a good chase while it lasted but looks like we may have to fight for a while now. Everything looks very good but the weather. I wouldn't be surprised if it doesn't get kinda cold this winter if this thing doesn't end. I have been in five countries. But no where have I seen anything to compare with the USA. I believe the homes are newer and cleaner in Belgium than anywhere I've been. Only in the best of homes and building do you find modern plumbing and fixtures and they are few and

36

far between. Maybe I should make an exception and that is Paris. Paris is truly a beautiful place and in my opinion it is France. Without it there would be nothing. You get about as much news about the war as we do but I don't see how Germany can last until Christmas.

If only George knew the extent of his understatement concerning the winter weather, I doubt he'd have mentioned it for fear of sending home a dark cloud of worry. Though the Allies had pushed the Germans back more than 360 miles toward their own border, the Allied optimism concerning the war's end, eventually proved near fatal, blinding the Allies to the massive

The beginning of an unknown grave site. I wonder how many more crosses rest there today?

German build up for the surprise counter offensive forever known as the Battle of the Bulge.

Postmark on the envelope is December 1st, 1944
Belgium
Dear Mother and Dad,
*   I don't guess you've heard from me in a long time, but I haven't been in much position to write. I was lucky enough to get to come back on a three day leave. We are*

"Hitler youth somewhere in Germany, German boys taught early." GWL. According to my mother, GWL strongly disapproved of the execution of a Hitler youth by an American officer for spitting on another officer.

living in a hotel just like a king. So far it hasn't been so cold but we did have a little snow the other day. We are going to have a big turkey dinner tonight and a dance afterwards. Don't know how I'll get along with these Belgium girls yet. Everything okay.

Note, over one month since his last letter home but the quest for survival will monopolize the best of men's time. The war's darker side was now practically riding in George's jeep but he still managed to tickle the light and sound more like a man vacationing than dealing with the brutal weather and terror of the Hürtgen Forest. Though George evidently saw a three day break in the action, I believe the previous correspondence was his most misleading to date.

During the most frightening of frightening times and though separated by the Atlantic Ocean, a mother's intuition told her something was amiss. George had written on the letter's envelope that his mother had mentioned her dream/nightmare of receiving a letter from him with a dirty patch on it. And the preceding letter's envelope contained exactly such a stain.

In only two days from the letter's postmark date, George,

George's convoy crossing a 1,370 foot bridge made by American engineers on the Rhine.

separated and left behind by his battalion, would earn his second Bronze Star for leading the ten walking wounded from the death trap of Hürtgen, including toting one GI on his back who was unable to walk and trying to surrender.

I found the following on the Hürtgen in George's private stash of notes by his bed after his passing: *Cut off for 3 days. It was from this position that 2 soldiers were sent out on patrol in the night. One stepped on a mine and blew one leg off. Another patrol was sent out to recover him but they were fired on and had to return. You could hear this boy pleading for help. The day we pulled back he was recovered and still had presence of mind to tell them his body had been booby trapped and he was disarmed before he was moved. I had gone out the night before with the 10 walking wounded. Am told he survived.*

For those American soldiers, fortunate enough to survive, most echoed the following sentiment: *The Hürtgen Forest was the worst.* Tom Galloway from Ken Burns "The War." The Bulge was just around the corner when Hell would turn inside out.

January 3rd, 1945 Germany
Dear Mother and Dad,
I know I didn't write very often but I wasn't in much of a position to write about that time. The Germans are trying to cause a little trouble but don't think they will get very far. The last few days have been pretty nasty. It is either foggy or trying to snow. Has been fairly cold a few days and nights too. We carry a stove with us and are getting to where we can build a log hut in nothing flat. I received a box of cookies from Wanda yesterday. Carmen's box came the other day. I have had plenty to eat anyway. Yes, Himmelman and I are still together. There are four officers in the battery and we have the same four that started out together in December of 42.

"More German prisoners of war. Good Germans." GWL. For many German prisoners, capture was a relief. Food and shelter and no more fighting. Rations were meager for American POW's and GIs suffered heavy weight losses during capture.

With Germany close to surrender, George observes the streets of Leipzig, Germany after his assignment to the Military Government Security Force in February of 1945. "We took a good home for my office here with the Military Government. I had command of one unit and placed guards at important installations, post offices, banks, food warehouses." GWL.

"What's left of a bridge and city after bombing in Luxembourg." GWL. Luxembourg abandoned its policy of neutrality during the war and joined the Allies.

(Himmelman, Scholze, Boren and Looney) I'll be seeing you before next New Year's Day.

Again, over a month since his last letter but only one day after George escaped the Hürtgen Forest, he found his battalion at Kalterberg, Germany, a small town near the Ardennes sector, to settle down for the winter. Now in a supposedly quiet area, George could barely dry his boots so to speak before 500,000 Germans attacked on 12/16/44 and kick started The Battle of The Bulge. George's reference to the Germans trying to cause a little trouble reinforces his crown as master of the understatement, as does his mention of the pretty nasty weather since temperatures dipped well below zero before the thaw of spring. Predictably, George's words provide no clue to his precarious situation the previous weeks, or his vital role at nearby Höfen, Germany during The Bulge. Though danger would still shadow George's

German prisoners. "We had 54 prisoners which were placed in one circle and told not to move all night. They did not," wrote GWL after the bombings of St. Lo.

The MGSG on the side of the helmet stands for Military Government Security Force. Best guess—George took these pictures (above and below) in or near Leipzig, mid February to April of 1945.

trail for several more months, he was now personally seeing the worst of the war in the rearview mirror. Much, much more on The Bulge later.

January 8th, 1945 Germany
Dear Mother and Dad,
    We have really had a white Christmas. In fact there is still plenty of snow around. To say the least we have had plenty of snow cream to eat. I went deer hunting today. Didn't get many deer but did find several fresh tracks in the snow. Several of the outfits have had fresh deer to eat. Well mother I hope you all have had a good Christmas and a Happy New Year. We didn't do so badly over here. At least we've had plenty to eat. Well mother

I'll be home before next Christmas. Just keep my clothes in shape.

    While still fighting, a military ceremony is stilled performed. Before Christmas, the German tanks had given up on penetrating the little village and had gone around to the south.

February 1, 1945 Germany
Dear Mother and Dad,
    Our snow is about gone. I hope to see the sun again some day. Don't look like the Germans are going to be able to stop the Russians now. Haven't heard anything from Fletcher yet. But I'm sure everything okay.

Though unknown to George at the time, he records history here as Russians prepare to enter a building at Leipzig, Germany to discuss terms of Germany's inevitable surrender.

George claims a car near the war's end. "They said we had to register them so I put some numbers on it and went on driving it." GWL.

George and friends discover an abandoned German hanger and airfield. This picture perfectly symbolizes the German Lufwaffte during the war—crippled. Within two weeks of D-Day, Allied fighters outnumbered the German fighters 8-1.

Yep, the Germans were up to something but (pun) never got off the ground.

George stands between some unique German engineering. Note the German helmet on the ground in the picture's far right.

More of the German's experimental aircraft.

To borrow from George Harrison: "It's been a long, long lonely winter but here comes the sun." Many boys, as George referred to young GIs, would still stay behind and populate new cemeteries in France and Belgium, but the Germans were whipped and once again fleeing toward the homeland.

March 2, 1945 Germany
Dear Carmen,
Most towns don't have electricity but I guess we can manage to get along without that. I wasn't in the place you spoke of at the time the massacre took place. Thank god. But was later on. They can do things like that but believe me most of them are pitiful creatures when they get cornered. Haven't heard from Zolon but don't think you need to worry. He is not up where the fighting takes place.

He's referring to the Malmedy Massacre when the Germans murdered 83 American prisoners at Malmedy, Belgium in the snow on 12/17/44. Word of the massacre infuriated American troops and some battalion commanders returned an eye for an eye, refusing to take German prisoners in the Ardennes. And yes, the war gods spared brother Zolon from combat in the Pacific and he would eventually return home safely.

March 22, 1945 Germany
Dear Mother and Dad,
Had a letter from Fletcher the other day. He seems to be doing okay. I see where his bunch is on the move again so he may be seeing a little fresh action now. The weather has been beautiful the last couple of weeks and believe me we sure do appreciate it. I wouldn't stay another winter where I did the last one if they gave me the whole damn country. Nothing but rain, fog, snow and mud.
I don't blame Papa if he can get $2500 for the farm. I would sell it. Land will be high for a few years but it will go down after some of the money happy people spend what they have made. I picked up a long barrel .22 target pistol the other day. Might even get to where I can hit something one of these days. Well I'm doing fine eating two meals a day. Too lazy to get up for breakfast. Hope everybody is well.

In charge of fifty men, George was now working for the Military Government Security Guards in Eastern Germany. His primary mission: to keep law and order in a country now without a functional governing body; also, apprehend German soldiers who'd tried to infiltrate civilian society by shedding their uniforms. And like a burlesque dancer in Paris revealing a bit more, for the first time, his words revealed a tad of the misery dealt by the past winter.

March 31, 1945 Germany
Dear Carmen,
You can tell those people over there who are taking so good care of those Kraut eating bastards, if they had seen what I did the other morning they would change their attitude. Some of our boys escaped from the Germans and our kitchen was the first place they came to. They were absolutely starved to death. Some of them have lost fifty and sixty pounds in six or eight weeks. I saw that with my own eyes. I just wished they would bring some of the boys over here who have been doing

the fighting back over there to guard the Germans we have over there. I'll tell you one thing, they would get their ass in high gear and a damn sight less to eat. I did get the package with the popcorn in it.

His sister, Carmen, had either worked at or visited a German P. O. W camp and George's words accurately reflect the feelings of many G.I.s in Europe who resented the relatively plush treatment German P. O. W.'s received back in the States. Thankfully I only saw my dad this angry once—after I'd broken into a grade school at age eleven. Reading this letter, I feel the bass rumble of his voice and the heat from his laser stare as if I were eleven years old again.

April 11, 1945 Germany
Dear Carmen,
This non fraternization law is killing me. There are some good looking girls in Germany but we can't have anything to do with them. At times they will go out of the way just to see if they can get a little consideration. We went out of our way the other day to make one clean up our hall and latrine. That took the grin off her face. You can tell all those Kraut eating bastards over there they had better make good of their time while there because they don't have a damn thing to come home to.

In March alone, Allied war planes released 67,000 tons of bombs on Germany. With no more targets, the bombings stopped by mid-April. Allied bombings had killed 600,000 German civilians, mostly women and children.

April 30, 1945 Germany
Dear Mother and Dad,
Everything sounds very good tonight so maybe it won't be very long now. I don't see how and by all means why they have held on as long as they have. I'm in the heart of Germany. Most of the German people have been very nice to us, contrary to what you might think. However, there is another way to look at it. How

A historic picture of sort. Taken in Coburg, Germany on V-E Day (Victory in Europe Day). The act of military surrender was signed on May 7 in Rheims, France or May 8 in Berlin so not sure which date. Ironically, during the Cold War years, Coburg became part of Western Germany though surrounded by the Iron Curtain or East German territory on 3 sides.

41

could they be any other way? I actually think they think we are going to help take care of the Russians when they come in. Just have a lot in store that they don't know about. I may end up in the Pacific.

George could not know that on the day he wrote this letter, Hitler would shoot himself in the mouth. With the Allies now moving through one German village to another, civilians would drape sheets and towels from windows as sign of surrender.

The Germans concern for the incoming Russians was justified. In retaliation for Germany's attack of Russia, upon arrival, the Russians looted and burned villages and gang raped hundreds of thousands of women. Many young people of today actually believe the U.S. fought with Germany against Russia. Remember, George and friends, casting a narrow eye toward the Pacific, knew nothing of the big bomb in the works.

May, 1945 Germany
Dear Mother and Dad,

I bought a few things but not a lot. Everything was very high and I was rather limited on money. I'm sending it all in one big box. The set is for you and papa, the pipe Andy, one piece of lace to Arness and one to Jesse. There are two small brass articles. Give one to Carmen and the other to Jesse. The two pieces of lace are very small but as Belgium is noted for its hand lace, I thought that would be okay. I hope to get everybody something fairly nice before I come home. I'm writing this by the light of a fire in a log house we built. Everything okay. Had a good chicken dinner today.

George and the Allies had already discovered the concentration camps and Germany's internal collapse was total and complete with virtually no utilities, or running water or food, and no form of government. Throughout all the chaos and with Germany's formal surrender only days way, George still displays his generosity to his family of yesterday, reminding his family of today that some things, in fact, do not change. He absolutely never and I reiterate never, thought of himself before family.

May 14th, 1945 Czechoslovakia
Dear Mother and Dad,

Yes, the damn thing is over here. If the Japs had enough sense to surrender, everything would be okay. As you can see I have added another country to my list. The main difference here is the lack of mechanization. Well mother, I don't mind telling you now. I felt very badly for Jesse and the boys last November when I heard that Fletcher was on his way over. A man in the infantry where I was a few times, just didn't hang around very long. Any part of it was rough. There is little to worry about now cause I think the German people are so glad we are here instead of the Russians that nothing will happen. I'll let you know when to have my clothes cleaned.

Nazi Germany, proclaimed by Hitler to endure for thousands of years, was toast after twelve years of terrorizing Europe while George finally admits to his long time concern for his brother-in-law, Fletcher. In the later part of 1945, George's sister, Jessie thought she saw a mirage—a vision of some sort while shaking her dust mop on the front porch of her quaint one story frame house in Charleston, Arkansas, a one street light, one policeman type of town. A mystery person, reed thin in proportion, was slowly walking through low clouds simmering above the street's

blacktop. Jessie's small children, Gary and John Ike, rushed to the front yard to the sound of a loud wail only to find their mom, still wearing her nightgown, embraced as one with a man in an army uniform. It was no mirage—it was Fletcher who beat the

Another postcard from the war, location unknown, though this looks like a castle in Coburg, Germany. George was in Coburg on VE Day. "I lived in this house about a week." GWL. The man grew up in a frame house in the hills of Arkansas without an indoor toilet and drank from a water well on the screened side porch. He must have felt awed and right at home simultaneously.

odds and had come home to Charleston where he remained until his death in 1999 at age 87. Fletcher served as the local mailman for approximately 35 years. I remember going on his mail route with him as a youngster.

George eating only minutes before crossing into Czechoslovakia shortly after VE Day. "I had charge of a city when Russian communists came to take over. I stopped them for one day but then headquarters said hands off and I gave it to them the next day." GWL. He'd already collected all the guns in the town from the locals.

Chapter Six

My Baby Wrote Me A Letter

On May 22, 1945, with the war over in Europe for approximately two weeks, my father sent his first letter home without the restraint of censorship. Shortly thereafter, the newspaper in Ft. Smith, which is located seventeen miles from his hometown of Charleston, saw fit to print the entire letter. I feel the same way six decades later.

Dear Mother and Dad:
I am now able to tell you a lot of things I have never told before. You can keep this letter and let the rest read it because I don't think I will try to write it to everybody. I left New York on February 10, 1944, and landed in Scotland February 22. (His birthday) Boarded the train

George near St. Lo France—before or after his near death at the hands of American bombers? On July 24, 1944, 3,000 Allied war planes were to carpet bomb the St. Lo area. Bad weather forced cancellation but not before 1,600 bombers had already left England and following the smoke lines, accidentally killed 25 men of the US 30th infantry. The next day was worse.

at Grenock and rode to a little town near Wolverhampton, England. Left there around the first of July and landed in Normandy the 8th. Went into position the 9th and fired our first concentration of 20 mi. until eleven o'clock the morning of the 20th. From then on, the picnic was over.

My battalion is a separate unit not attached to any division. We were always in the First Army, but shifted from one division to another as we were needed. Of course we weren't needed where there was no fighting, so you know what that meant. I was a forward observer, so therefore I spent a lot of my time up with the infantry.

Took a few trips up in a cub plane but crashed up landing one day and decided that it wasn't too healthy. (Yea, yea I know.)

When we first landed we were attached to the 9th Division, which was just outside of Carenton. Here the fighting was rugged and slow. Sometimes you would wonder if there was any future in it, then came the St. Lo breakthrough.

I was with the 3rd Battalion of the 60th regiment. Our mission was to bypass everything, get to our objective, and hold at all costs. We jumped off at 11:00

On the way to Paris from George's privately operated vehicle. Could the Americans have possibly imagined the Super Bowl champ like reception awaiting?

Frank Williams manuevers George's jeep into Paris. Soon Frank will accept one too many "dranks" and turn over the trailer hitched to the rear of the jeep.

A sign tells George, Frank Williams, and James Everett Allen that Paris is just around the bend. "We crossed the Seine River here on August 24, 1944." GWL. The liberation of Paris remained less than 24 hours away.

A youngster wearing his birthday suit greets the Allies' jeep in Paris? (Another of George's notes say this was Germany.)

and evidently found somewhat of a weak spot in the German line. We fought and walked 4 and 1/2 miles and were at our objective by 3 pm, only to find out that the other two battalions had been held up and could not reach their objective that day. Just in case you don't realize what that meant, one battalion is supposed to protect the other's flank. Well, there we sat away out in front with nobody on either flank. That night the Germans closed in all around us, but the next morning an armored cavalry unit fought through to us and I was relieved and went back for a rest.

If you remember St. Lo is where the big bombing took place. It was all planned for July 24th, but due to poor visibility it was put off until the 25th. However, it was not decided to put it off until the last minute, so therefore, all the preparation had taken place. In fact, a few of the bombers appeared and dropped their bombs. Just as a precaution against getting hit by our own bombs we had pulled back about a thousand yards. When we started back to our old position we found that the Germans had moved into our foxholes. They were soon run out again though.

A prelude of the hoopla to come, a mademoiselle applauds the sight of George and friends entering Paris.

Lt. Looney celebrates with more Parisians. George quickly developed amnesia concerning the women of England after meeting their counterpart from France.

The celebration begins! GWL, the master of the understatement, wrote "quite a show." Unfortunately the break in the fighting lasted only 3 days and the worst was still ahead.

Party on! Don't know that I ever saw a brighter smile on George. "I have never seen in any place such joy as radiated from the faces of the people of Paris this morning." Unknown correspondent as quoted from the book: "The War."

A wounded but smiling GI, headed for medical attention, receives rock star attention as the Americans enter Paris.

Like milling the streets after their favorite team's victory, Parisians enjoy freedom after 5 years of German occupation.

After maneuvering through the streets of Paris, Allies approach the Arch de Triumph, arriving at approximately one pm.

George, Frank and Everett at the Arch. Within hours, maybe only minutes, George will narrowly escape death, avoiding one German sniper's bullet by inches—twice! If George did not have nine lives during the war, he was close.

GIs look to the sound of German sniper fire from a nearby building. American casualties were incredibly light as the Allies claimed the city.

The French converse with a GI, admiring his hardware almost as much as their newfound freedom.

Toward the picture's top center, a French woman receives a burr haircut, the symbol of a German sympathizer, courtesy of the angry French resistance.

Free haircuts for all friends of the Germans in Paris after the liberation of Paris.

The results—not the best haircut but in the words of author Cormac McCarthy: "Whatever you do in this life will get back to you—if you live long enough."

Another mark given to the German sympathizer was the Nazi swastika on the forehead. Note the GIs watching in the background.

On the way back up to the company command post, that afternoon my radio operator and myself were walking up the road. As we rounded a curve a sniper shot at us, so we took to the woods. Being unable to find a hole in the thick hedge, we decided to try the road again. When we got back out to the road again we found a vehicle and a driver there. I looked up the road and saw a man walking along by himself. I asked the driver who it was and he said, "General McNair." Well I knew that was no place for him, but who was I to tell him to go back, so I just followed him up to the CP. He just talked and looked around for a little while, then went on back. The next day he was killed in almost the same spot.

I am sure you read about the bombs falling short on the 25th. There were a few clouds but visibility was fair. There was a slight wind blowing in our direction. We pulled back as the day before, but gave any Germans trying to get into our fox holes a warm reception with artillery. The bombers began to appear. As far as you could see there were more planes. The more bombs they dropped the darker it got from smoke and dust, and that is where the trouble came from. As the wind was blowing in our direction the clouds moved toward us. It seemed that the bombers were bombing into the clouds, so they kept getting closer and closer. One bunch hit about two hundred yards from me and that is when I took off. I don't think any came any closer than that, but anyway I put about three hundred yards behind me in record time. I later found out that Gen. McNair was up where the bombs hit.

About the most exciting run we had was with the French 2nd Armored into Paris. About the middle of August we were down around Maganne, not doing much fighting, but just holding. One day we received orders to move back to a rendezvous point and were told we were going to be given a special mission. Of course everybody was kinda tense until we found out what it

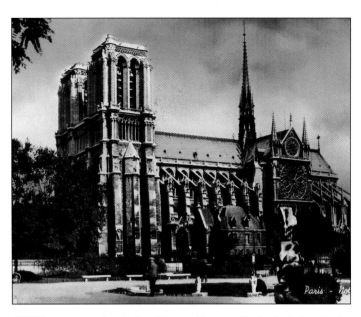

GWL's postcard of the Notre Dame Cathedral in Paris, purchased during his visit from 8/25-8/27/1944. His battalion parked across courtyard of Cathedral during this time. "I've never seen people so happy in my life to really be hungry." GWL 8/28/44

Postcard purchased by George in 8/44. "Our machine gun fired over my head at men upon arch as we went in Paris. I later heard they were shooting at two Frenchmen, trying to put up a French flag." GWL

Postcard of Eiffel Tower purchased by George in Paris, 8/1944.

was. As soon as we found out we were being attached to the French 2nd we thought we knew where we were going.

We later found out that we were supposed to have gotten a few days' rest, but the uprising in Paris changed the plans. About 4 the next morning we were called out and started on our way. There we were in open trucks and jeeps, and most of the French were in tanks or armored vehicles. It was another one of those missions of bypassing everything and reaching your objective. Well, that is just what we did. The French people would guide us around the Germans through fields or any way. The end of our column would get shot at every once in a while, but no serious damage was

"Near the Hürtgen Forest." GWL. The 196th entered the Hürtgen on November 10, 1944. GWL earned his second Bronze Star there for his actions on December 3rd. During that time, weather conditions went from mostly cold and rainy to freezing with hard driving snow.

A town in France near the Hürtgen Forest. When the snow melted in spring, hundreds of bodies would still litter the nearby forest floor.

"Taken 3 days after the most uncertain days of my life in the Hürtgen Forest of Germany, Nov. 44." GWL. He received his second Bronze star for his rescue of the 10 walking wounded in the Hürtgen. Note the aging process of Lt. Looney compared to earlier photographs. Statistics showed Lieutenants had only a 17% chance of surviving two weeks in the Hürtgen.

done. On the night of the 24th we pulled up to the Seine just outside of Paris and it was decided we would stop there for the night and go on in the next morning.

The next day was beautiful. I don't know what time the lead vehicle started out because I was too far back, but I went across the bridge a little after noon. The people were near hysterics they were so proud to see us. It wasn't hard to find a girl to kiss you-in fact there were too many of them. Every once in a while firing would break out, but usually didn't last long. A few of our boys were hit but only one in the battalion killed.

That night we set up camp just a little way down the street from the "Arc de Triumphe" and slept on the sidewalk that night. Naturally, we set up our kitchen too, but it was hard to eat with so many hungry people looking on. The second night the Germans gave us a little scare with a few bombers, but didn't do much damage. On the 27th we moved back out into the woods.

After leaving Paris we were attached to the 5th Armored Div. That is where I met Alonzo Pierce. (From his hometown of Charleston.) We had a fairly hot battle one afternoon in the edge of the campaign forest, but that night most of the Krauts pulled out. The next day

GWL travels the quiet Ardennes forest which blanketed much of Belgium and Luxembourg and stretched into France. And "you could spit into Germany," Ray Leopold, "The War." After the misery dealt to the Americans in the Hürtgen Forest, like many GIs, George surely relished the thought of settling down for the winter in a supposedly quiet sector. Prior to the Bulge, life was so uneventful in the Ardennes, it was called the Nursing Home and the Ghost Forest.

"I wouldn't be surprised if it doesn't get kinda cold here this winter if this thing doesn't end." Foreshadow from George on 10/25/44. No kidding! Freezing GIs gather for chow along the Eupen Highway, only a short distance from Höfen. Temperatures reached twenty below zero before winter surrendered to spring.

"Natives found bodies stacked four deep in the Valley," wrote GWL, referring to when the snow melted around Höfen. Hemingway's wife, columnist Martha Gelhorn, thought the landscape area around The Bulge looked like a "scene for a Christmas card."

This peaceful setting near Höfen betrays the facts of The Bulge: 2,000 American casualties a day, 20,000 dead and 60,000 wounded.

we moved on through, but ran into another convoy and had to wait an hour or two. During that time I saw a major standing in a halftrack and my first impression was that it was Alonzo, but after looking at him I decided it wasn't. Later I saw him again and decided it was Major Pierce. We were together for several days, but haven't heard from him in some time.

Just outside of Sedan we left the 5th and combat for a while. Our trucks were used to haul engineer equipment and ammunition on the famous "Redball" Highway. We drove night and day for about five weeks. Around the first of November we were called back into the line to support the 4th Division in the Hürtgen Forest drive. That was by far the roughest thing I have ever seen. Somehow a hundred dead Krauts didn't mean very much to me, but every American soldier I saw fall really hurt, and there were a lot of them that fell there too. Aside from the fighting and shelling, the weather was miserable. Snow, rain, sleet, freezing and thawing with men lying out in foxholes for days at a time without

blankets, fire or anything warm to eat. Those days were dark, then about that time I received word that Fletcher was coming overseas. About all I could think of was John Ike and Gary, (Fletcher's sons).

For some unknown reason, about the first of December we were transferred from the 7th corps to the 5th and placed in support of the 395th Regiment of the 99th Division at Höfen, Germany, due east of Eupen, Belgium. Everybody was happy. This was a quiet sector and how. On December 16th, the breakthrough came. (The Battle of The Bulge.) They struck with everything they had. Had they gotten through us to Eupen the entire war might have been changed, but they didn't. They tried to get through at night, blow up the houses we were in, push through with tanks, but every time they failed. After about three days and nights the attacks weakened because we were taking a heavy toll at a surprisingly light cost. We never left a single house that we occupied (much more on Höfen later).

Again in February we were attached to the 9th

Division to support their drive to the Rohr River. During this drive I never was up with the infantry so I had it pretty easy. Toward the last of February we were pulled out of actual combat and I have been working with military government ever since.

At the present I am stationed about 30 miles south of Pilsen but hope not to be here long. You can be sure if I go to the Pacific it will be because I have to.

I hope to be seeing you soon.
Love,
George

I showed this letter to a friend and business acquaintance of mine, Buddy Wagner, a bomber pilot in the war. When Buddy read the part about the bombing in St. Lo, his eyes erupted into flying saucers.

"That was me dropping those bombs that day at St. Lo!" Buddy cried. "That's the day I got shot down and captured by the Germans!"

Buddy was a good salesman, convincing his captors of his German heritage which conceivably contributed to the lax attitude that allowed him to soon escape. Buddy, Jewish and with roughly the same amount of German blood as Churchill, eventually made his way to Paris and lived underground with the French until George and friends arrived to liberate the city.

During his stay in Paris, Buddy frequently enjoyed the night life in French pubs with German soldiers actually on the premises but that's another story. Regretfully, Buddy and my father never met.

A few comments on George's big letter. No way he wrote a rough draft and the original handwritten letter contained no errors so his mind was sharp as an officer's bayonet at the time. Furthermore, my father, though unknown to his family, did write about the war during the last few months of his life. His notes reveal an interesting boat ride from New York to Scotland. On the second morning, his ship blew some engine gaskets and lost power, sitting idle in the ocean for the better part of a day. Anxious moments for thousands of American GIs who became sitting ducks for German wolf packs roving the Atlantic ocean at the time. Thankfully nothing happened except some anxious moment for nervous GIs. *We had a few pretty sick boys in the bathroom that day,* wrote George.

George wrote in more detail on General McNair too. On July 24, 1944, the day before American bombers accidentally killed General McNair, McNair's aide asked, "should the General be out there?" George replied "No, he could only get shot." The aide then asked Lt. Looney if he would "go get McNair and bring him back in?"

George's message was stern. "No. He is your responsibility."

And a significant responsibility indeed. McNair had appeared on the cover of Time Magazine on December 28, 1942 and was known as "Educator of the Army" and trainer of some three million troops. If the aide passed on George's advice to the General, it was ignored. On the previously mentioned war map of Normandy, George marked the ill-fated spot with his words: *This is where the bombs fell all around us. General McNair killed there by air bombs.* Identified only by a fragment of his collar containing three stars, McNair was the highest ranking US casualty of the war and was supposed to take command of Allied ground forces in Europe under Eisenhower.

By now George's admiration for the women of France, especially Paris, is well documented. Evidently the women of France harbored similar feelings for the Lieutenant from Arkansas.

Guibon Georges wrote George from Mendon, France near Paris on June 30, 1945, her wispy dramatic penmanship enhanced by the use of a pen dipped in an ink well from days gone by.

June 30, 1945
I was very sorry you could not come to my house but I was pleased when you passed by to see your Jeep and how nicely you waved your hand out. Since then I often thought of you daily and how your life in danger and tried to follow on the maps the progress through Belgium, German, Austria of the 1st Army.

Not surprisingly, the horrors of war bled onto the page.

Unhappily many of my friends died in Germany in concentration camps and we have no news from veterinary, surgeon, native of Brittany, mayor of this little town who was an old friend of all my family and has been in prison at Rennes since last August. Please send me a word, (she concluded with what I perceived as a heavy emphasis on the word please.)

On the back of a wallet sized photograph, another mademoiselle of an undetermined name also wrote in English *I will remember always of this very nice Lieutenant with whom I have passed a very good evening.* Though the photo of the young woman, set in a wooded area with a light snow covering the ground, was black and white, I imagined her hair, which was both thick with waves and swept back from her high forehead, as reddish blond—a young Lucy, I decided. (See picture below.)

Did Lt. Looney sleep with the women of France or Europe? Not according to another garage confession he shared with youngest son, Dean. Amid the sounds of wrenches and sockets clanging against motorcycle metal, our dad volunteered that the threat of disease fortified his vow of abstinence during the war. An obedient soldier simply adhering to his Pocket Guide to France held out against temptation.

"I will remember always of this very nice Lt. with whom I have passed a very good evening." George's letters to his sister, Carmen, spoke highly of the French Women. The notion of my father as a ladies man is a difficult concept to grasp.

Chapter Seven

Japan?

June 9, 1945 Czechoslovakia
Dear Mother and Dad:
Getting plenty to eat, even a little lettuce, onions and a few eggs. These people are working and doing the best they can but they have very little to do it with. It looks like they are going to get pretty hungry before it is over. Don't worry I'll see you before fall.

The key to George's heart still clearly ran through his stomach. So much for his concern for the Czech people. On the same date, he wrote Carmen: *The people here are full or crap. Too far behind.*

June 12th, 1945 Czechoslovakia
Dear Carmen:
I don't know how long I will be over here or if I will go to the Pacific or not. The picture with a hole in the house was taken at Merseburg, Germany near Leipzig.

They hit the house on each side of ours, but missed it. So happened I was down the street a little way at the time of that shelling. That was all in a day's run though. I had several homes beat up while I was in them, but I was in the basement of course. Had about the first hard rain I ever saw in Europe the other day. Went to Pilsen the other night to a dance. Had a date with a girl that I couldn't even talk to. About as much fun as a one legged man at an ass kicking. She could dance very well though.

The bombing incident George refers to would have occurred sometime between mid-February-April, his last known close brush with his maker. With the fighting still fierce in the Pacific, George, like so many seasoned war veterans in Europe, could only hope for a miracle to avoid re-entering the drudgery and uncertainty of combat. The estimated human cost to invade the mainland of Japan: one million American lives.

"Höfen OP 6 with German 88 shell hole, near the window I used." GWL

Czechoslovakia, immediately after the war. Looks like horses were still a prime source of transportation and George mentions in his letters the Czechs were behind in the time.

Refugees wondering through Europe.

Probably French hoping the situation safe enough to return home.

"Looks like Poles going home." GWL. Americans will never truly comprehend the suffering endured by the people of Europe during the war.

More refugees longing for home or what was home. 60 plus years later, the uncertainty of the future bleeds from their hollow expression.

June 15th, 1945 Czechoslovakia
Dear Mother and Dad:

I don't know what is going to happen, but looks like I will be over here some time yet. It looks like the ones going to the Pacific will be home first. In that case, I could afford to wait awhile.

Say, let's don't be rushing me into marrying so fast. I've got to have time to look around a little when I get back. How do I know what has grown up over there since I left? These chicks don't speak my language so I don't get along so well, even though fraternization is legal. We had ice cream for supper last night. We furnish the stuff and got a man to freeze it. Not bad either. Powdered milk is okay. Have had two fresh eggs the last two or three mornings so I'm doing alright. If it wasn't for potatoes there would be plenty of people to starve over here.

July 4th, 1945 Czechoslovakia

Would have been having plenty of cherries to eat. Cherry and apple seem to be about the only thing they have here. It has been raining every day lately but it doesn't rain hard. They really treasure grass. You can go out in the ditches and cut it by the basketful and carry it in for feed. Nearly everybody has a flock of geese. They are having a big parade in Pilsen today, but I have seen enough parades. Have a nice room with a big feather bed and I'm doing alright. The women clean up the room every morning and make the bed.

The daredevil we never knew. George takes a ride on a high wire in Czechoslovakia. The war was over. Boredom and or the need to let off steam probably fueled this stunt.

July 11th, 1945 Czechoslovakia
Dear Mother and Dad:

I'm afraid it will be a few months before I get home. Better that than going to the Pacific I guess. We have a big dance twice a week and a show three or four times a week so it isn't so bad. We may move into Germany before long which would be better. This country is too far behind.

George could not know that in 4 days the USS Indianapolis, while docked for repairs in Mare Island, near San Francisco, received orders to pick up a piece of special cargo at Hunters Point Naval Shipyard in San Francisco and deliver the mystery package to Tinian, an island in the Pacific close to Saipan.

July 16th, 1945 Czechoslovakia
Dear Mother and Dad:

We have a good place to swim so that is how I am spending most of my afternoons now. It is still a little cool here but not bad. The shortage of soap is quite apparent, but other than that, everything is okay. If you get one at the dance that you can't dance with you just woller around until the music stops and then take her over and sit her down.

In ten days the USS Indianapolis would arrive in Tinian, carrying it's top secret cargo...two atomic bombs. Four days later,

the Indianapolis would take a Jap torpedo and split in half, killing 880 crewmen; 321 survived.

August 5th, 1945 Munich, Germany
Dear Mother and Dad:

On my way back to Czechoslovakia from a three day leave in Paris. I tended to buy some things to send home but when it comes to paying $8 to $10 for handkerchiefs, $60 to $100 for handbags, that ain't none of me. Well, I am getting along and I hope you do the same.

At approximately the time George wrote this last letter from Europe, an atom bomb was placed aboard a B-29 plane named the Enola Gay in Tinian. At 8:15 the next morning, the bomb passed through the bomb bay doors, over Hiroshima, Japan; 46 seconds later, not only Hiroshima, but the world would shake with destruction. On August 9, after an American plane dropped another atomic bomb on Nagasaki, the Japanese finally quit, sparing George from adding another country to his resume. After three years of active duty and one year, seven months and ten days overseas, George, older than his twenty seven years, returned to the United States on September 20, 1945. Making good on his promise to be home for Christmas, the Army of the United States discharged him from active military service at Camp Chaffee, Arkansas on December 6, 1945, his life and the way he would look at the world forever transformed.

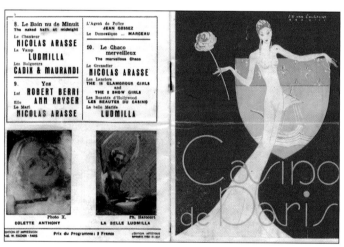

George visits a Paris nightclub. George's letters indicated he returned to Paris on leave after liberation day so this may be from post 8/44.

56

Chapter Eight

Höfen

In the spring of 1997, an incident occurred that ushered in a tidal wave of family emotions and longing for George. My mother asked me to meet her and my two brothers, Phil and Dean at my parent's home.

"What for?" I asked innocently enough.

"You'll see," Mary Looney replied in a surprisingly suspicious tone.

As I entered the den, their sly grins poorly concealed the conspiracy weighing heavily in the air. My mother handed me a present wrapped in an elongated jewelry sized box.

"We took a vote and decided you should have it—since you are the oldest," my mother said. She was a small silver-haired lady now but her wide smile caught a glimpse of a world ago when as the nineteen year old homecoming queen of Arkansas

I'll never know whether George took this before or after the Battle of Höfen. "I saw this again on 10-5-90 just outside of Höfen near Elsenborn Ridge". GWL

A&M in Monticello, she found herself courted by George Looney. Ten years her senior, George was A&M's Dean of Men at the time, the courtship probably was a scandal of sort until the two married a year later.

It's pertinent to mention that when our father crossed to the other side, his children were stumbling about in a forest of economic pitfalls. Several business deals of mine were going south. Phil and Dean struggled with career changes. Loaded with concern, George started entering the Reader's Digest Sweepstakes in an effort to bail his sons from financial harm's way.

To improve the odds, George filled out the sweepstakes paperwork on a daily basis and sometimes multiple submissions on the same day—for over a year! Not without substantial ribbing from his family members.

Sure enough, after unwrapping my gift, the words Reader's Digest seemed to flash in neon letters on the cover of the box. Inside the box, a big gold eye stared back at me—not the million dollar sweepstakes, but a Wittnauer watch. I now wear that watch almost daily, protecting it as if it controls my children's happiness. If life's clock hadn't run out on George, he probably would have hit the jackpot. Once again, I heard his chuckle. Maybe the watch brought good karma; financially, things improved for George's sons.

During the initial phase of my World War II exploration project, I stumbled upon the single most significant bit of information, like discovering gold the first day in the mine. In that giant mess of paper rubble in the room of my youth, I found a complete copy of the previously mentioned history of The 196th Field Artillery Battalion. Also printed on the inside cover: Lt. George W. Looney, Reconnaissance Officer and Forward Observer. Discharged at Rank of Captain. It was George's handwriting on the book's cover that leaped out at me with all the warning of a surprise attack.

First night hell—several nights of torment in Höfen

George revisits the Elsenborn Ridge near Höfen on 10-5-90.

OP (Operating Precinct) My brightest star by me. I helped save the day. Lt. Starter (not his real name) first night cracked up. Lt. George W. Looney-2nd night. Peiper was ordered to run over us. He did not. (Colonel Joachin Peiper whose 1st SS Panzer Division had earned the nickname the "Blowtorch Battalion" for its enthusiastic approach to burning villages and butchering civilians.)

My brightest hour was in Höfen, Germany. I helped stop the Germans there on their second night trying to run over us. We had too much artillery. They could not get over us. Had they done so, it would have opened up all Elsinborn Ridge to Germans and possible disaster for all. Fact by Historians.

My brightest star. I helped save the day.

The words caught in my brain the way a phonograph needle catches in a groove. Since his family seldom heard George brag on himself, I immediately knew the magnitude of his accomplishment exceeded his actions that resulted in two bronze stars. Though he received the written history of his battalion at the end of the war, I suspect he recorded his comments much later—after revisiting the battle site in 1990 and realizing the importance of the battle.

Why would George all but bury the details of the most significant day in his life? My hunch is because he would resist discrediting another officer regardless of the circumstance. (Lt. Starter will serve as the other artillery observer's name for this book—a good synonym since even the best starting pitcher occasionally needs relief.)

With the war letters still in hiding, I had never heard mention of Höfen, Germany. History tells us the most significant portion of the Battle of Höfen took place in the bitter cold from December 16th through December 20th—a critical part of The Battle of The Bulge, so nicknamed because of the 40 mile salient the enemy had begun to carve in the American lines. The blanks in George's notes left me crazed with curiosity, desperately longing for more. Thankfully, the mystery of *Höfen* would unravel in practically chronological order.

I soon came upon the following letters from a man named Thor Ronningen.

July 24, 1992.
Dear George,
    You probably don't remember but we met on the Battlefield trip to Krinkelt in 1990. I hope this finds you in good health.
    I'm currently engaged in writing a history of the 3rd Battalion-395th Infantry. As you know, The 196 Field Artillery Battalion was a very important part of our successful defense of Höfen during The Bulge. To help complete the story, I would like to contact one or more of the following from the 196th: (he lists several men here including Lt. Starter)
    If you can help me at all in locating these fellows, I would sure appreciate it. I want to tell a complete and accurate story of what actually happened and feel that the only way I can do this is with help from the men who were there.
    Sincerely,
    Thor

George obviously replied because Thor Ronningen's second letter was dated:

August 7th, 1992.
Dear George,

Thanks so much for your very prompt reply to my letter. Since I neglected to make a copy of my letter I may repeat myself some. Please excuse. (I will make a copy of this letter.)

I am in the process of writing a history of The 3rd Battalion – 395th during WW II and of course the fight in Höfen is a big part of it. I have obtained a copy of a report Starter made as well as a commendation addressed to him from Lt. Col. Butler, CO of the 3rd Bn. I have a copy of the Bn's S-3 Journal as well as Lauer's book etc., but still have questions. (Major General Walter Lauer was commander of 99th Infantry Division that included The 3rd Battalion-395th.)

You mention George Himmelman. (One of the officers in the picture with GWL in the New York City night club.) Do you have his address?

I am enclosing a map of Höfen. Can you mark on here where you were on "the south side?" I have no information at all about observers any place other than the 3 story building. Can you mark on the map about where the bunkers were that you refer to?

You refer to Lt. Starter being sent up to our area "that afternoon" and that "all hell broke out the next morning." Since the Germans first hit us the morning of 16 December, I take it that he came up on the 15th. Do you agree? You also mention Lt. Starter cracking up. I have heard some reports of this, but do not have any details I can check. Can you furnish any details? (Rest assured that in my book there will be nothing about any American that denigrates them in any war.) If I have the details I can tell the story better.

You say you replaced Lt. Starter "early next morning" which I take to be 17 December. Right? (Was the 16th) According to my records the German tanks were a part of the attack on 18 December, but they never got into Höfen. A number of infantrymen penetrated behind you and surrounded the Bn. HQ, but were all killed or captured. I have reports from the 612th TD Bn that they had a 3" gun in or right next to the 3 story building. Can you confirm this?

Anything at all that you can tell me about your experiences in Höfen during The Bulge would be most welcome. A number of the men who were in the 3rd Bn have sent me information and I now know a lot more about what went on, but still keep learning more. You mention that we have 40 battalions of artillery tied together in support. How many guns would this be? What sizes? The artillery really saved us and I want to give them full credit. I look forward to hearing from you.
Warm regards,
Thor

I found this third letter from Thor in the same stack.

September 13, 1992
Dear George,

It was good to hear from you, but I was sorry to hear about your shortness of breath. I don't know about you, but taking a stress test is one of my least favorite things. Stay well. (I remember the exact day George

mentioned the less than ideal results of his stress test but he offered no hint of his WWII discussions.)

I appreciate the information you gave me but am still in a quandry as to what happened at Höfen as well as just when it happened. I am confident that there was a major German attack early on 16 Dec. On the 17th we received artillery but the major attack was on the 38th Cavalry in the Monschau area. On the 18th they again hit Höfen, this time with tanks and armored cars.

I have heard that Lt. Starter had broken down on the 16th. You say, "To be honest Starter must have kind of cracked up a little." I also gather from your letter that you took over the OP on the 17th. Is this correct? My problem is that Starter chronicles his actions on the 18th (copy enclosed.) I also have a copy of a letter John Reid from HQ Co. 3rd Bn wrote in which he extols Starter's heroics on the 18th. I enclose a copy of this letter. I am also enclosing a copy of the Commendation Co. Butler wrote to your CO which I thought you might enjoy.

I would appreciate it very much if you would answer some questions for me so I can be correct.

1. What day did you take over from Lt. Starter?
2. Was Lt. Starter evacuated?
3. Who took over from you when you left after 5 days?
4. Does the 196th have anything written on these events?
5. Do you know how I can contact Lt. Starter?
6. You say, "I also pulled those big guns off of us one night." Do you know the date? Whose guns were they?

We all realize that the artillery saved our necks at Höfen and in my book I will give them full credit, but I do want it to be factual and as complete as I can make it. I hope this finds you a picture of health and look forward to hearing from you.
Warm regards,
Thor

Who was Thor Ronningen? I had no idea only that a book was in the works and Höfen seemed a whirlwind of controversy.

The following is Lt. Starter's report mentioned in Thor's third letter that placed him as the forward observer at Höfen on December 18th, 1944.

(Specific Data),
(1) Character of terrain; of hostile observation and of enemy fire: Our front line elements were dug in within the town of Höfen, Germany between houses and barricaded within houses and cellars. The terrain over which the enemy attack was launched was hilly and the road into the town was utilized by the enemy. Hostile observation was from tanks, and infantry accompanying tanks from points within two hundred yards of our front line positions. Enemy fire was indirect from artillery and rockets, and direct from tanks and accompanying infantry mortar and rifle fire.
(2) Visibility, time of day and atmospheric conditions: Visibility poor; 0525 hours; cloudy and foggy.
(3) Location of enemy: Infantry supported by tanks in attack against our infantry defensive positions.
(4) Morale, that of our forces and of the enemy: Morale of our forces, excellent. Enemy, determined to take our

positions at Höfen.

(5) Casualties sustained: Unknown.

(6) Effect or result of dead in questions: Cp. Webber's part in this operation played an important part in maintaining the efficiency of the observer party. The artillery fire directed by this party was a major factor in repelling the enemy attack, enabling our forces to hold the town.

(7) Detailed Resume: On 18 December 1944, while acting as forward observer for the 196th FA Bn, I had as members of my forward observer party, five enlisted men of my Bn, one of whom was Cp. Webber. My observation post was in a three story building located on the main line of resistance in the town of Höfen, Germany. (See overlay for 18 Dec.) From this point I was observing fires of my battalion in support of the 3rd Battalion, 395th Infantry. At approximately 0400, 18 December 1944, information was received that the enemy was preparing to launch an attack. All personnel of the observer party took up positions to cover approaches to the building. The attack commenced at 0525 hours with small arms and machine gun fire on the observation post. It soon became evident that the enemy had infiltrated the thinly held lines of our flanking infantry and that our positions were completely

George returns to the Siegfried line on 10-2-90. "There were concrete houses as well as major pill boxes all along border." GWL. Referred to by Hitler as the West Wall, by 1944 it had fallen into disrepair. Keys were lost to some pillboxes; farmers stored vegetable in others. No mines or barbed wire guarded the approaches; no gates closed off the roads running through it.

surrounded. It was further realized that the building in which our observation post was located must be held in order to hold control of roads which were the one route of supply and communications to the 3rd Battalion, 395th Infantry. In order to accomplish this, it was necessary to call for artillery fire from the 196th FA Battalion on our observation post. Artillery fire was adjusted by radio as our wire communications were cut early in the attack. Shells hit on and near the observation post blowing gaping holes in the roof and sides of the building, showering plaster, bricks and shrapnel on the men as they stayed at their posts at the windows, often knocking them to the floor. The men stayed at their posts and returned the small arms fire taking a high toll from the attackers, keeping the observation post from being taken. Cpl Webber and Pfc Roach, relayed commands to the radio from the third story from which the observer had (did?) his best though most hazardous observation. These two men, although the large room was constantly swept by fire from automatic weapons, relayed all commands to the radio operation, despite the fact that they knew that often times the fire called for would hit their own position. In addition to relaying commands they fired small arms from the third story window, probably the most dangerous spot in the building, and inflicted several known casualties on the attackers. After about eight hours of defense of our observation post, Cp. Webber delivered covering small arms fire to protect the approach of relief columns on our rear and flanks. He exposed himself many times informing the relief party of the location of enemy positions in the vicinity. I personally observed his movements and his disregard for his own safety in defense of our position. The acts of courage displayed by this enlisted man were a credit to himself and was in keeping with the highest traditions of the armed forces. Cpl Webber was not wounded in the performance of this act or service.

Lt. Starter's report sounded a far cry from a man that "cracked up" during battle. Neither did John Reid's letter to John Toland describing Lt. Starter's actions during the time in question. Excerpts from Reid's letter to Toland who wrote several books on WWII are as follows:

January 18, 1958
Dear Mr. Toland,

In Höfen Germany I was member of a front-lines observation post, OP 6. It was on the 3rd floor of a house with stone walls that had been an orphanage, I think.

But in late December (1944? 45?) when the Krauts made their big push they fired a lot of rockets one night. Dec. 17? During a major attack by German foot-soldiers about Dec. 17 or so, their soldiers started up a road "following the leader." From our outpost a Lt. Starter, a field artillery forward observer, called for artillery fire which saved the day (or crushed the advance.) We were raked by small arms fire so that every window on the third floor was dangerous as hell. A tripod arrangement for artillery sighting was shot to bits, but Lt. Starter slithered around on the floor using the busted stove-pipe or "periscope" like tube to see

60

over the window sills. That took real nerve, to look and call for fire close to us.

In the meantime the Jerries were advancing up the road, in both ditches. By now Lt. Starter had started to bring some 105 Howitzer fire closer to our cross roads. The cross roads lay about 75 or 100 yards to our right. Starter knew that the Jerries were swarming around the base of our outpost trying to break in (while we were up on the top floor.) So he started moving the artillery (now joined by 155's) down into our laps. Finally, he got them (our guns) to hitting practically on the cross roads. Some of the rounds landed only six feet to the right of our building, and practically in our yard. Woohie!!! As our artillery with times fuses started hitting near the road I could see Jerries diving into the tiny ditches along the road although the water was ice-cold.

Anyhow, I saw a German band set up a machine gun post and start to fire interdicting the road. Very soon a battery of artillery shells from our rear completed annihilation of the brave little German band.

The Germans retired in confusion and hurt.

In the margin of Reid's letter, adjacent to his description of Lt. Starter's heroics, I recognized George's handwriting *me and James.* Though vague to me at the time, James referred to James Everett Allen, George's radio operator.

Within minutes, I found a handwritten reply from George to Thor:

February 16, 1995
Dear Thor,
I had on occasion to get out some of my old paper today and ran across your correspondence. I did this a couple of years ago and you answered back. I am sure I found the sheet of my last letter that you thought I left out of your letter. I also read Col. Butler's letter. Everything I read in your letter, and his, is correct as best I know. I remember the body of the boy that was killed was still on the floor when I got there. That was about 8 am the 17th.

I have no idea how much artillery we had but with Division-Corps-Army and our BM plus whatever else may have been there I know it was a lot. Of course it was all surveyed in position and could be brought to bear on any one target on call—boy did we call.

I well remember the night it seemed all of it began to fall on top of us. When it hit on building I ordered everybody to hit the stairway to basement, my radio operator also. I grabbed the radio and called our gun position and told them they were falling all over us and to stop it quick. They had it stopped in a few seconds.

Thor it is obvious I am not very well organized but

On 10-3-90, George enjoys the breathtaking beauty of Monshau, Germany located only a few miles from Höfen. Hitler ordered no shelling on Monshau, sparing the famous honeymoon capital of Germany from the destruction of war.

at 75 I guess I do ok.

Incidentally I guess it (the sheet) had this on it. I requested you to send me a copy of book COD if you ever get it published.

I don't know whether I told you or not but we received a wonderful citation from Col. Butler. He gave us a lot of credit for the defense. I did not realize it was from him when we were over there or I would have thanked him.

I don't know about you but I lay awake in middle of night reliving a lot of those incidents. Just glad to be here to do that.

I don't expect to get back over there anymore. (No, he never made it back.)
Wish you and yours the best.
Sincerely,
George

Notice the date—over two years since Thor's initial correspondence! With no typewriter, computer or copy machine in my parent's home, it's doubtful George ever mailed the letter since I held the original. My other hand, a hand trembling with sadness, held an announcement dated April 1993 from Brunswick Publishing Corporation of Lawrenceville, Virginia advertising the release of Thor Ronningen's book, "Butler's Battlin' Bastards." Time to contact Brunswick and hope suspicion detoured from fact.

I immediately wrote Thor, care of Brunswick Publishing, and received the following reply from Walter Raymond, publisher emeritus of Brunswick.

February 28, 1997.
Dear Mr. Looney,
Received your letter addressed to Thor Ronningen which I sent to him. I was sorry to hear about your great father passing away. Your father, Captain Looney is mentioned several times in Thor's book. (George was promoted to Captain at war's end.) It makes a very fine and real contribution to family history and your great-grand children will be able to benefit with pride.
Wish you all the best in your noble endeavors,
Walter J. Raymond

I promptly dialed the telephone number for Brunswick displayed on the letterhead. After speaking to Mr. Raymond for several minutes, an elderly gentleman who proved most understanding, a copy of "Butler's Battlin' Bastards" was on its way and I had Thor Ronningen's home phone number in North Carolina.

During the time that elapsed following my letter to

Thor Ronningen took this picture of George reuniting with OP 6 in 1990. George mailed this picture to his radio operator James Everett Allen shortly after his return along with the following note: "This is where the OP was. You looked out those windows a lot. BAR man shot patrol just across street in front of burning embers from burning building. That tree in front probably saved my life. They shot at me one morning. I saw flash and shell hit a tree limb and exploded."

Thor Ronningen, author of "Butler's Blue Battlin Bastards" and who wrote the forward of this book, during war time. Thor fought with the 395th infantry at Höfen while George was directing artillery fire. The initial German ground assault was so intense that on at least three occasions, Germans, shot at point blank range, fell into foxholes on top of GIs.

Brunswick Publishing and Mr. Raymond's reply, I had uncovered most of George's private writing's on the war—private in that he never disclosed them to his family. He had plenty to say about Höfen but practically the same thing over and over.

For example, an undated scribbled passage on the back of a map that he brought back from his reunion tour in 1990. *They tried to come over us two nights in a row. I came up to OP on 2nd day. They tried to come over that night. Could not. Too much artillery. Went around down south the third night and on out with breakout. We never gave up our position.*

Or his similar notes concerning Höfen, written on page twenty four of his copy of the previously mentioned book: The 196th Field Artillery Battalion, *This was my day.* (Referencing December 18th, 1944) On page twenty five he wrote in the margin, *I relieved him on the second attack the next morning. I took over at 8:00 am after the first attack on Höfen. Lt. Starter cracked up during the first attack. I relieved him and helped stop them the next morning. It was reported Hitler told them to take Höfen at all cost. We held. The actual fact was we had too much artillery. They just could not get through it. The world may never know that Hitler gave Colonel Peiper orders to run over my position in Höfen. He did not, but lost thousands of boys trying.*

Or his passages found in a blue spiral notebook; *6th December 1944-196 FA Battalion was placed in direct support of 3rd BN 395th Infantry Reg. 99th Division. It is a long story. In the big push the German made two major attempts to come over our position. I missed first attack, but had to relieve Lt. Starter about 8 am on 17th. They made another major effort the next morning but we had too much artillery and they did not cross.*

The following handwritten letter contained no address or date or closing, trailing off into nothingness.

Dear Sir,

I was a forward observer for The 196th FABN. On the 15th of December I was with the 395 Reg. I was relieved late that afternoon and went back to gun position. Got a good night's sleep, but the Germans attacked early in the morning of 16th. Our observer with the 395th in Höfen had some trouble and I was told to report up there as quickly as possible. I got there about 8 am. Not too bad the rest of the day but they came back the next morning. The infantry did a wonderful job but

Höfen today from a slightly different angle. Note the steeple in both pictures.

The town of Höfen during wartime. If the Germans had broken thru at Höfen and opened the highway toward Eupen, the war would have lasted longer and with even more loss of lives on both sides; it's that simple.

The Gasthaus Schmidden at Höfen, which was Batallion headquarters and located across the street from OP 6, during the war.

according to reports, we gave them more artillery than they could take. I do remember the fastest call I ever made was to get them to lift their fire because it was falling on our OP and infantry outside. Fortunately it only took ten to twenty seconds to get it stopped.

Check out the date on the following letter to The Battle of The Bulge, Inc. Only nine days before his passing. Written shortly after my doubting remark concerning his crash landing in the airplane, it too contained no formal closing and I'm sure was never mailed

Dallas, Texas
November 30, 1996
Chief Editor
Battle of The Bulge, Inc.
P O Box 11129
Arlington VA 22210-2129

Dear Sir'
I was a first lieutenant artillery observer for the 196 Field Artillery Battalion, First Army. I've had something on my mind for all these years, but finally decided to write about it.
My battalion was firing artillery support for a division in France when we received rush order to the Belgium Bulge area. I was left cut off with infantry regiment. We got out next day. I was told my unit (196 Field Battalion) had been transferred to the Elsinborne area. I found a jeep from our unit, went back to First Headquarter. I came to and found the location on the map of 196th Field Artillery Battalion. We had been assigned to the 99th Division for artillery support. We had it fairly easy for a few days. Then all hell broke out.
On the 16th, the Germans made their first direct attack in Höfen. Prisoners said they had orders to take objectives at all cost. Lieutenant Starter was on duty during first attack. Germans succeeding in penetrating Höfen defenses but were repulsed in the end. It so happened I was called to rush up to replace Lt. Starter. I arrived on post at 8:00 am December the 16th. During this first attack our battalion, 196 Field Artillery was giving credit for firing fifty-eight missions in fifty minutes. The 196th remains in place for several days.

To be sure, George had carried a dark secret too long, making no attempt to unburden himself with so much as one spoken word on the subject to any family member. Any anxiety I felt about calling Thor disappeared shortly after he answered the phone in a voice both warm and strong as artillery cable. At least, I had stumbled into a friendly camp.

"Those of us who fought have a very close bond on what we went through," Thor said, saddened to hear of my Father's passing. Thor expressed further remorse to learn that George evidently never knew his book was published. Thor spoke fondly of their meeting on the reunion tour in 1990, even leading my father to that now all too familiar three story building in Höfen and taking his picture. Thor served with the 3rd Battalion-395th Infantry under Colonel Butler, fighting only a matter of yards from the building that contained George. "It is very possible that your Dad and I met face to face in December of '44, but neither of us remembered it" Thor said. "The field artillery literally saved our lives. They put up a wall of almost solid steel between us and the Germans and we could never have held our positions without them. Höfen was the only place on the entire front of the German attack that did not yield a foot of ground," he added pridefully.

In an upbeat tone, Thor informed me his book recognized Captain Looney for his role at Höfen—and without discrediting Lt. Starter. Yes, he and my father had discussed the incident but George did not seem overly concerned and by no means haunted that somebody else took the credit. But based on George's writings, I suspected different and contrary to our conversation, I suspect Thor felt the same way.

Thor's book, "Butler's Battlin' Blue Bastards" arrived a couple of days later. Hand written on the inside cover *Best wishes to Mike Looney in honor of his Father, my friend, Captain George Looney, who was an essential part of the successful defense of Höfen, Germany during The Battle of The Bulge in December, 1944.*

The prologue from "Butler's Battlin' Blue Bastards" explains best the opening day of what will forever be known as The Battle of The Bulge. *At 0525 on the morning of December 16, 1944, men of The 3rd Battalion-395th Infantry-99th Division were in their usual positions. Guards manned each position and the off-duty men were sleeping. It was cold and dark and quiet. Five minutes later the world seemed to come to an end as ten battalions of German artillery opened fire on Höfen, Germany. High explosive shells whistled in; Nebelwerfer rockets, aptly called "Screaming Meemies," came in with an ear-piercing, almost heart-stopping, shriek before they exploded thunderously. The very earth trembled. Houses burned. Debris filled the streets. All communication lines were severed. Each position was cut off and in each hole the men prepared to defend themselves, to the death if necessary, not knowing what was happening around them. For twenty minutes the 3rd Battalion endured one of the heaviest artillery barrages the German Army had ever fired prior to an attack.*

When the artillery finally stopped firing, three battalions of the German 326th Volksgrenadier Regiment began their attack. It was an eerie scene as the Germans shined aircraft searchlights against the low hanging clouds to aid their troops. Of course these lights also aided the defenders, as the enemy was silhouetted as they plodded through the snow towards Höfen. Remembering their training, the defenders held their fire until the oncoming Germans were almost on top of them and then opened up with every weapon they had, inflicting massive casualties on the enemy.

The Battle of The Bulge had begun. This was a last, desperate effort by the Germans to regain the offensive and became the largest pitched battle the American army had ever fought. Over 600,000 Americans were eventually involved and they suffered 81,000 casualties.

Thor wrote on page 56 of his book *a large measure of the successful defense of Höfen was due to the large volume of accurate and timely artillery fire supporting the defenders. From December 6th through January, the 196th Field Artillery Battalion was in direct support of the 3rd Battalion with their twelve 105 mm guns located near Kalterherberg. A forward switching center was established in Höfen to coordinate the forward observers in each of the rifle company areas. In the I Company area, the Forward Observer Team set up shop on the third floor of the highest building in the village where they had a commanding view of the area. This was designated as OP-6 and there were observers for the 81 mm mortars here as well. Initially led by Lt. Starter, Captain George W. Looney assumed command of the team on December 17th.*

A mist clouded my eyes. It would have been enough.

Chapter Nine

Donald Zinngrabe

George at the Gasthaus Schmidden on 10-4-1990. "A Browning Automatic Rifle (BAR) got 5 Germans on patrol just in front of this site," wrote GWL.

Showing Thor's book to my mother and two brothers stirred a flurry of cerebral blows to the brain. Regret ultimately lost a hard fight to the pride we felt for our own flesh and blood. Thor's recognition of George would hopefully heal our heartache generated from his repeated and troubled recount of the events of Höfen.

Not so. Without any conscious tendencies for masochism, I kept stumbling into publications about The Bulge that would hurl literary artillery into my own mind field with disturbing accuracy.

One such book, when describing the battle of Höfen on December 18, 1944, the author writes *Colonel Butler phoned the forward observer of the 196th Field Artillery Batallion, whose little party was fighting off Germans around its observation post (a three-story brick building right in the forward line) and asked for three-five minute concentrations on his own position. The*

shells came in promptly

Not bad so far, but then a brain shattering rattle came from a footnote at the bottom of the page, practically shouting that the artillery observer was 2nd Lt. Starter, who later received the Distinguished Service Cross for the defense of the observation post!

Lt. Starter's citation for the Distinguished Service Cross, later forwarded to me by Thor Ronningen, reads as follows *First Lieutenant Starter (then Second Lieutenant), 196th Field Artillery Battalion, United States Army, for extraordinary heroism in action against the enemy on 18 December 1944, in Germany. Under cover of darkness, a strong German force completely surrounded First Lieutenant's observation post located in a building along a vital supply route. Intense enemy fire was being directed upon him from all directions. Realizing* the importance of maintaining the communications and supply route at any cost, First Lieutenant Starter requested artillery fire upon his own position. Stunned by several direct hits upon the building, he unflinchingly requested an intense artillery concentration upon himself and the immediate area, which repulsed the attack. At daylight, approximately two hundred enemy dead were found lying near his observation post.

The subject matter slid downhill from there. During the summer of 1997, my mother mentioned receiving a military book addressed to my father. "I thought you might want to look at it," she said in a tone still colored grey from the loss of her husband.

Within hours, I held in my hand a book entitled "The 196th Field Artillery Battalion" by Donald L. Zinngrabe, Sturgeon Bay, Wisconsin. Written in hand on the first page: *To – George W. Looney. I hope you enjoy reading my book. Sincerely, Don Zinngrabe.*

The dedication page read *This book is dedicated to all the men who served in The 196th Field Artillery Battalion during World War II and the Korean War. It is also dedicated to the men who served in the First Tennessee Infantry Regiment and the115th Field Artillery Battalion which are direct descendents of The 196th.*

I quickly surmised that Zinngrabe, though a Northerner, had somehow landed in the Southern laced 196th during Korea and served as a radio operator. And the 196th's descendent, the 115th, fought for the confederacy during the Civil War! Furthermore, the father of the 115th, the first Tennessee Infantry Regiment or the "First Tennessee" fought in the Revolutionary War. A Yankee writing the history of a Southern battalion, a sure indicator of a man fueled by passion. I would soon learn the word passion fell shorter than misplaced artillery in describing the fire that burned within Donald Zinngrabe's gut.

By now, I understood that Höfen held the key to The Bulge's northern shoulder. One of George's pride filled passages summed

Donald Zinngrabe during his stint in Korea with the 196th Field Artillery Battalion as a radio operator.

up matters best. *I'm glad to think that I may have played a small part in helping stop them on the north corner of Elsenborne Ridge. I did not get much sleep for five days and nights, but it was worth it. I have no reason to believe the final outcome would have been any different, but if the Germans had broken through the first or second night, it would have been very costly in lives and suffering.* In short, the Allies impenetrable defense prevented the Germans from easy access to the road network all the way to Eupen, Belgium and forced the enemy to circle around to the south, providing the good guys more time to organize defenses that ultimately thwarted the massive German attack and hastened the end of the war. The battle at Höfen was the only sector of the entire battlefront that the Germans never penetrated the American original line of defense. I repeat—the only place the Allies did not bulge during The Bulge.

Armed with this war history, I flipped the pages of Zinngrabe's book, starting with the year 1774, but rapidly applied the brakes on December 16, 1944, the first day of The Battle of The Bulge. My eyes anxiously scrolled down the page, quickly finding mention of December 18th, the day of the second massive offensive at Höfen—after Looney purportedly replaced Lt. Starter. Zinngrabe's description of that fateful day jarred my insides like a hand grenade in church. *The enemy again launched a very heavy attack on this position at 0430 hours on 18 December and succeeded in penetrating the front line in three places, gaining entry into the town of Höfen. Once again, the battalion observers and the Liaison Officer were active in directing the fire of the battalion. In one instance, 1st Lt. Starter, one of the battalion observers, was surrounded and called for fire to be directed on his own position. This fire killed or drove off the Germans, but no casualties were suffered by the men in the OP. The battalion fired almost continuously until this attack was repelled at approximately 1130 hours.*

Lt. Col. McClernand Butler's report (The Butler of "Butler's Battlin Bastards") concerning Höfen appeared in both Thor and Zinngrabe's book. An excerpt: *When it is taken into consideration that the German mission was to take Höfen, Germany, at all costs regardless of price and that to the south the enemy had been successful in making some penetration of the Allied lines, this unit (196th FA Bn) disregarding reports that came in and the confusion that existed around them, fired efficiently and accurately when and where they were requested and in a volume that is credit to any outfit, if not a record. I believe that they deserve a commendation for their noble efforts and efficient work.*

Now familiar with the details of George's war medals, I knew he never received the commendation Butler mentioned in his report. The military in essence, maintained no record of the most important week of George's military life—a very important week indeed.

Both artillery observers agreed that friendly artillery fire blasted OP 6 on December 18th but the common thread quickly severs. Lt. Starter's report claims it was necessary to call for artillery fire on the observation post, while George's writings in the previous chapter repeatedly indicate the direct hit on OP 6 was a surprise.

My head was full of more static than a military radio during battle. Evidently, only one man directed artillery fire from the third floor of OP 6 on December 18, 1944. One question fueled another. If Lt. Looney replaced Lt. Starter, where did Starter go? What was Lt. Starter doing on that day? Who was with him? How did Lt. Starter gather the information to file the report? Who were the men who corroborated with Lt. Starter's report?

Chapter Ten

Enough's Enough

Some might consider my letter to Donald Zinngrabe as clever; others might think it the work of a scholarly buttocks. I enclosed copies of George's writings with the following note: *His name was George Washington Looney. He was born on George Washington's birthday. You tell me he told a lie.*

Within a matter of days, my assistant, Adrienne, announced with whispered excitement, "it's the man who wrote the book on the phone."

"Z" cut straight to the heart of the matter, speaking in a high pitched raspy voice, its strength camouflaging his near 70 years. "I took the part about Höfen from government records," he said darned near apologetically. "No historian likes to record history wrong. I have no doubt your Dad was the man at OP 6 on December 18th." True, hand written notes speak with authenticity but Z, unknown to me at the time, had already discovered discrepancies in Lt. Starter's report. In fact, Z already knew the full details of my package which contained probably forty pages of George's notes. As I would rapidly learn, an army of elephants would envy the memory or eye for detail of Donald Zinngrabe.

"I guess you know this is quite controversial," Z added in a voice lined with both care and concern. "Why don't you look through more of your Dad's papers? See if you can find names and address of anybody that served with him in The 196th," said Z, the former radio operator's investigative antenna already sending out signals.

Our conversation eventually revealed that Z was a retired high-school principal, currently teaching art at a junior college and moonlighting as a security guard at a local manufacturing plant in Sturgeon Bay, Wisconsin. He wrote the history of The 196th as a labor of love and at his own expense, mailing it to any known survivors of The 196th. His passion to accurately record history became as apparent as his willingness to battle any uncooperative "government bureaucracy or politician." His voice would rise an octave in frustration anytime he said the word "politician." As Z already believed George's account of Höfen, I already suspected Z would either see my father receive his proper credit or die trying. Back to the paper heap of my old bedroom; the place of George's last stand.

Toward the end of his life, the war began to trail George like a dark shadow. References to the war surfaced almost daily in most any conversation with George, as if the "War Gods" had finally granted him permission to discuss, in earnest, the matter, before he became heavenly bound. While searching through his papers, I discovered recognizable names like Norm B. Cohen, or fellow officers, Sinkler Schloze and George Himmelman, even uncovering the picture of both men with George wearing their military uniforms while dining at a New York City restaurant the night before sailing for England. All eyes stared hard at the camera, but through confident expressions, as if to say we know what's coming but we can handle it.

I was also familiar with the names of James Everett Allen, George's radio operator from Memphis, Tennessee and Frank Williams, his jeep driver from Jasper, Alabama. After finding addresses for all the men, I sent copies of his obituary from the paper, also asking for any details of Höfen. Donald Zinngrabe followed with similar letters of his own, regarding Höfen. My journey into World War II was about to accelerate faster than one of Lt. Looney's artillery shells.

We'd already received a letter from Everett Allen, dated January 29, 1997, a result of my mother notifying him of her husband's death. Wistfulness streaked the barely legible handwriting of Everett Allen's initial reply. *As you probably know by now, I was his radio operator and was with him all his observation missions. Only once did I see him just a little confused as to where we were. He found out in just a few minutes. I really believe he was the best forward observer there was in the battalion.*

I never saw him get excited about anything. I guess you would say he treated Frank Williams and I about like brothers as an officer could an enlisted man. Although I haven't seen him in many years, I have thought of him anytime I think of the war. I know I will miss him also.

Donald Zinngrabe forwarded a copy of his letter from Everett Allen.

April, 1997
Yes, I was there with Mr. Looney. Whenever he was called to go forward, which seemed to me, like every time things got hot, Lt. Looney was the one who got called. Being his radio operator, I went also.

I've never been one to remember names, dates, or places, but Höfen, Germany I will always remember. As I remember the attack by the Germans, Lt. Starter was observing and in less than half a day, he cracked up and Lt. Looney replaced him. No disrespect for Lt. Starter but that is what happened. Lt. Looney was definitely the FO. I don't remember how many days we were there at that time but I do remember it was several.

I hope this will clear up some things about Lt. Looney, he, to my opinion was the best in the battalion. Sincerely,
Everett Allen

Responding to my letter, Everett Allen provided additional comments in his reply dated April 24. *Now I don't know what your Dad may have said about Höfen, but you count on it being right. The commanding officer must have known he was the best forward observer because anytime the infantry would jump off on a hot mission, your Dad was the one to go.*

If it bothered your Dad, at all, that Lt. Starter seemed to get all the honor, if that is what you want to call it, because as I understand it at the time from some of the infantry men, Lt. Starter absolutely did crack up.

Mike, if there is anymore questions I can answer let me know, either by letter or phone. I am here most every night.

My response from George Himmelman, who ultimately achieved rank of Lt. Colonel.

April 23rd, 1997.
Dear Mike,
Sorry, I waited so long to answer your letter. I don't know what happened in the case of Lt. Starter, but I remember Looney having to take off in a hurry to get up to the front to replace someone at the observation post.

Lt. Himmelman and his men stare hard into George's camera, as if remembering the past and dreading the future.

Mike, Looney and I spent the whole time together while we were assigned to The 196th all the way through World War II. I consider him one of the best friends I ever had-as close as brothers. I always promised him I would come to Texas and see him and am sorry I never did get there. He did come to Virginia to see us. Sincerely,
George Himmelman

By long distance phone from Florida, Sinkler Schloze, regretfully admitted to a failing memory, remembering only that Höfen was a bee hive of activity. "Go by what Allen and Williams say," he said in a warm voice still strong as the bond of men in combat. "They were with your Dad every step of the way."

Somewhere during this letter writing campaign, I forwarded to James Everett Allen in Memphis, a copy of John Reid's letter from 1958 that touted the heroics of Lt. Starter. James Everett's reply came dated 5-28-97. His literary voice continued to speak loud and clear—brutally honest with simplistic reason, uncensored grammatically or emotionally, remindful of the innocence of a child.

May 28, 1997
Dear Mike,
I received your communication yesterday. I hardly know how to answer it, but will start some place. I do not know anything about this Reid. As for Reid's letter, I can not vouch to much on what he has said, but I sure don't go along with his making Lt. Starter such a heroe. He sort of makes my blood start boiling.

I don't think any book or anything else can now be written that are true facts after over 50 years since it took place. You have your Dad's writings and mine. Put them together and compare then as best you can and see how close we are together.

Mike, I appreciate your sending me a copy of Reid's letter, although I do not agree with everything he has said. You know two people can't see things alike. That happens to be the way he saw them 13 years afterwards. Sincerely,
Everett

Reflecting on Reids' letter, I considered its accuracy. He's cloudy on the dates; maybe the heroics described in his letter to John Toland occurred on December 16th—before Looney relieved Starter. Since the first German attack was repelled on the 16th; somebody must have performed bravely.

Oh, to wrap a tidy ribbon around the battle of Höfen and detour from controversy. It's the Looney way as sure as the inevitability of mankind's unflailing ability to engage in war.

I received a letter dated May 30th, 1997 from Norm B. Cohen in New York City. Norm expressed his sympathy stating *I'm sure I'm not the first to tell you what an outstanding gentleman George was. A man's man. About your questions about Lt. Starter. I can't give you any information.* Norm went on to write that I should contact Frank Williams, mentioning that he was a happy go lucky guy and James Everett Allen who was a good churchgoing farmer.

His letter also described the story of a Battery Clerk from The 196th, Larry Buck. It seems Larry turned a column around under fire during an ambush, but someone else received the credit. Norm wrote, *I was invited to his 50th Wedding Party last year and took the opportunity to decorate him with the Silver Star*

Norm B. Cohen during the war—a Yankee in a primarily southern battalion, who distinctly remembered George at OP Six during the battle at Höfen. George visited NBC in the late 50's in New York City. NBC lived in the same location during my visit in May of 2005.

he really deserved. I obtained this medal with no difficulty (bought at a pawn shop.) Unfortunately he passed on a few months later. I feel a bit happier. Unfortunately these injustices happen in the turmoil of combat. I am saddened, but this is life.
    Sincerely,
    Norm Cohen.

On July 20th 1997, the letter arrived from the happy go lucky jeep driver, Frank Williams. *I would like to tell you what a wonderful father you had. I was sorry to hear about his death. Myself, like James Allen, will never forget Höfen Germany. I was always the jeep driver. I remember Lt. Looney having to go up and replace Lt. Starter who could no longer perform his duties in Höfen. The date was between December 16th and December 20th, 1944 when this happened. Hope this statement will help.*
    Frank Williams

I perceived a common thread of regret in the men's correspondence. Maybe a regret of aging or death, or possibly a regret that the men seldom and in some cases never saw each other after the war. A Christmas card to George from Everett Allen, written on an undetermined date, supported this notion.

Dear Mr. Looney,
    I don't have anything really to say. My health is still in good shape. I hope you are as well. I would sure like to see you but don't guess I will.
    Sincerely,
    James Everett

The inside of the card read: "Thinking of you at this beautiful season, just as you're thought of so warmly all year."

On the card's cover design, a blue grey sky touched mountain tops stretching across the horizon. In the foreground, three evergreen trees towered above a small red barn resting peacefully on a ridge throwing off the illusion of the tree tops rivaling the mountains in height. Below the barn, an ocean of snow wrapped around a frozen pond.

Staring at the serenity of the drawing, I wondered if the radio operator ever escaped the war. His salutation to my father reminded me of the way an enlisted man would address an officer. I also wondered if James Everett thought of the same place as myself when staring at that scene—Höfen, Germany in December of 1944. Before or after the turmoil of the storm, I could not say.

Frank Williams, the swashbuckling dare devil jeep driver from Alabama. "My jeep driver and a good one. He took chances to see that James Everett Allen and I had our bedrolls and equipment when needed." GWL

Mining a road, an engineer lowers a 10-pound antitank charge into a hole and prepares to scoop dirt over it. Sometimes two mines were buried together to increase chances of disabling a heavily armored Tiger tank. U.S. Army Signal Corp

Chapter Eleven

The Radio Operator

Drawn by the warmth generated by his cards and letters, I decided to first call James Everett Allen. George's radio operator answered the phone in a high pitched Southern accent as thick as the forests of his war years. His dialect could have passed for that of a black man in the Deep South from a time long gone with the wind. All within the same sentence, the volume and intensity of Everett's voice would rise and fall like a tidal wave, as if torn by the choice of calmness or turbulence. Ironically enough, the cadence of Everett's speech at times triggered thoughts of black comedian Richard Pryor's impersonation of a white man.

After accepting his heart felt condolences for my Father's passing, Höfen quickly became the subject matter. Everett remembered lots of snow on the ground and the bitter conditions.

How cold was it? A revealing post war Christmas card to George from fellow officer George Himmelman that mentions The Bulge comes to mind. *The snow was very deep and I remember Sgt. Iglay's gun froze up and when I went down to his gun, the wind would blow me back two steps every time I took one!* Everett further verified that he and George occupied the third floor of that three story building (OP 6) on a ridge with about thirty other men.

"Yeah, it got kinda hot in Höfen but you know when that bomb hit our buildin, yo Daddy, he grabbed that radio and he started telling everybody to stop it and he stopped it right quick. He knew that was an American bomb. We'd all hit the deck but the lieutenant. I'd lost my helmet and was crawling across the floor to get it when I saw yo Daddy just standing there holding the radio."

An image of the lieutenant standing erect and tall daring the Germans to take a shot at him played in my mind. The master of the understatement, his calm voice came over my internal headphones. "That's a little too close," said George.

I could hear the radio operator smile over the phone. "I knew when I didn't see him excited then, I'd never see him excited." Everett's smile was now, no doubt, wider than before. "Yo daddy was as calm as calm can be."

Everett, fueled with the adrenalin of yesteryear, continued. "Yo Daddy did get a little irritated with me once in the Hürtgen Forest. It was at night and there was a bunch of infantry men in front of me. We walked across this pine log across this creek and I had my rifle across my shoulder. I turned it loose somewhere along the line to catch one of those limbs to keep me from falling in and I got across the creek. I was reaching for my rifle and I couldn't find that thing so I started to crawl down the creek, but somehow or another he found out I wasn't with him. And he yelled out to come on. I said, 'I lost my rifle.' He said, 'we can get another rifle! Let's get through this mind field while we got

George looks tired, thin and haggard. I'm guessing this is the Hürtgen Forest before the snow, so first part of November, 1944. (Or about the time Everett Allen lost his rifle.)

somebody to get us through it.'" The phone line went silent for an instant before he added, "And we did."

Everett went on to describe some unique sleeping habits to say the least. "Ever time those bombs started hitting, I'd just crawl in my foxhole and go to sleep. I did it ever time. God was lookin out for me then and I thanked him then and I thank him now."

In the absence of incoming bombs, Everett had a more favorite place to sleep. "I'd stretch out on that jeep and I'd take me a nap. I was a short guy then, only five foot four."

I wondered if Everett had grown, but didn't ask. Brokaw would love this guy, I thought. I further learned of his career as a farmer until 1955, until he went broke, then entered civil service until retirement. Now, age 77 and divorced with one grown daughter, we never mentioned Lt. Starter.

"I'll buy you a hamburger for lunch if I come to Memphis," I said.

"No, you can't buy me a hamburger, but if you visit, I'll make us a home cooked meal from the garden."

James Everett inhaled audibly, a sort of reverse sigh. "Yo Daddy was the best observer and those commanding officers knew that." Everett's tone turned melancholy and the phone line from Dallas to Memphis bowed from an overload of regret. "I thought about coming to see yo Daddy in Dallas and I thought well, I'll get there and I'll say 'Mr. Looney; good to see you' and I'd say 'goodbye.' I just wasn't much to talk. Knowing what yo Daddy did in the war, he should have gotten more recognition. No doubt about that. He did not get the recognition he deserved."

Ditto for James Everett Allen.

Members of the 196th Field Artillery Batallion at Stratford on Avon, England. An unknown GI separates the diminutive Everett Allen and Lt. Looney. "Was in the room where Shakespeare was born. I had tea and cookies in Shakespeare's daughters' room." GWL 4/26/44

Chapter Twelve

The Jeep Driver

I next called Frank Williams, my father's jeep driver from Jasper, Alabama. I'd found a picture of Frank sitting driver side, his left hand dangling down the side of the jeep, clutching a bottle of wine. A look of sparkling mischief beamed from his eyes and spread all over his face.

Frank answered in a tired ragged voice, but warmed to the subject matter quicker than his commanding officer once stopped American bombs. Like Everett, he pronounced each syllable in an accent only heard in the Deep South.

"At Höfen, German paratroopers dropped everywhere. One landed right beside me. I took your Daddy and Everett Allen about eight the second morning," Frank said, further reinforcing Lt. Looney's presence at Höfen. "Colonel Cross wouldn't let me go back. I had to think about it, but after a week or so, I went back to get your Daddy and Everett. My jeep got shot all to hell. I got three sets of tires shot off that jeep. I remember a shell went off right in front and shook the jeep pretty bad."

The fatigue temporarily returned in Frank's voice when he mentioned witnessing "a hundred and fifty American bodies that the Germans had stripped for boots and clothes." Frank then seemed most anxious to discuss the good times. "Did your Dad ever tell you about HE?" he asked, his voice percolating with youthful delight.

"No."

"HE stood for High Explosive—was a mutt dog picked up by a guy named Flynn from Monroe, Louisiana in France. That dog stayed with us all throughout the war. He'd go flyin every time a bomb hit. As far as I know, Flynn took that mutt dog back to Louisiana after the war."

Sure enough, later I found a picture of HE with George's war pictures.

Frank was on a roll now. "We had a little trailer behind my jeep. We'd gone into Paris, France. Those French people lined up all along the streets givin' us cognac, wine and champagne. I guess I had one drank too many. I turned over that dern trailer. It's the only time your Daddy ever got mad at me and he told me I better not be takin' any more dranks from those French people."

We both laughed, his good spirits feeding the illusion that I'd known Frank much longer than a few minutes.

"Did your Daddy ever tell you about my little pony horseshoe that I had on the front of the jeep?"

A kinetic burst of energy invades H. E. (High Explosive)at the sound of gunfire.

"No."

"It was a little pony horseshoe that I found in a barn in a castle in England. Put that on the front of every jeep that we had. That horseshoe's right over my kitchen door today. Looks like it belonged to a little pony."

I resisted the urge to ask Frank if I could buy that horseshoe when his time came to visit Lieutenant Looney.

"We wound up in Pilsen, Czechoslovakia," said Frank. "Me and another old boy went to the opree."

I assume Frank meant the opera. Without warning, a brittle pause delivered a chill all the way from Alabama and the jeep driver's cheery outlook turned melancholy in an instant.

"Mike, I don't want to talk about the war anymore," Frank blurted, the weight of his tone smothering the happy-go-lucky in him.

And he never did, later refusing my offer to visit him.

George on the left and an unknown GI (possibly Louis Flynn) with the wonder dog! HE or High Explosive that Frank Williams referred to the night of our phone conversation. Frank said Flynn took HE home with him to Monroe, Louisiana after the war.

Chapter Thirteen

The Herman's

During my time travels to World War II, I constantly bumped into the Herman family from Jalhay, Belgium, finding several pictures of husband and wife with their four teenage children. My Dad wrote on the back of the pictures; *Stayed with the Herman family after The Bulge,* or *Mrs. Herman made us cookies,* or *I traded coins with Leon Herman.*

But it was a barely legible handwritten letter dated in October of 1990 from Marie Herman that left me reverberating like a struck bell.

Hello Lt. Looney!

We hoped you enjoyed your trip in Europe and am back home with a lot of deeply revived memories of the war years you lived over here, specifically about the terrible Battle of The Bulge. We should never forget the valiant GIs of the north flank of the battle and we are deeply grateful to them all forever. It's because you were there by Höfen, we were just outside of the battlefield. Those events are still so alive in our memories, we should never forget and our thankfulness will fail never. All of us (the four Herman children) *still remember you. You came at our little village right back from the frontlines for a couple of days or a week for so needed rest. Poor boys, you all looked so tired, covered in mud, just coming out of the hell. Well, we should be so pleased to get the opportunity to share some moments with you but we were busy that Saturday evening as you couldn't get in touch with us. We are so sorry, so disappointed. All of us remember you very well and should have been pleased and proud to have you even for a short while in our homes. Let us hope the opportunity will come again and we will meet each other.*

That Saturday evening everything seemed to be against your good idea to get in touch with us. Jalhay has many Hermans, only they are not of our family. I'm the elder of the Herman family and the only one who lives in our native village. As I married, it's my husband's name in the book. The lady you got the call with gave my brother's phone number in Spa. Several people in Spa are named Herman. My husband and I were so surprised and excited to come home for calling the hotel. We were down when we found out you left in the morning. (Evidently the lady that received George's call did eventually call Marie.) *Before calling the hotel,*

I called Henri (Marie's brother.) *They were at home that evening and no call came from the Holiday Inn.* (Where George was staying.) *Now we know why! The girl at the reception office at the hotel were very kind for giving to me all the information they could but they didn't have your address. On Monday, I called again, hoping the bookkeeping office would know it. They didn't. However, your travel agency gave us the vice president's name of The Battlefield Association in Los Angeles. We hoped this way could help.*

Josett, my sister, who lives only 5 miles from Henri-Chapelle Cemetery, had a good idea. She said the superintendent (of the cemetery) *could have information about your group or we could find your name and address in the visitor's book.*

Last Tuesday, we went there together and the superintendent had a list of all you with addresses. Luck! So it's why I can be able all of my family can get in touch with you! All the family was looking after something which could help. Josett's daughter had another good idea. Call the travel agency in England for knowing your schedule. The hotel said you were gone to Bavaria. We guessed your group to follow your war way back to north France probably. We did hope to catch you in Luxemburg or France or even at the airport or at the harbor if you go back to England. We were up again because we were sure the niece's ideas would be the good one.

We were down again and completely this time when the British agency said part of the group has gone to Remagen and 80 members went to Brussel's Airport on Sunday morning! While you were flying home and getting a good rest after a certainly tiring trip, we were still thinking you were not far from here. Well, you are far from here, but close to our hearts and memories specially revived right now. In nearly a half century so many things happened that I don't know how to begin! With you in my parent's home were Lt.s Rebec, Coyne, Dimitropoulos. We never heard from them. We are still in correspondence with Captain Corcelius and Lt.Starter. They came visiting us in '65 (Capt) in '63 (Lt. Starter)

Our parents are gone. Father died suddenly in 1981 and Mother in 1983. Her mind was completely gone almost 12 years before. She was just like a baby I had to nurse. When Dad was gone, she was in our home. The house where you came in February '45 is still ours and I live with my husband just outside of the village.

Marie goes on to list the address of her sisters, Yvonne and Josett and her brother Henri, then closes with, *We are hoping for an answer from you and it would be the start of correspondence between Texas and Belgium. With all our faithfulness and love; for all the family, Marie.*

Did my father respond to the request for a reply? Another letter from Marie, dated December of 1993 would indicate yes. Her descriptive passages provided an insight into world history greater than any text book with her concerns extending beyond the borders of Belgium.

December 1993
During the war, in May 1943, an RAF plane crashed on the side of the little lake, two miles from the center of Jalhay (her hometown) *coming back from a mission over Germany. Four men had time to bail out before the crash. Two were saved. One wounded and one found dead. They were helped by a secret organization. One of my husband was so not to be taken by the Germans. They reached south of France and were captured near the Spanish border. They were prisoners in Germany in a POW camp and the two Belgians who led them, died in camp. The wounded airman (who didn't travel with the other two) landed here in the area which is now the national park. After three nights living on the ground not being able to stand up and to walk because his pelvic bone was broken, he was able to*

cross this area and reach a farm. The fourth dead airman was carried further in the woods and buried there not to awaken the German border officer's attention. As the plane was all burned, they didn't find the bodies easily. Fortunately! By that way, they didn't search all over the village. Well a lot of talk to say that the wounded airmen's daughter came visiting here last October. Her husband was with her. They are from Winnipeg. He's in the mounted police and six months ago signed an engagement to Yugoslavia for humanitarian aid. He was stationed in the building in Sarajevo and he couldn't hide his tears when he talked about the awful misery there. The Serbs shot anywhere and at the UN peace troops as well. Their visit was a real emotional one for us all. I hope my story is not boring you too much. Let us hope that the Christmas season brings peace. In 1994, it will be the 50th D-Day and Battle of The Bulge Anniversary. We suppose many veterans will come back. We wish you will be coming then and be assured you are always welcome here. With love and best wishes again, All the Hermans.

Reading Marie's letter, I thought of Mick Jagger's comment from the documentary movie, "Gimme Shelter," during a Rolling Stone's performance at Altamont, California in the late sixties. "People, why are we fighting?" he lamented through that thick British accent moments after a Hell's Angel member, brandishing a large knife, sliced up a spectator near the stage. Anybody from any time period might ask the same question.

I found seven more letters from Marie, dated not only toward the end of the war but for several years afterwards. Her first letter was:

The Sagehomme sisters—Josette, Marie, and Yvonne. An exhausted and weary George stayed with their parents in Jalhay, Belgium for almost two weeks after The Bulge.

March 20th, 1945
Dear Friend,
    We wish you were far from the line of battle. We send you a lot of good lucks. We should be very glad if we should see you again.
Good luck and so long!
Family Herman.

Marie's next letter, was addressed to Carmen, George's sister.

August 12th, 1945
    It's with the greatest joy we have heard of the Japs surrender. For us, the day which brought the greatest change in our life was September 11th, 1944, day of our liberation. We have found again our freedom after watching the valiant Allied troops five years under the Jerry's occupation. Last December, we were afraid to see them again but God Bless USA, they were stopped before reaching here. (Marie is referring to The Battle of The Bulge.)
    You are wondering about my age. You know, I am nineteen, my sister Josette, fourteen, my brother Henri, fifteen, my youngest sister, Yvonne, thirteen and a half. I give you my best friendship and the best regards from my family to your mother and your entire family.

Marie wrote Carmen again.

September 23rd, 1945.
    Long time ago we have no more hear from your brother. We wish now he left Europe and he is again among you for these last weeks. Many soldiers are returning to states and doubtfully he had this happy luck also.

Freed from the fear of rejection, Marie responded to Lt. Looney's long anticipated correspondence.

January 15th, 1946.
    It's with the greatest joy I received your beautiful picture. We are glad you haven't forgot your Belgium friends. Several times, we have spoken about you and would have just liked to know whether you always were in Europe.
    Soon it will be one year ago you were stationed here. At this time nobody could believe the end of this conflict so near. Lt. Coyne and Dimitripoulos from who we never heard. If someday you get an opportunity to visit, we invite you with open arms among us. Oh it would be with great pleasure we'd like to see you again.

Marie's next letter lifted my eyebrows a notch or two.

February 23rd, 1947
Dear Friend,
    We have been very surprised receiving your package. We believe we were out of your thoughts since long time you left us. We are very happy we are wrong and we thank you again for the wonderful chest of fruits which are delicious. It's proof you still remember of that we are very pleased.
    Sometime we go with my school friends to the cemetery of Henri-Chapelle. We pray for the valiant

soldiers who gave their life for us. Everyone has adopted a grave. If you have some of your soldiers buried there, let us know their names. Sure their families would be happy to know we don't forget them and we'll never do it.
    It's a large cemetery—17,000 little white crosses are dressed there and it's not possible to realize 17,000 GIs are resting there forever. We holy wish that all your fellows came safely out of this terrible war, but we doubt it for the field artillery outfits were often under the fire of the front lines. I am sorry to write you so sad words which perhaps remember you the terrible days you spent in the hell over here.
    We wish to hear from you again. We shall thank you very, very much for the lovely package as a loud as you can hear it on the other side of the Atlantic Ocean.
    That would be wonderful if someday we could see you again. We really wish it would be true.
    With all our heartfelt friendship
    Best regards

Marie's next correspondence came almost one year later.

February 19th, 1948
    So three years ago at the same time you were living here and if our memory is good, it's your birthday. You'll know during you were celebrating your birthday we were thinking of you and we have talked about you and your fellows of The 196th FA. You were living all together nearly like brothers and now you are back home in different states. We sure you promised to write each other and you do it from time to time and not as often as you expected.
    We received a Christmas card from Lt. Starter but we rarely hear from him during the year. We've had a special good winter comparatively to when you lived fighting along the Roer River.

    I was stunned by Marie's undying appreciation of the Allied war effort, expecting her views represented the nation of Belgium. (A correct assumption, I would later learn.) When she spoke of the Belgium Liberation Day of September 11th, 1944, her passion poured from the page and arguably exceeded the pride many Americans display concerning July 4th.

    Her insightfulness regarding the GIs lack of communication with each other directly after the war displayed wisdom far beyond her years, pre-dating my own suspicions by over a half century. A very wise lady, I decided.

    Lt. Looney left an indelible mark on the Herman Family. Marie remembered his birthday three years after he departed her tiny village of Jalhay! Her family's effort to locate my Father on his return trip in 1990 fell nothing short of Herculean. Yes, the thought crossed my mind that the nineteen year old Marie harbored a flame for the twenty-six year old lieutenant, also causing me to wonder if my father returned this hypothetical heatwave with the precision of well placed artillery fire. But mostly I felt proud of my father for remembering the Herman Family when other war time house guests forgot them the way he once forgot to fill a swimming pool.

    The lives and now remains of George and Lt. Starter, scattered since the end of the war, had come to an intersection in Jalhay, Belgium, reminding George's family of what precious little they really knew of his life as a soldier.

An American jeep passes the smoldering ruins of buildings in Bastogne soon after the siege was lifted on December 26. German shelling made the town uninhabitable and created 250 more civilian casualties. Of the several thousand civilians trapped in the contested area, 782 had been killed. U.S. Army Signal Corp

In England, the U.S. massed weapons for invasion. Here, rows of 105-mm Howitzers are surrounded by hooded antiaircraft guns.

Chapter Fourteen

Marie's Reply

I don't remember the specifics of my letter to Marie, only of informing her that a lieutenant who once stayed at her parent's home had crossed to the other side. I'm sure I mentioned the wonderful old pictures of her family and of her warm letters to my father and his sister. Along with Marie's condolences, a fascinating description of The Bulge arrived in her reply.

April 21, 1997
Dear Mr. Looney and Family,

Thank you so much for your letter. All my family has been so sad to hear your Dad has passed on. When the post man brought your letter and I saw your name, I was sure the content wasn't a joyful one. We are becoming old and fate is pitiless! All the members of my family joined me to send to you and all of yours our fond sympathetic thoughts.

All of us still remember your father as a brave soldier, a very reserved, tactful, shy itself man. We

A somber George at the American cemetery in Henri-Chapelle, Belgium on 10-2-90 during his reunion tour.

appreciated him so much. It's why each of us has been deeply shocked to hear the dreadful news. Please tell your dear Mam we share her grief with her and with all of you.

More than 50 years after those terrible war years, we are still heart felt grateful to all of them who came from so far and fought so hardly in snow, cold and mud for our freedom and we'll never forget the thousand and thousand young boys who gave their life for a free Western Europe. All these soldiers (I mean GIs) who were killed in action here, were buried in Allied soil so no one in Germany. Right after the war, 17,000 little white crosses were lined up in Henri-Cheplle located 15 miles from here near the Dutch and German borde, and 19,000 in another World War II US cemetery in Holland just beyond the Belgian border.

After having been so unlucky missing your Dad's visit in Belgium in 1990, my sister and I went to this cemetery hoping the superintendent could help us to know your Dad's schedule and so expected to get the opportunity to join the tour somewhere. We were sure they visited the cemetery as all tours do and they did. The superintendent didn't know however where they were gone. We were lucky he had the tour members addresses. It's why you received my letter.

Now let me come back to war time. We were occupied by German troops for 4 years. They were not very many, but along the ocean and Nordean Sea specifically opposite to England. After 41 they had a second front in Russia after D-Day (still so alive in heart) and the fantastic Allied advance. Germans went back to Germany in disorder and without fights over here. We were sure war would be surely over when we have been liberated by US Army in September 44.

Arriving in view of the German border, the Allied troops slowed down waiting for more troops, fuel, ammunition. Meanwhile, German army gathered the troops and the 16th of December '44 rushed across the Belgium and Luxemburg borders at the great disappointment of everyone. It was the last energy jump of the German Army and it was terrible and destroying one! German Pancer SS were awfully hard and mercilessly killed soldiers, civilians and advanced pretty

George's 1990 view of the cemetery at Henri-Chapelle; over 17,000 tiny white crosses.

far in south Belgium. They wanted to reach Antwerp our harbor at the Dutch border, northern of Belgium. The shortest way for them was north direction. It means through our area. Fortunately the airborne troops dropped in an area nearly like forest. Couldn't make the junction with their troops and were nearly inefficient.

The 99th Infantry was there with The 196th Field Artillery. (George's unit) *They never withdrew though they had very, very hard fights. Face to SS Pancer division and others who were just like wild ferocious animals knowing their mother country was in extreme danger. All the US companies being of artillery, infantry engineer had very heavy casualties. The front line was about 15 miles from here and continued to south along the border and southern inside of Belgium. From here to Elsenborn Range* (said the historians because our area is softly hilly) *we heard artillery all along days and nights and in darkness. The sky was all red in that direction because of the artillery and fire and houses and forest. It was just hell every where and your Father was into it. It lasted seven or eight weeks. During this time we were very lucky to be behind the front. We had no casualties, no damages. However a German Pancer Division Armored went through the Allied lines and rushed to so close to here. Killed a lot of GIs and civilians and were stopped and out of fight.*

Here and all around just behind the lines, a lot of GIs, soldiers of different units, were packed to make just

like a human wall when the enemy attack could come and they couldn't come. These so brave defenders in Elsenbourn range area didn't let them go through their lines. It wasn't without terrible casualties. Some units or companies lost a lot of their men. One half said a 196th man to our neighbor where he slept. And it here your brave Father was.

During these weeks, we had an engineer headquarters in my native village which was located one mile west of the road. Our main village is gone through by that road. Another hamlet is 14 miles east. Many soldiers of the 99th were there and went to the front lines for a few days and came back for a couple of days rest. (When they came back.)

When The Battle of The Bulge was over, the engineer unit went to the battlefield to rebuild bridges and roads to allow troops to go ahead. As our village had no damages, US soldiers leaving battlefield came for a rest. A how much needed and won one! They were from The 196th Field Artillery. Soldiers arrived in trucks and officers with their jeeps without their heavy equipment. They were all muddy and terribly tired. Their faces had nearly the same color as their battle dress. Snow was melting and mud was mixed with snow. It was raining. It was so sad to see them so exhausted. Your Father wasn't with that group. He came a couple of days later in the same conditions.

As my Parent's home was across the school and the

80

house beside was empty, the school was the canteen and the empty house was the officer's and a shelter for sleeping. My Parents home was open and officers came to find a bedroom or a room to sleep on their camping beds. All the people opened their homes for the soldiers. Many families let all their bedrooms for the soldiers because these families were frightened all along the battle time and frightened also of the buzz bombs so they slept in their basements. I remember Mam did pies for them and they were so pleased. Lt. Starter said they didn't sit on a chair for six weeks. They lived with us for 2 weeks and were no more of 196th because they had done more then their duty and had no more to go to the front. They were involved into a military police but Lt. Starter asked to go back to front.

Were at our home: your Dad (when Lt. Starter left) Lt. Ward Coyne, Lt. Mike Rebce, Lt. Pete Dimitropoulous and their Captain Lynne Corcelius. They were all so happy to find rest, quietness in Belgium

The picture of George that Marie Herman of Belgium mailed to me when responding to my letter informing her of George's passing. Neither myself or my family had ever seen it before.

hamlet, in a friendly people whom hearts and homes were wide opened for them all. You can't feel what has been our feeling when the US soldiers liberated our villages. It was September 11th, 1944. We were so happy and so thankful to them. We couldn't say to them ,just say thank you, thank you because we knew few English language and had no time for gathering our poor vocabulary. The reason was that Sherman tanks, light tanks, half trucks didn't stop. Two days before, German soldiers were very many in Jalhay. They built block roads, gave instructions to civilians, living close to the crossing, to leave immediately. German soldiers were lying in ditches along the roads and all around with guns and machine guns ready to shoot. They planned for a severe defense and hard fights. Probably orders were received and during the night, they left shortly leaving a lot of military documents, maps - opened on tables. So the US troops found a quiet village fortunately and passed through just in a while. The US advance was so quick and the same events development occurred in many areas.

We don't know where the 196th FA was in September, probably not far from here if they were already a support for the 99th Infantry. This 99th liberated a little town about 15 miles north of us very near the US Cemetery of Henri Chapelle named Aubel. Before the German attack in the Ardennes, round October '44, I know 196th was close to here in the vicinity of a little castle named Liberne.

The whole family over here especially pleased to hear you plan to come on a trip. Be assured you and yours are the most welcome in all the Herman's homes. Now, our homes are more comfortable than during the war when everything was scarce as well as coal and wood. By the way, we had only stove in the kitchen. For soldiers we lighted heaters in the dining room and bedroom.

In thankfulness for their hospitality received at our home, your father sent to us from States, a wooden box filled with fruit, pastries. It was very kind from him and we were grateful to him for his remembrance of a few days spent with us while we were so indebted to him and all GIs. That box was made in red cedar I think. It was decorated with pyrocraftings and Mam saved it forever and saved the family old pictures into. (Man, where is that box today, I wondered?) Naturally, our parents are gone forever for several years.

We were in correspondence with some of the 196th and with your family for a few times. We never heard from Mike Rebce. Neither from Ward Coyne nor from Pete Dimitropoulous.

All the along this one half century we have been in correspondence with Lt. Starter and his wife. They came for a couple of days visit in winter 61. In 1987 we visited Lt. Starter. Lt. Starter died suddenly in July 1991 three months before my so dear husband. Like with Lt. Starter., we are still in touches with Capt. Corcelius.

No quite special event happened while your dear Dad was at home.

Thank you so much for your letter although the contents hurts deeply our hearts and memories and by now we more regret to have missed your Dad's visit in 1990. Please convey all our friendly regards to your dear

George with Pete Dimitropoulos and Ward Coyne in the backyard of the Herman home in February of 1945. Coyne, who lost the boots in a shooting contest with George, rode in one of the two observation planes to land in Paris on 8/25/44, the first Allied planes to land on liberated Paris soil. George was now personally looking at the worst of the war through the rear view mirror and would never be the same.

Mam to yours and brothers families. Excuse the long delay. Thank you for your kindness to write us last month.

Two black and white pictures of Lt. Looney tumbled from the envelope. I'd never seen either picture before. Wearing Army fatigues, Lt. Looney stood by the Hermann Home in one picture and his condition perfectly matched Marie's description in her letter— frail, tired and haggard but alive. He managed to look old and young simultaneously. The second picture, obviously taken at a better time, was virtually a head shot of Lt. Looney dressed in his officer's uniform. For the first time, I took note of his near matinee idol looks. Strong, brown eyes peered hard from under the bill of the officer's cap. A jaw chiseled of granite, perfectly symmetrical mouth. Smooth elongated face and a slightly pointed nose.

It occurred to me that George and his oldest son occupied opposite ends of the checker board at that particular time of our lives. At age twenty-six, my father had endured a depression and survived enough combat to haunt him for a lifetime. At the same age, I had survived enough rock concerts and softball tournaments to develop a pleasant tolerance for cold beer. As mentioned, I'd never thought of my father as young. My kids have probably never thought of me as old as if he sacrificed his youth for his future family (okay, maybe sort of old).

Since Lt. Starter evidently left Höfen before the hostilities ceased, it made sense that he also visited the Herman home before Lt. Looney. But then Lt. Starter asked to return to the front, conveying the image of a proud rider bucked from a horse but aching for redemption. A right or wrong assumption, I'll never know.

Chapter Fifteen

Heroes Are Hard To Find Revisited

The documents would take a few weeks to prepare—just the time I needed to make another journey. With a revived optimism that thankfully overflowed into my outlook concerning George's medal, I booked a flight for Europe. My mission: To retrace my father's war steps, in my mind's eye, pushing the Nazis from the beaches of Normandy, through hedgerows too thick for passage of soldier or tank, then survive the bitter cold and snow of Europe and ultimately force the German retreat to their border; also to pay a visit to the Herman family in Jalhay, Belgium, especially to Marie, the family spokesperson as a nineteen year old during the war and now as a seventy-two year old in 1997.

Z was busy conducting his own campaign, preparing to battle the US Government with an arsenal of paperwork in an effort to win my father recognition for his actions during The Bulge. Z's submission featured a portion of his just rewritten book that now prominently featured George's role at Höfen. Excerpts: *First Lieutenant Starter, one of the Forward Observers for the 196th, who was stationed at OP 6 when the area became virtually surrounded by Germans, called for fire to be directed on his own position. At approximately 0830 hours on 16 December 1944 a new OP party consisting of First Lieutenant George W. Looney and radioman James E. Allen, who had been relieved at OP 2 south of Höfen, were ordered to relieve Lt. Starter on OP 6. A fire fight then erupted between the Germans in the junk yard and the Americans in OP 6. Lt. Looney called for The 196th to fire on the Germans located in the junk yard then coolly "adjusted" the fires of the battalion when some of the rounds fell on the OP.*

The enemy again launched a very heavy attack on this position at 0430 hours on 18 December and succeeded in penetrating the front line in three places, gaining entry into the town of Höfen. Lt. Looney and the Liaison Officer were active in directing fire of the battalion. Once again, OP 6 became surrounded by German troops and once again, Lt. Looney called for fire to be directed on his own position. This fire killed or drove off the Germans, but caused no casualties among the Americans stationed in the OP.

During this phase of the battle, The 196th was the only artillery outfit firing in support of the Höfen front. At one time during a night attack, the battalion fire direction center handled fifty-eight fire missions in fifty minutes.

Z's package included letters from Everett Allen, the radio operator and Frank Williams, the jeep driver, both supporting Lt. Looney's presence on December 16, 1944 at OP 6 in Höfen,

Germany. Z also forwarded the excerpts from Thor Ronnigen's book that acknowledged Lt. Looney replacing Lt. Starter along with a letter from Lt. Colonel Himmelman addressed to me dated April 23 of '97 stating: *I don't know what happened in the case of Lt. Starter, but I remember Looney having to take off in a hurry to the front to replace someone at the observation post.*

Even a letter from Senator Dale Bumpers of Arkansas strongly recommending George W. Looney for the Silver Star for his duty during The Battle of The Bulge. To reiterate George's credibility as a soldier, Z provided copies of my Father's citations for his two previous bronze stars. No intent to slander the man, Lt. Looney replaced, assured Z; only for the US military to properly recognize George for leading artillery fire from that three story building on the hill.

Z's own letter to the government provided a peek at his zeal for justice that I already knew would provide the fuel to complete this journey wherever it may lead. Citing the previously mentioned documents as proof of Lt. Looney's role at Höfen, Z wrote *it was Lt. Looney who manned the Observation Post (OP 6) for The 196th and attached units for a period of approximately seven days from 16 December to 22 December, 1944. Lt. Looney's courage and attention to duty while at OP 6 greatly exceed those acts for which he was awarded the Bronze Star. His life was in far greater peril at OP 6 than it was during the incident for which he was awarded the Oak Leaf Cluster to the Bronze Star.*

I did not serve with Lt. Looney. I had never met Lt. Looney or his son, but I believe his service and bravery deserve greater recognition than he has thus far been accorded. On the basis of my research which sought only to find the truth, Lt. George W. Looney should be awarded the Silver Star for his role in preventing the German Army from capturing the town of Höfen, Germany.

Give em hell Z.

A castle in the countryside of France.

George records the carnage of St. Lo. On July 25, American bombers returned to St. Lo and once again, following the smoke line, killed not only another 111 men of the 30th division but also General MacNair. The bombings mangled about 1,000 Germans.

St. Lo, believes George. Despite the worst friendly fire incident of the war, after St. Lo, the Americans were able to advance up to 70 miles a day. Prior to that about 1,000 yards a day.

According to George's notes, more St. Lo, but I wonder? Too much left standing. Oh, the questions I would ask today.

With the worst over, a native rides his bike through the remains of St. Lo, France on a beautiful summer day in 1944.

Chapter Sixteen

Following GWL's Trail

My traveling companion for Europe was George Monteith, a delightful neighbor and entrepreneur about my age and recently settled in Dallas by way of Canada. No way I could take Sandra and the kids with school in full swing. George lost an uncle in the war, a pilot, shot down in the vicinity of the German/Belgium border. Bonded by the passion to explore liberation highway, we boarded a 747 for France on September 25, 1997. George, also a pilot and the designated travel guide for our journey, had regretfully come to the conclusion that we could not land at Normandy and fight our way across France. With no flight from Dallas to Normandy, we would land in Paris, drive to Normandy and then follow Lt. Looney's path back to Paris, then to Belgium and Germany.

After a smooth and uneventful flight, George and I checked into the Paris Hilton about 4 pm (9 am Dallas time) on Friday, September 26th. Our room overlooked the Eiffel Tower and a school with kids playing soccer on an artificial grass surface. Beside the soccer field, more kids played basketball; with a backdrop of gray domes and towers capping off ancient buildings, historical Paris looked like a giant postcard.

It was the most beautiful day imaginable, similar in feel to the day Lt. Looney traveled to eternity. From our high rise balcony, a turquoise blue sky stretched to eternity; temperatures hovered in the seventies while an occasional slight breeze stirred memories from another lifetime. The busy sounds of traffic and Parisian chatter, mixed with sidewalk café aroma, floated up to

Lt. Looney's 1944 photograph of the Eiffel Tower. "I was allowed to go to 1st floor elevator. Not running in August 1944." GWL

I'm standing near the Eiffel Tower—and in the exact location my Father stood in 8/44.

I'm holding a picture that GWL took of this spot in Paris in 8/44. George Monteith and I found the site while touring the city—like finding a needle in a haystack.

Lt. Looney's shot of same plaza from 1944.

our room. I closed my eyes and recognized similar sounds from New York.

My first dinner in Paris, pepper steak, cottage fries, pate and sorbet—wonderful! The sidewalk café offered or should I say denied service in a most peculiar manner. Patrons would sit at a table and management would promptly remove the table, thus

That's me at the Notre Dame Cathedral shortly after George Monteith and I arrived in Paris on 9/26/97. "I did eat lightly because there were hungry people standing by," writes GWL of his discomfort when eating at the Notre Dame Cathedral over a half century ago.

denying service. This happened twice during our dinner.

That night, the Eiffel Tower glowed with the spender of a giant electric Christmas Tree. We walked to the top of the Arc de Triomphe and predictably the view was spectacular, a never ending centipede of pedestrians and vehicles, weaving effortlessly throughout the streets and walkways of Paris. I tried to pinpoint my Father's location at the Arc when that German bullet whizzed by both of his ears.

We left for Normandy the following day and hostilities started early, barely avoiding a wreck on the French interstate. Two cars directly in front of us managed to merge their front and rear bumpers. One of the cars went toppling end over end, surely severely wounding the driver or worse. Other cars immediately stopped and rendered aid; George and I quickly decided that two foreigners better keep moving.

During the drive to Normandy, the French countryside was a sea of green mesas with castles, country villas, and cobblestone houses, all dating back centuries ago. Cows and horses dotted the landscape. Flower boxes, loaded with all colors of the rainbow, were in full bloom in most of the houses. The air smelled as pure and clean as fresh clothes on the line. I felt as if we should be on horseback, wearing knight's armor.

Without warning, guilt pounced heavily on my shoulders. Why hadn't I made this trip with my father? He never saw Paris or Normandy again, only primarily Belgium during The Battle of The Bulge Reunion Tour—a thought as sobering as the realization that one cannot change the past anymore than know the future.

As we neared the Normandy beaches, in spite of the balmy gorgeous weather, the sight of German bunkers nestled in the countryside threw off a chill. With dark rapidly approaching, we checked into our hotel, the Best Western in Cannes. A dog met us in the lobby, also joining us for breakfast the next morning in the hotel cafe. With no showers and only a free standing tub, the ancient four story structure had about four or five rooms to a floor; if carrying luggage, only one person could ride the rickety elevator that moved slower than my kids on Sunday morning. To save energy, the hall lights would turn off automatically once we entered our room. A huge castle, located directly across from our room, still showed nicks and bullet wounds from the war.

We drove along the Normandy Coast the entire next day,

A German's point of view from a gun emplacement at Juno Beach. Canadians took Juno on D-Day, 6/6/44, though the Germans destroyed 90 of their 306 landing craft and one in nineteen of the 15,000 Canadian invading force lost their lives.

Massive German gun stands ready, inland of Gold Beach. Though the fortress is nicked a bit, Allied fire power failed to destroy this mass of concrete. The giant gun remained in remarkably good condition.

George takes a breather from the top of a gun emplacement inland of Gold Beach. The British took Gold and Sword Beachs with little difficulty and light casualties on D-Day. Note the fortress of defense sprinkled through the country side.

What's left of a home along Omaha Beach, standing as if the destruction occurred yesterday. We saw several homes in this condition.

I've discovered a passage to the intricate German underground bunker system that ran along Omaha Beach.

The remains of a tattered and torn German gun emplacements along the Normandy Coast. I'm not sure which beach.

Wow! George Monteith checks out the size of this bomb crater just inland of the Point du Hoc section of Omaha Beach.

Bomb craters sprinkle the landscape inland of Omaha Beach. 450 American pilots roared over Omaha on D-Day, but for fear of hitting American landing craft, released their bombs too far inland, and not one bomb hit the beach. More French cattle were killed than enemy soldiers.

As seen in the movie "Private Ryan," the cemetery at Omaha Beach. White crosses as far as the eye can see.

The entrance to the American cemetery at Omaha.

visiting all the beaches of the Allied invasion, also entering a couple of the German pillboxes. The concrete bunkers smelled of damp must and was dark except for the bright sunlight entering through the slit for shooting. I imagined D-Day from a young German soldier's point of view—a low sky thick as grey wool, the obscene enormity of the 5,000 Allied ships slashing through the turbulent ocean waters, the barrage of pounding artillery, leaving the German deaf from the ringing in his ear. Looking through the same peephole I was looking, did he see Allied soldiers fall at his hand? Was there remorse for taking a man's life? Did the German survive? If not, how many minutes or hours remained in his life? How many American soldiers did he take with him? What was his last thought?

Beyond the countless pill boxes and bunkers, American bombs from over five decades earlier had left the countryside sprinkled with green moon craters. Featured in the movie "Private Ryan," the Allied Cemetery at Omaha Beach left me breathless. As far as the eye could see, little white crosses stretched over a rolling green lawn more manicured than Augusta National.   On the first grave I approached at Omaha, date of death, July 4, 1944.

This is the first grave I approached at the American cemetery at Omaha, date of death, July 4, 1944.

Omaha Beach in October of 1997. On D-Day, 1,200 German troops lined the ridge, while GIs leaving the landing crafts proved easy target practice. By 10:00 am, one German commander even reported to his superiors that the invasion had been stopped. The infamous Point du Hoc looms at the western edge of the beach.

Point du Hoc in the fall of 1997. Imagine the Americans scaling toward the crest while the heavily armed Germans fired on the Americans coming up from the rocky beach. Many survivors of the invasion of Omaha Beach thought the day had been a failure.

Point du Hoc from the German's point of view. Some figures peg the casualty rate on the first landing at Omaha Beach as high as 90%. The initial reports that filtered out to General Bradley, aboard his flagship, were so discouraging he considered halting the invasion of Omaha and redirecting further troops to Utah Beach.

A panoramic view of Omaha Beach taken from Point du Hoc. For more than two weeks after D-Day, the English Channel continued to cough up the dead, with bodies washing up onto the sand below the 100 foot cliff.

Due to the detail of my Father's war maps, I'm able to take a picture of the precise location at Omaha Beach that Frank Williams drove Lt. Looney's jeep from the landing craft to shore. Note the fresh tire tracks leading to "GWL's Trail." I took three vials of sand from the beach by the tracks.

The church at St. Mere Eglise, Normandy, France. Made famous in the movie "The Longest Day" when Red Buttons portrayed the American paratrooper stranded on the roof of the church during battle. The war in Europe started here in the early hours of 6/6/44.

A lonely gun emplacement on Omaha Beach slowly sinks below the beach surface, as if trying to disappear and forget the carnage of D-Day once and for all. Despite the carnage of Omaha, 150,000 Allied troops were on French soil within 24 hours of D-Day.

We could view the beaches for miles from the high cliffs of Omaha Beach, providing a clear understanding of the terrible American casualty rate on June 6th of '44—the bloodiest day in US Military History since the Civil War with over 2,500 American deaths. In museum pictures of the landing at Omaha, white flashes from German guns practically blinded the GIs before they ever left the coffin shaped boats for shore. Custer had better odds. In spite of Omaha's gory history, the panoramic view below, the blue skies, the sound of rolling waves, all left me feeling invigorated.

Evidently, the French don't believe in age discrimination on the beaches. On one beach, a rifle thin lady of at least sixty years of age sunbathed topless. We arrived at Utah Beach, the site of my Father's landing, around dusk and spent the night in a quaint little hotel at St. Mere Eglise, the first French town my Father saw, which is located just inland from the Normandy Coast. The

Overlooking Utah Beach, the indestructible Crisbecq Battery, (above and below) contained three 210 mm cannons and housed 400 men. Allies dropped over 800 bombs on Crisbecq prior to June 6, including 598 tons of explosives on June 5. Crisbecq answered the bell by sinking an American destroyer on June 6, D-Day. The battery endured hand to hand combat before the German commander ordered evacuations on June 12. Glad Lt. Looney arrived a tad late to Utah Beach for this get together.

I am literally dismantling a gun at Omaha Beach. I got the impression no one cared if I drug it off.

war opened there with paratroopers dropping in before dawn on D-Day; one US paratrooper dangled from the church rooftop while watching so many of his comrades die—a scene immortalized in the movie, "The Longest Day."

Thanks to Z's map, the next day we found the exact spot of my Father's landing. We arrived around 1:30 under a lazy fog. I envisioned Frank Williams, a mischievous twinkle in his eye and

A German cemetery near St. Mere Eglise, France. Any symbolism in the black crosses?

hankering for one "drank," slowly navigating the jeep from the landing craft to shore. Lt. Looney sat front seat shotgun, calm but a laser intensity consuming his expression. Innocent to danger, Everett Allen and his radio, one not significantly larger than the other, occupied the back seat.

The weather cleared and the sounds of the gentle waves blended perfectly with the distant fog horn and a deluge of blue sky. It seemed the most peaceful place we had visited so far. With the burble of ocean birds floating thru ocean air, I filled up three little vials with sand for myself and my two brothers and thought of the massive contrast of June 6, 1944 vs. today.

Just out of St. Mere, we toured a German cemetery. Though equally maintained as the American cemeteries, black instead of white crosses lined the green meadow. From St. Mere, we followed my Father's route to Mont Martin En Graignes, the town of Lt. Looney's first action as an artillery observer. We next proceeded to another small village, Goucherie; Lt. Looney received credit at Goucherie for knocking out a German gun battery while observing from a Cub plane that I had come to

That's George Monteith at the hotel bar in St. Lo, France, flanked by the owner on his right and a local patron on his left. The bar owner remembered clearly the American bombings of St. Lo that leveled the city. These same American bombs barely missed Lt. Looney and killed General McNair.

I'm enjoying a peaceful moment by the Meuse River at Charleville, France. Lt. Looney won his first Bronze Star at Charleville for directing artillery fire from a building across the river. Germans came out of a cave with their hands up.

know well. As we approached an even smaller town called Amigny, I'm fairly certain we found the ditch where Lt. Looney was crawling beside an American tank when German artillery blew the tank and its crew to Smithereens.

We arrived at St. Lo around 6 pm, the site of the worst friendly fire incident of the war when American bombers mistakenly killed 111 GIs and wounded over 500 more. I visualized my Dad in a dead sprint, attempting to escape the bombing, no easy scene to imagine since I saw my Dad run as often as he used the Lord's name in vain which is to say none at all. Only the church survived the bombings at St. Lo, a town of over 25,000 people during the war.

We stayed at a hotel with approximately thirty rooms; though fairly modern by French standards, the two story structure still seemed older than its fifty years. George and I struck up a conversation at the tiny bar with a slightly odorous rather frumpy always smiling, lady of sixty five or so who owned the hotel. According to the owner, when the American bombers darkened the sky, most civilians went underground for three days and nights with little food, water and no light. The sound of battle was deafening. When all was quiet, the natives of St. Lo dared to venture out like nervous birds from a cage only to discover their town was gone—a bomb made pile of ruin, sewn together by solid rubble! An unfortunate consequence of war she assured us, but necessary because the Germans were so very mean.

During our history lesson, the regulars huddled around the bar's television, watching a soccer game the way Americans watch "Monday Night Football." A dense fog cluttered the air since everybody in the bar, but George and I, were reducing the lengths of cigarettes at a frenetic pace.

Finally, we arrive at OP 6 on 10/02/97, the scene of so much controversy. I'm holding the picture Thor took of George standing practically in the same spot in 1990. I see the reflection of a young George, strong and with laser focus, taking in the action from the middle window on the 3rd floor. It's a healthcare facility today.

George's view from the top floor of OP 6-a much more peaceful day in the fall of 1997 than in mid-December 1944. "50 Germans surrendered. 500 dead. We had 5 killed and 7 wounded." GWL. Norm Cohen's words come to mind: "I think those Jerries were doped up because they were coming up in droves. The brain is marvelous, I smell the various aromas of combat right now."

I've made it to the third floor of OP 6! Marie Herman Sagehomme's communicating with the German nurse that finally allowed our access to the 3rd floor. "I stayed up here six days and night without relief." GWL.

Charleston Officer Gets Bronze Star

Charleston, Ark. – (Special) – Lieutenant George Looney, son of Mr. and Mrs. M. W. Looney of Charleston, has been awarded the Bronze Star for heroic and meritorious action against the enemy beyond the call of duty. Lieutenant Looney has been in service three years, and has been overseas 11 months. His award was for action in France, but he now is in Germany.

Looney

He is a graduate of the University of Arkansas, and was instructor in the agricultural department of the Monette, Ark., high school at the time of his induction.

Recognition of Lt. Looney's first Bronze Star as it appeared in either the Charleston or possibly the Ft. Smith, Arkansas newspaper in late summer 1944.

We left St. Lo the next morning, a Wednesday, and arrived in Jalhay, Belgium, the hometown of Marie Herman around eleven Friday morning. She lived in a large old farmhouse that was built in the 1800's.

As our rental car eased to a halt in her driveway, Marie, an incredibly spry woman, practically sprinted from her house to greet us. Through Coke bottle thick glasses, her big eyes traveled the length of my body. "You look like your Father," she finally said in fractured English, the tone of her cough drop voice, rich and deep.

She had lunch waiting for us—cheese, fruit, tuna and French bread. Over lunch we showed her my Father's pictures of her siblings and parents during the war. Marie never quit talking and truly possessed a photographic memory, remembering details of the war as if it happened yesterday. At times, her English drifted into Flemish, leaving George and I only slightly confused. We learned that Marie inherited the house from her husband, the past mayor of Jalhay for many years, who had passed away about three years earlier. The home of her youth and my Father's temporary resting place during the war was about a mile down the road.

Did she know of the three story building in Höfen that served as a major battle site during The Bulge, I asked?

Without hesitation, she replied, "Yes, and I will take you to it."

Within forty minutes, we gawked at that red three story building that had become a healthcare facility. A German nurse with eyes as sharp as a hawk, allowed us inside. Entering the building, I caught the familiar sterile fragrance of medicine and hospitals and my anticipation was flowing like electricity. She and Marie began to speak and though I understood neither party, the intensity of the conversation matched their sober expressions; I smelled trouble. Marie began to dominate the conversation and with her every word, the nurse's look gradually advanced from serious to one of frosty detachment. Tension hung in the air like the dense fog of the Hürtgen Forest. Without warning, the nurse's face broke open into a grin and with a slight wave of her arm, she granted us passage upstairs. Marie later told me that the nurse, born since the war, had been disavowing any knowledge

Seven years after the Bulge reunion tour, looks like George and I found practically the same spot where Lt. Looney revisited the Siegfried line.

George and I follow GWL's Trail to the cemetery at Henri-Chapelle, Belgium.

The home of Marie's parents rests peacefully in the fall of 1997, practically pleading to tell all that it saw during the war. Lt. Looney recuperated with the Herman family for almost two weeks after The Bulge and slept in the downstairs room with the light on.

Marie took this picture of George and I soaking in the beauty of Monshau, Germany.

of the matter. "Embarrassed by the subject," Marie said.

Soon, I gazed out the third story window, standing in precisely the location my Dad had once directed artillery fire; per his notes, I saw the tree branch that saved his life from a German sniper's bullet. On this day, the world was silent. A spacious deserted green meadow eventually met a distant Caribbean blue sky. If there was going to be a place on this trip to link with my Dad's spirit, to see what he saw, feel what he felt, this was it. Once again I beheld the battle scene from his point of view—a gun metal grey sky practically touching the small building's roof, the surrounding area humming with artillery, countless Germans advancing up the snow covered meadow like robotic ants only to be greeted by giant balls of fire dealt by my father's hand, dirt splattering high in the air followed by smoke clouds spiraling upward in great bursts, Germans dropping like bowling pins, screams of anguish, and finally the potent odor of gun smoke. Perhaps my Father saw similar sights when he returned to this spot in 1990. He almost certainly saw in the reflection of the third story window, the image of himself as a young man again.

As we prepared to leave, Marie pulled out a gift wrapped box of Belgian chocolates and presented it to the nurse who promptly smiled from ear to ear. Referring to the gift, Marie later said, "only if she let us in."

We finished the day by visiting Henri-Chapelle, the cemetery mentioned in Marie's letters. An endless view of white crosses triggered an all consuming thought. Why did my Dad return home and so many stayed behind? I'm sure Lt. Looney pondered the same issue more times than he called for artillery fire.

That night, George Monteith and I met Marie's brother, Henri and his wife, Matre, a petite blonde lady with a personality as warm as her smile. Henri, a retired teacher of agriculture at the university, looked to be in his early sixties. With his full warm face, similar build, and thin retreating hairline, his appearance actually reminded me of my Father. He spoke little English, but also told Marie of my strong resemblance to Lt. Looney. As we stood together in Marie's living area, Marie began to translate for Henri who was reenacting the time that my Father took Henri to shoot guns. "Rat tat tat," said Henri, holding an imaginary rifle, his face tightening with the strains of battle. Henri, about fifteen during the war, had never told Marie until that day.

Though the population of Jalhay was only a couple of thousand people, we dined at the equivalent of at least a four star restaurant—a converted barn no less. As we were entering the restaurant, the sight of several parked German Mercedes Benz angered Henri. "Henri's never forgiven the Germans for invading Belgium—not once but twice," reminded Marie.

Never before had I stopped to consider that I'd driven German cars for years without consciously connecting Germany to my Father's past. If my Father harbored any resentment for his son conducting business with the former enemy, he did so silently. In possibly a sort of forgiveness by association, my Father, after steadfastly refusing to buy any car other than American, drove a Honda the last few years of his life.

Henri later insisted on paying the bill. "He's thanking your Father for helping liberate Belgium," said Marie, referring to the free dinner.

After returning to Marie's house, my suspicions became fact. Her mind housed an endless supply of knowledge about the war and neither she nor her siblings grew up under ordinary circumstances. A few instances: a German officer, in full dress regalia complete with an officer's sword, demanded the use of the Herman home. Marie's Mother, a proud lady, but with limited

The Herman children in May of 1945 or a few months after Lt. Looney's departure. Henri, Josette, Marie and Yvonne. The family home is in the background.

Marie's sister, Josette sits between George and I at the dinner table at Marie's house, located only a short distance from their parent's home. Josette, who was making her first public appearance since the loss of her husband, 3 years prior, later surprised me with the gift of my Father's candy box—a gift from Lt. Looney to the Herman Family over 50 years ago. Josette passed away not long after our visit.

options, told the officer to remove his boots before entering.

Marie told of the Herman children racing to the site of three different Allied plane crashes, trying to reach the wreck before the Germans. One crash involved two Allied planes in a mid-air collision in fog. No survivors. Once, the children rushed to falling parachutes only to discover Allied guns and ammo, but no soldiers.

Reiterating her earlier letters, Marie said of The Bulge: "The night sky was orange from fires, but the battleground was ten miles away!" A huge bomb crater took up much of Marie's back yard. Her future husband had saved a piece of bomb shrapnel for a paper weight that once came hurtling through two bedrooms! No one was hurt.

We spent the night at Marie's house and the next morning I awoke to the sound of a neighbor's tractor engine churning. My upstairs window view overlooked the lush green pasture. Napoleon may have used the ancient free standing tub in my bathroom.

George and I soon left for our day's exploration, while Marie stayed home to prepare for the big dinner that night. We first went to Malmedy, infamous for the massacre of American prisoners in cold blood by the Germans who left them buried in the snow. We next drove to Remagen and saw the remains of the famous bridge that American troops used to cross the Rhine. It collapsed a few days after my Dad's battalion had crossed, killing many Americans.

On the drive back, we returned to Höfen and the three story building. While George filled up the car with gas, I went to the front door. No sight of the nurse from the previous day before, but a young smiling co-worker readily granted my passage to that third floor window. Probably expecting a box of candy, I thought. As I looked across the vast meadow in solitude, once again my Dad's spirit entered my insides with a dignified serenity. In my solitude, one question pecked at my mind like a hungry squirrel. Was my Father disappointed that none of his sons served in the military? During my time, Vietnam was raging and I was now acutely aware of the fact that we'd never broached the subject. To borrow from Scott Turow's wonderful novel, "Ordinary Heroes," it's my belief George had gone to war so that his children would not have to, not so they could take their turn. I walked away, leaving the room and its view of the former battle field, to the ghosts of Höfen.

Before dinner, Marie and I made a quick trip to her parent's home, now occupied by her cousin and husband, both gracious Belgians as I'd come to expect. Marie motioned to one corner of the den/living area with her eyes. "That's where your Father slept," she said. She took me to the backyard, pointing to the spot Lt. Looney stood in the picture that she'd sent me earlier. Marie explained that Lt. Looney arrived in February of 1945 a very quiet and reserved man, exhausted to the point of stooped posture. "He left in much better condition ten days later," she proudly declared.

After returning to Marie's house, I met her middle sister, Josette, along with her youngest sister, Yvonne and her husband, Andre a retired police investigator from Spa, a town in Belgium known for its natural bottled water. Marie's dining room table was the size of an indoor soccer field and set for a king's feast. An abundance of invaluable antiques filled her house, but she probably understood little of its value and cared less than that.

Josette's presence, a virtual recluse since her husband died approximately three years before, proved an unexpected treat for the family. A plump white haired lady, a seriousness surrounded her, certainly more so than her other family members, and then the unexpected happened. With her face void of any expression,

The box itself along with the vial of sand from Utah Beach. Both are proudly displayed in the dining room of my home.

Josette, who spoke no English, presented me with a dark cherry wooden box. I forced a smile and accepted, but felt more inadequate than a near sighted artillery observer.

"It's your Dad's box," said George, recognition inscribed on his face.

Too stunned to reply I just stared at the box.

"It's the box that your Dad gave to their Mother," George said.

Through mist welling in my eyes, my stare took in Josette and then the rest of the family. Josette smiled for the first time in three years, I'm told.

It was an unforgettable night, dominated by laughter and conversation. I longed to understand Flemish, though Marie gladly interpreted for everyone. I learned that Andre, the retired policeman, made hand crafted wooden bowls. In his retirement, Henri maintained beehives and presented me with three jars of wonderful honey to take back home. His wife, Marthe made beautiful silk pillows. Yvonne, the jovial type, laughed at everything and Marie just kept on talking.

After dinner, Marie disappeared, but soon returned holding an envelope. As she slipped the envelope in my hand, her mouth pointed north at the corners, exposing a youthful grin. It was a letter dated January 4th, 1991 from my Dad, responding to her correspondence when the two failed to correct in 1990.

Staring at his instantly recognizable handwriting generated instant thoughts of his jack-o-lantern smile, his chuckle, his warm country voice that to this day I hear randomly on most any day. My own smile took command of my face as the contents of the letter ushered in a tidal wave of wistfulness.

January 4, 1991
Dear Friend,
I just wanted to let you know I received your letter and I was very disappointed that we did not get to see

Henri, Marie's brother, who Lt. Looney evidently took to shoot guns during his stay, occupies the seat to my left at the same dinner. Youngest Herman sibling Yvonne and her husband Andre, a retired police investigator, flank Henri.

each other while I was in Brussels. The girl in the office tried to help me. I am sure we traveled around each of you several times on the bus. Guess I could have tried harder. Not speaking the language did not help.

I still have the pictures you sent and also still have the silver coins I traded with your Father. I never forgot your Mother bringing in tea and cookies at night.

I am retired from Dallas Government. Have wife and three boys, three grandchildren, nice home, two cars, comfortable income but most of all good health at 72.
Sincerely, George W. Looney
PS Made Captain before the end of the war.

Marie soon retrieved a sack of silk parachute remains from the area plane crashes during the war. With the care of handling a newborn infant, she then displayed exquisite embroidered silk handkerchiefs made from the same parachutes. "Not all is lost in death," Marie said. "Don't wait fifty years before visiting again," she reiterated as if I was Lt. Looney, as if reading his letter had made us one. Soon, George and I bid a heartfelt goodbye to all of Marie's family as they started for home.

After eating breakfast the next morning with Marie, we gave her a big hug, and piled in the car for the ride to the airport. As our car slowly eased away from her front yard, I could see Marie waving good bye, her massive grin exposing massive teeth worthy of a billboard ad. "I don't expect to make it back," my Dad once told Thor Ronningen in a letter, referring to his trip to Belgium in 1990. I questioned the same seven years later.

"I wouldn't change a thing if I had my life to live over," claim some. "Horse hockey," say I. My Father never returned to France or saw the Hermans again. Hell yeah, I'd rearrange the deck if provided the opportunity. Imagine the joy on George's face when taking in Paris or reuniting with the Herman siblings. Consider the history lesson to be learned while traveling Liberation Highway, with a man awarded a Bronze Star and an Oak Leaf Cluster.

It's now as clear as the French country sky in October that World War II was the defining event in the life of George Washington Looney and his buds of the 196th. Not all is lost in death.

Chapter Seventeen

Gateway To Readiness

I finally received acknowledgement of George W. Looney's application from the Review Board Agency of the Army on November 10th, 1997, in response to Z's submission in July. The agency further stated the evaluation process would take anywhere from eighteen to twenty-four months.

Per an earlier request by Z, Senator Kay B. Hutchison of Texas had already written The Department of the Army asking for an update on the status of our inquiry. The Army replied to Senator Hutchison on November 17, 1997. *We are continuing to inquire into this case, but it is taking more time than would normally be expected.* I could hear Z's howl of frustration all the way from cheese country.

In January of 1998, a letter arrived from the Department of Army, located at 9700 Page Avenue, St. Louis, Missouri, stating that in June of 97, the Army Board for Corrections of Military Records and Army Discharge Review Board were transferred to the Army Review Board at the same 9700 Page Avenue. Maybe a different department or floor, but hardly a confidence builder in the whole process. At the bottom center of the page, I noticed the slogan. *Gateway to Readiness.* By George's birthday of February 22nd, still no word from the Review Board.

With relentless passion Z stayed on task. "These politicians sure get in a hurry to send these kids to war, but can't find the time to get the records straight," Z mumbled over the phone. On April 5th, Z fired a verbal round of artillery to Senator Bumpers from Arkansas. *I am not, was not and never will be one of your constituents, therefore, I suppose you have every right to toss this letter in the can. I do hope that this letter will not be "canned" until either you or someone on your staff reads it.*

Z went on to quote Thor Ronningen's book. *For the defense of this town (Höfen) which is recorded in depth of almost every history of The Battle of The Bulge, President Roosevelt awarded The Battalion with the Distinguished Unit Badge, and every soldier was awarded the Bronze Star by special order of the War Department. That statement is not quite true because Lt. Looney and Cpl. Allen got NOTHING!*

I delighted in the concept of Z retrieving his uniform from the attic and paying a visit to the review board. We never heard from Bumpers.

Advancing through the dangerous Hürtgen Forest, mud-splattered infantrymen of the U.S. Division clamber out of a gulch clotted with barbed wire, felled trees and other debris. American GIs frequently lobbed grenades or small charges of TNT ahead of them in order to set off any mines or booby traps that German soldiers might have placed in their path. U.S. Army Signal Corp

An American studies a captured Nebelwerfer, the conventional artillery. Its projectiles made a horrifying screeching noise that earned them the GI nickname "Screaming meemies." U.S. Army Signal Corp

Almost a full month after the massacre of American soldiers by Joachim Peiper's SS troopers near Malmédy on December 17, a U.S. Graves Registration team performs the grim task of location and identifying the victims. The fall of snow had preserved the bodies until Graves registration could do its work. U.S. Army Signal Corp

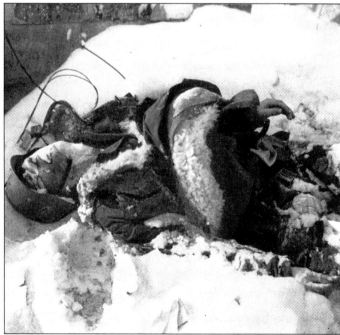

German looters enjoyed U.S. cigarettes only a short time; one died in the snow with a box of American matches under his left hand.

Chapter Eighteen

Little Big Man

Early that summer, my youngest brother Dean and I, consumed with the need for frontline duty, decided to travel to Memphis to meet our Father's radio operator, James Everett Allen. Though Everett welcomed our visit, he again warned us by letter of his inability to remember names, places, or dates, and also volunteered that *I just don't have much to say.* But some things the human memory bank stubbornly refuses to delete so it speaks out anyway.

I never saw the town of Höfen but it sure made history for us, Everett wrote in the very next paragraph. *I will say I saw some terrible sights,* he continued, referring to the area surrounding Höfen. *I came upon this curve in the road and saw all these dead Germans laying in the ditches and one tank on one side with a dead German hanging out of it, and man the odor was terrible. I covered up my head as not to see them and that helped me with the odor.*

If Bob Seger once told us, "Rock-n-Roll Never Forgets," George and his buddies of The 196th might say: neither does war—the indelible stain of blood on life's canvas.

After arriving by air and renting a car, our map skills paled in comparison to our Fathers' during wartime and we were unable to find Everett's house. Mindful of our Father's disorientation toward the end of his life, we found ourselves hesitant to call Everett for directions. An awkward moment for all, if George's former radio operator's memory lost its signal. A few minutes later, more hopelessly lost than George and the ten walking wounded in the Hürtgen Forest, we called Everett for help.

Everett answered, his voice throaty from the years, but his tone, still high and birdlike, was loaded with energy; he immediately identified our location which proved further off course than a good spy plane. Through a Southern accent rich enough to conjure images of the Civil War, he provided directions that MapQuest would envy, his attention to detail remarkable for a man of any age.

Nearing Everett's neighborhood, we passed recently built brick homes with manicured lawns, lush green in color from automatic sprinkler systems. We soon spotted Everett's address; the sight of his dwelling sent my heart into a free fall, leaving a hollow feeling. Dean and I exchanged troubled looks. In the midst of an upscale residential development, Everett Allen lived in a small frame house, its condition rapidly advancing from worn to dilapidated.

A 1970 faded blue Pontiac Catalina and a '64 rust colored Chevy quietly occupied one side of Everett's bare yard, like old boats abandoned on shore. Throwing off a delightful smell, row after row of fresh vegetables, all lined militarily erect and precise, completely filled his two acre backyard which dwarfed the size of any neighbor's yards. As if quietly providing guard duty, a tractor, its former red color also eroded from the years, was parked in a tin shed toward the rear of the garden. Progress had totally surrounded Everett, leaving his residence more out of place than combat boots with a tux.

Everett greeted us in his front doorway, his round soft face gleaming with delight; his posture was slightly hunched, taking on the shape of a wooden stick warped from the weather; his height no longer reached the five foot four of his war years, more like five foot two with a frame slight as a bird. Throw in the droopy eyes, pointy ears and an off center nose rising at the tip and Everett could easily have passed for one of Santa's elves in off season. After the proper introductions and handshakes, we soon occupied his modest, but tidy living room. With his dated furniture and hardwood floors, I thought of Grandma's house. His eyes, which seemed incapable of hostilities, began to travel my entire body, then Dean's.

"Which one of us looks the most like Daddy?" I asked, realizing the reason for such scrutiny.

Once again, his heavy gaze alternated between Dean and myself. "You do," he said to me after a modest pause. "Yo Daddy was the finest man I ever met durin the war," he suddenly blurted. I'm sure a blind man could have read the pride written on Dean's and my face. But Everett wasn't through. "I guess it was because he didn't treat us like some of the other officers did. He treated us like equals." We'd been with Everett less than five minutes, a good start like scoring the first time with the ball.

I briefly wondered if the emotion of the moment was causing a heat flash but then noticed tiny beads of sweat on my brother's forehead. The place was a furnace. A quick survey of Everett's near hairless dome and high forehead revealed no signs of perspiration or discomfort.

Everett noticed our meltdown. "I sent the air conditioner out to be fixed, but it's not back yet," he said sheepishly, motioning with his eyes to the spot for a lone window unit in the quaint living area. Everett later admitted that the air conditioner had not worked in years and he'd sent it for repair only because of our visit.

Without warning, the tiny kitchen area bordering the living room delivered an aroma that overpowered any discomfort from the heat. Smoke signals were rising from pots on his tiny white stove, percolating with the inviting fragrance of fresh okra, cream

Myself and George's radio operator, Everett Allen at his home in Memphis during the summer of 1998.

corn, and black eyed peas—all from Everett's garden. Breathing hard enough through my nostrils to inflate my chest, I also took in the welcome scent of homemade bread, fried chicken and fresh apple pie rising up from the stove top.

With a table fan stirring a welcome breeze in the kitchen, we sat down to lunch. Everett said the blessing, as heartfelt a thanks I've ever heard—thankful for his guests, the food, and to be alive. No doubt, a small man with a giant heart. Clearly energized by the purpose of cooking for his lieutenant's offspring, the pride from Everett's smile blanketed the room as we devoured the home cooked meal of a lifetime. Is there any doubt that most men need a purpose in life—especially during the twilight years? A dose of purpose would stretch across the Atlantic on this day.

Over lunch, Everett confirmed that he tilled his garden with his 1946 red tractor from his farming days—purchased with military paychecks from the war. "Eight hundred dollars. That's all I saved," he said, laughing heartily. "Give most of it to the neighbors," he announced. Oh, the irony I decided. Everett, his spirit richer than his pocketbook, provided food for his more affluent neighbors.

Everett broke into Everettese reminiscent of Casey Stengel, the ancient New York Yankee Manager of the 50's & 60's, when discussing the massive Allied bombing of St. Lo. "I thought at that time that I saw one of those B-24's or B whatevers they was, them big bombers, blew up in the air—and go down in smoke. I thought at that time, I saw that. I'm saying now, I thought it. And then I was sure I saw what I saw, but uh, nonetheless…Why I say now I thought that I saw it? I won't say I did."

A life long resident of Memphis, the retired civil service employee had left home, only for the war. Everett held strong beliefs concerning the murder of Martin Luther King. "No way James Earl Ray did it alone," Everett adamantly declared, echoing the thoughts of many Dallasites when discussing Oswald and JFK.

Everett briefly mentioned his divorce of several years ago; something in the inflection of his voice led me to believe this was not his idea. A comment from one of his Christmas cards to my

Dad, written shortly after the way, flashed across my mind. *Say, now don't fall down, but am making plans now, undercover to get myself a wife the first of the year some time. She sure is a nice girl to.*

When asked if loneliness ever stopped by to visit, he replied with conviction, "Nope," adding that he saw his daughter regularly and remained active in his church. Was Everett truthful here? Maybe, maybe not. But one thing's as obvious as German war crimes. A man filled with the pride and dignity of James Everett Allen would swallow tank fuel before admitting loneliness to the sons of his former lieutenant.

His eyes danced with mischief at the mention of Frank Williams, the jeep driver. "Some French people gave yo Daddy a case of champagne when we liberated Paris. He was goin to give it to some American officers for a big shindig, but then those bottles turned up empty." Everett abruptly stepped on the verbal brakes, seriously pondering the issue. "Ever last drop," he continued, now speaking slowly enough to spell the words.

"Did Frank drink the champagne?" we asked.

Everett's face broke into a massive grin, revealing several teeth gone AWOL. "Well, yo Daddy and I had no use for it so yes I believe it was Frank. Made the Lieutenant mad, but I never heard him say anything to Frank about it."

Everett reiterated his disdain for alcohol later in the day while reflecting on the time he became separated from his outfit and was running short on water. A Frenchman offered him some cider, but in spite of his thirst, Everett declined. Thinking of yesterday, an infectious smile spread across Everett's face today. Everett also shunned tobacco. "Don't remember yo Daddy using it much either," he threw in for an exclamation point on clean living.

After lunch, we all took a seat on Everett's sofa in the living area. Though the heat and humidity in the room melted my jeans to my skin, I was relishing every moment. As we looked through my Dad's scrapbook, memories would crease through Everett like rifle fire through smoke. "I know one thing. England's the darkest place in the world I'd ever seen at night. Of course, during the war, you see, there were no lights shinin. They had been cautionin us about the razor gang which was English young men cuttin throats of the GIs for takin their women away from 'em." Everett belched a quick explosive laugh. "That's what they told us when we went there. One night I was goin down this road and these trees—I got in my mind, they was pines and crows g-a-l-o-r-e. Man them things. When one moved, they all moved. Man, they scared the scee wad out of you," said Everett, who was forever expanding his vocabulary. "Especially dark as it was. When I walked by this guard one night, he said, 'Be careful don't let the razor gang git you.'" Everett laughed again, his wide eyes remindful of a kid telling his favorite scary story.

"Was there really a razor gang?" we asked.

"No, I don't think so," he answered with a dismissive wave of his hand. "I say that today. I don't know what I thought then. But anyway, I didn't go very far down that road when those crows made a move. I turned myself around and I went back up there and said to that guard, 'you oughten tell me about that razor gang. You're gonna have to go down there with me!'" Everett cried, his tenor pitch managing to rise an octave.

As inevitable as the destruction of war, we all knew our discussion would inevitably center around Höfen, Germany. We showed Everett a picture from my recent visit to the three story building in Höfen, the place of George and Everett's "Finest Hour." He stared hard, as if to remember it all but then a flash of recognition illuminated Everett's face. Dean and I turned mute, clinging to his words like a life preserver, mesmerized by his link to such an important time and place.

"Now our observation post, if I'm looking at this picture right, was up in the attic of what I'll call it. We were told at least, I heard it, I don't know where I heard it but any way I heard that it was an orphanage. Now our room that I was talkin about would be somewhere along about there." Everett dotted the picture with his index finger to mark the spot. "About midways of it. All right then," Everett said hesitating as if to allow his mind sufficient time to reel back through the years. "Ah go upstairs up here and look out these windows goin over here into Höfen," he said pointing to the massive green meadow that had not changed since the war. "If we see something that we needed hollerin about, well, we'd call on officers and they'd come up and check it over. But I was up there one morning—ah, kinda early and ah..." The old radio operator took a longer pause than before, his eyes narrow in reflection of another lifetime. "I saw these dudes where there was snow on the ground. They had on snow suits, white, I understand that was sheets or something over them. They walked up against the black hedgerow." Surely thinking of the enemy's ineptness, Everett cackled with such vigor, his body trembled. "That's how much they were stickin out and these two guys were carrying a pole," he continued after drawing a deep breath. "Now I hollered at the Lieutenant and he came up there and he saw what I saw. He opened fire on em. And I said then,

"The people are really glad to see an American. One man gave me 10 quarts of champagne," wrote GWL on 9/12/44 in a letter home. Uh oh, maybe Frank Williams really did take the champagne given to Lt. Looney by the French and intended for an officer's party?

now whether I did or didn't, I can't vouch for that forty-five, fifty years ago, but I said that when he dropped that registration down on them. I saw one of 'em guys flyin up in the air. Now I said that. Now whether I saw it or not, I can't say today."

My own mind retreated to my childhood, when I'd innocently asked my Father if he'd ever killed anybody in the war. While I cannot promise that what I remember now is what I remembered then, it's my recollection that George tiptoed around the truth the way he would tiptoe around an enemy minefield, eventually replying in a vintage combination of Everettese and Clintonesque. Something to the effect of, "No...well maybe...well, it depends on the definition of killing somebody," to finally concluding that his orders and direction caused the death of German soldiers. His tone, I expect, revealed no satisfaction or shame.

Was George haunted by his death dealing hand during the war? I think not, at least not to the extent of self destructive tendencies. Judging by his writings toward the end of his life, George was certainly more disturbed by Lt. Starter's recognition for defending Höfen.

Makes perfect sense. Why waste precious senior years, trudging through mental quicksand, fretting over a commandment of his religion that if he violated, he did so under orders from his government. In the twilight of George's life, his thoughts returned to his emotional life raft—the big war, for another reason. To a time when American war heroes enjoyed the status of today's rock legends, movie stars and athletic studs—all rolled into one. To a time when enough purpose filled George's life to overflow one of Everett's cooking pots. Except during George's only return trip to Europe in 1990, he came to the startling conclusion that a fellow officer evidently took the credit for his most important contribution to the free world.

To spread more gloom, it's no secret Americans often treat its senior citizens with all the respect of a sore armed relief pitcher. Beside my regrettable airplane faux pas, one specific incident, in my mind, defined George's low point as a senior citizen. It occurred during his part time tenure at a sporting goods store—a job he held for a few years to ease his transition into retirement. I happened to visit the store one day and overheard the store manager, a much younger man and oblivious of George's past, chastise him for ringing up the register incorrectly. Though I battled the urge to wring the supervisor's neck, the embarrassment lingered in my father's eyes like a search light. Quite a comedown for a decorated soldier who later served as Dean of Men for a college and ultimately retired as head of the Dallas Juvenile System.

With such sobering senior moments, is there any doubt George spent some time in the depression tank during his last years? Heck, like an old jock, he evidently even dreamed of a comeback. At age 72, and surely by mistake, George received a letter from the Army informing him of a job opening as Company Commander of the 588th Engineer Battalion, a Corps Combat Company. Interesting, he wrote in bold letters above the Army letterhead. Who knows? Maybe this lack of purpose, in his own mind's eye, is why God brought him home on December 9th, 1996. But back to the home of Everett Allen in the summer of 1998.

"Did you know Lt. Starter?" I asked. "

"Oh yeah; I knew him," Everett answered automatically.

"You know, he got a medal for Höfen," I volunteered.

"I didn't know he got anything," he replied quicker and louder than before, practically vomiting the words. Everett's eyes briefly went to another place, taking his thoughts along for company. "Your Daddy got a dirty deal in the sense of the word," he then said, his voice now mellow and sorrowful.

"You were there too," Dean and I promptly protested in stereo.

More reflective silence before Everett replied: "Yeah, but I didn't think too much of it. But come to find out, right after they gave Starter all that attention, kinda made my blood boil."

"I guess Lt. Starter at least performed well during the first attack at Höfen," I said, referring to before George and Everett reported to OP 6.

With slits for eyes, Everett's face tightened and his disposition suddenly became more kin to a machine gunner than a radio operator. I could smell his disapproval over the smell of the food. "You can believe that if you want," he said through an abrupt hoarse laugh that conveyed no sign of humor. I decided against asking Everett's opinion of Lt. Starter's report placing himself at OP 6, even after Frank Williams had stated delivering George and Everett to relieve him.

After a couple of hours on Everett's sofa, we took a tour of his garden. Beneath a fading orange sun, the three of us were soon downing his cherry tomatoes rapid fire; as if a truth serum, the tomatoes seemingly triggered the most emotional response of the day from George's radio operator.

"One thing I always said," Everett announced between bites, his voice now foreign, suddenly melancholy. "It was always a lie. I didn't intend for it to be a lie, but it was. If you gonna be a farmer, don't need no education. Don't need no education," he repeated. "Well, I found out different. You got to know what you're doin to be able to farm. Ah, just no two ways about it. A stupid man can't farm." Though he managed to say this in a way that started out sounding nostalgic before leaning towards regret, the intensity in his voice scared away any potential tears—from him or his guests. He paused, swallowing his memories, the remorse from a failed career reducing him to silence. Everett was now staring upward, possibly considering the often razor thin difference between a job done well, and a job done poorly. "You got to have some knowledge about what you're doin," he concluded, the pain in his look as clear as the pale blue sky.

In the same Christmas card Everett had mentioned his upcoming marriage, he also eerily foreshadowed his farming destiny. *It was all very low grade,* he wrote, referring to his harvest. *I still have a year under the GI Training Bill and if it weren't for that I sure would have been sunk this year.*

Dean and I glanced uncomfortably at each other. I wanted to give the little man a gentle hug and say: "Hey, I've been stupid a few times in my life." Like the time I broke into the school or when I doubted my Father's airplane story. Or how about when I invested in cattle semen for the Chinese; yes, I was capable of doing this.

"Man, those tomatoes are good," I announced. It was the best I could do.

With our day drawing to a close, we slowly meandered toward the rental car. As we passed Everett's shipwrecked automobiles, Dean admired the relics one last time before commenting, "Guess you got your money's worth out of those cars."

Everett threw Dean a sly look which Dean immediately translated. "They still run?" Dean asked incredulously.

"Sure do. Pull that tractor. Pull a cord of wood," Everett declared, as if boasting on proud old warriors. Just like the cars' owner, a proud old warrior.

When I invited Everett to visit Dallas and stay at my home, he gave a hearty laugh that unexplainably made me realize he'd been through more than most during his lifetime. As I shook his hand, I read this in his look: the regret he felt for never seeing my Father after the war. And I knew he would never leave

Memphis again, especially since he'd previously left only for the war. I wondered—no make that doubted that I would see Everett again and I'm certain he read this in my look easier than George read war maps. With our car moving further and further from his home, the Little Big Man seemed to grow taller while waving goodbye. Finally, the old radio operator began to sink behind the horizon.

Later, Dean and I reflected on the trip; Everett's apparently meager financial situation and less than five star living conditions tormented Dean. "The man's a hero but look at the way he lives," lamented Dean, "Practically living on social security. He deserved better. It's depressing."

I tried to focus on the positive. Everett was at peace with his maker and he damn sure ate better than anybody else. I volunteered to send Everett a new air conditioner, claiming the unit was free, courtesy of my cousin in Memphis who was married to a commercial contractor. A mini-lie since I would buy the unit at cost. Everett refused; "Don't need it," he said firmly over the phone. I mailed him a $100.00 for Christmas, asking him to take his daughter to dinner for my present. The check came back with a note saying thanks, but he'd rather eat from his garden. The proudest of warriors I would say.

A colonel and some soliders of the 62nd Volksgrenadier Division drive through Vielsalm, Belgium, in a captured American jeep. U.S. Army Signal Corp

Two Germans salvage clothing and equipment form the muddy bodies of two machine-gunned American soldiers. The trooper at right checks the fit of socks and boots that he has stripped from one corpse. U.S. Army Signal Corp

Chapter Ninteen

Private Ryan

Shortly after our visit with Everett Allen, I took my Mother to see "Private Ryan." I'd already seen the movie and suspected the similarities between the Tom Hanks character and my Father would stir her emotions into a mini-storm. Both men landed at Normandy; both were captains, though George achieved the rank later in the war. Both also taught high school before entering the military.

To my relief, the movie lifted my Mother into her best spirits since my Father's death. The coward in the movie reminded her of an incident that I'd never heard before, involving the three story building in Höfen.

One night during a lull in the fighting, George ordered a young private to stand watch at the front door; George, exhausted from sleep deprivation, crawled into his sleeping bag on the third floor and promptly fell asleep. In spite of his exhaustion induced slumber, George soon sensed something peculiar, as if the stars were out of line. He awoke to find the young wide eyed private practically crawling into his sleeping bag. From past experience, I would say with conviction that my Father was not the best I've seen in dealing with unwanted surprises. I would guess, therefore, that his manner fell far short of pleasant.

"What are you doing here?" asked the Lieutenant, hoping his eyes were failing him.

"I heard something," said the teenage private, his voice unstable, his body trembling with fear.

George, the master of many chuckles, was capable of a particular classic chest rattling type that would convey more disgust than humor. A strong possibility, the young private heard this chuckle before Lt. Looney drew his officer's pistol and presented the private with three options: (1.) Take a bullet from the pistol staring him straight in the eyes. (2.) Leave the premises and join the German army. (3.) Stand watch as ordered. Is there any doubt which option the private chose?

An engineer equips a jeep's front wheel with a "mud shoe," improvised by his company to give vehicles better traction and flotation in deep snow and mud. U.S. Army Signal Corp

Opening a blocked road, an engineer employs a bulldozer to topple a German Rappenschleper cargo vehicle into the woods. Lacking bulldozers, sometimes engineers often called on tanks to clear debris. U.S. Army Signal Corp

The End of The German Spies
During the Battle of the Bulge

A captured commando doffs his American disguise—to reveal a German uniform.

MPs tie Manfred Pernass to a stake for his execution.

With blindfolds in place and targets pinned onto their chests, the commandos wait for the fatal volley. Billing died shouting, "Heil Hitler!"

On December 28, 1944, three men, dressed in GI clothes and driving a U.S. jeep, were stopped at an American roadblock. When they could not say the password, GIs investigated and discovered that they were Officer Cadet Günther Billing, Corporal Wilhelm Schmidt and Private First Class Manfred Pernass—one of the nine teams sent out by Lieut. Colonel Otto Skorzney to spread confusion in the American rear areas.

The price of their daring was a sentence to be executed as spies. But they turned their capture into a coup of sorts by spreading alarm through the American high command with an invented tale of a plot to assassinate General Eisenhower.

Before their executions, the commandos were granted a last request—to hear German nurses in a nearby cell sing Christmas carols. The next day they went before a firing squad. This is a U.S. Army Signal Corp. photo used for press releases by the Army. George Looney did not attend this event.

Chapter Twenty

"Sorta Makes My Blood Boil"

Any somber mood remaining from our trip to Memphis, bled into our paper battle with the Army, arriving in the form of a letter dated September 24, 1998 from the Review Board Agency in St. Louis; the salutation alone proved enough to torpedo our spirits. Addressed to my Father, George W. Looney, the message delivered a direct hit to my nervous system.

Your records were destroyed in a fire of July 1973. Although there are no records available, your application has been forwarded to the Military Review Board Agency in Arlington, Virginia.

A month later, the response, addressed to Mike Looney, came from the Chief Screening Team of the Review Boards Agency in Virginia, thus at least acknowledging George's passing. The guts of the reply,

Since his records are not available and since your application does not contain enough information to allow the Board to make a determination, the Board cannot take any further action at this time. You may reapply at any time if you can submit the necessary documents and/or information.

At Z's insistence, I pleaded our case to that same department in a letter dated November 9th, by basically restating the facts of the case. If all else fails…beg. All remained quiet on the battlefront until a letter dated July 7, 1999 came from the Review Board in Virginia. The Army made no mention of the previous application or any records lost in a fire, simply stating,

In order to process your application you must submit a copy of your late father's AGO Form 53-55. We will hold your case for 30 days from the date of this letter.

Throughout this process, Z's impatience and frustration stemming from the Army's inability to act in a timely fashion constantly battled his belief that justice would eventually prevail. The Army had waited a mere eight months to answer but we were back in the battle and Z wanted nothing more than front line duty.

Exactly one week later, Z fired a two page salvo back to the Army Review Board in Virginia, explaining that he would shortly provide a package of documents supporting our medal request.

(The same package as before.) Z also stated his role with the 196th as a radio operator in Korea and subsequently as the author of the offical history of the battalion.

Further excerpts:

Lt. Looney was a victim of what could best be termed a clerical error! The evidence shows that in the early morning hours of 16 December 1944 Lt. Looney and Cpl. James Everett Allen were enroute to the Battalion area, in a jeep driven by Frank Williams when they received orders to relieve the FO (Lt. Starter) at OP#6. They arrived at OP#6 and relieved Lt. Starter at 0830 hours on 16 December 1944. Lt. Looney and Corporal Allen remained at OP#6 continuously throughout the effort of the German Army to dislodge the Americans from Höfen, Germany—until 22 December 1944, when they were relieved. Given the confusion that was existent in that sector at the time it is easy to understand why the Baker Battery clerk failed to enter the fact on the Morning Report that Lt. Looney and Cp. Allen had relieved Lt. Starter and his party at OP#6.

Lt. Starter received a Distinguished Service Cross for action at OP#6 on 18 December 1944. We are not challenging Lt. Starter's right to a medal but, we have incontrovertible evidence that it was Lt. Looney (and Cp. Allen) not Lt. Starter who were present at OP#6 on 18 December 1944 when the action occurred for which the medal was awarded.

Lt. Starter may have been eligible for a medal for an earlier action, but he clearly was not present at OP#6 subsequent to 0830 hours on 16 December 1944. The information gathered from my closer examination of the record caused me to produce a second edition of my book which contains the new facts regarding Lt. Looney.

I pray that the evidence thus presented will convince you to recommend that Lt. Looney (and Cpl Allen) receive the recognition from the people of the United States they so richly deserve.
Sincerely,
Donald L. Zinngrabe

By that fall, still no word from the Army and the patience Z so carefully displayed in his previous correspondence had grown thinner than the initial Allied defenses during The Bulge. On October 25, Z wrote the Review Board Agency;

More than 100 days have elapsed since I mailed my initial letter so I don't think I am being hasty or advocating a "rush to judgement" by sending you this note seeking your response. I believe a strong case has been made for these two heroes who were and are too modest to pursue their rightful awards themselves. I ask you to render a decision on this matter as soon as possible.

On November 7th, Thor Ronningen, author of "Butler's Battlin Bastards," whose original correspondence to my father started this journey, joined the fray by sending his own letter direct to the Review Board.

You have previously received requests that 1st Lieutenant George W. Looney of the 196th Field Artillery Battalion be awarded a Silver Star for his actions while he was a Forward Observer in Höfen, Germany, 16 to 20 December 1944.

At this time I was a PFC rifleman (MOS745) in I company-3rd Battalion-395th Infantry Regiment-99th Infantry Division and was stationed in a house about 50 yards from Lt. Looney's position so I was an eye witness to all the happened. The Germans attacked us at 0530 the morning of 16 December 1944. They outnumbered us at least five to one and we could never have held our line had it not been for the outstanding support we got from the Field Artillery.

Lt. Looney directed his guns on critical points time after time. At one time he laid down such a wall of fire that the enemy could not retreat to their own lines and surrendered to avoid death. Every man there is happy to acknowledge their debt to Lt. Looney and the 196th.

I trust the above will be taken into account and that Lt. Looney's family will soon receive the Silver Star he so obviously earned by his heroic actions and professional skill.

The urgency in Z and Thor's letter generated a prompt response from the Army albeit a different department. The Board for Correction of Military Records in Virginia sent a form letter dated November 19, 1999, the words piercing my insides like bullets.

Dear Applicant:

I regret to inform you that the Army Board for Correction of Military Records has denied your application. This decision is final. You may request reconsideration only if you can present newly discovered relevant evidence.

The Board for Correction included a several page memorandum that served as a rebuttal to our request for George's medal.

Lowlights of the memorandum:

Evidence of Record (General Orders awarding the Distinguished Service Cross) shows that a fellow officer, not the FSM, was at OP 6 during the enemy attack early on 18 December 1944. The Board also noted that the statements by the driver and the radio operator do not substantiate that the FSM's forward observer party was on OP 6 from 16 December through 22 December 1944 as alleged.

However, the unit chain of command was present during the period that the FSM and his forward observer party manned OP 6 and the chain of command had the opportunity to recommend the FSM's forward observer team for personnel decorations. However, the chain of command chose not to do so based on the facts at hand.

The contention that the FSM was not recommended for the Silver Star due to "chaotic and uncertain conditions" is without merit, particularly in view of the recommendation for award of the Distinguished Service Cross prepared by the chain of command for a fellow officer.

I imagined Everett's response:

"Well I can't say for sure but it sounds to me if I'm readin that right and I'm not sayin I am but if I was, ah...I'd say that Board or whatever you call it, ah...they don't believe us. Sorta makes my blood boil."

A First Army engineer employs wire and cord to bind dozens of half-pound charges of TNT to the side of a tree destined to be knocked down for building a roadblock. U.S. Army Signal Corp

A cloud of snow and ice erupts as the 276th Combat Engineers resort to dynamite to clear packed snow. U.S. Army Signal Corp

Chapter Twenty One

Purpose

"I think we're done," I told Z over the phone, my voice lined with resignation. "We put up a good fight but unless we've got some new evidence, the decision's final."

"We're not done. Not even close," fired back Z. If his voice was a measure of determination and strength, the man would dispose of Tyson in the first round. The long distance line went silent, allowing Z's conspiratorial grin the time and space to travel all the way from Wisconsin to Texas. "I've got new evidence!" he declared. "I talked to Norm Cohen. (Norm B. Cohen, also known as NBC, had bought his dying buddy the Silver Star at the pawn shop.) He was with your Dad on December 18 at OP 6. The date stands out in his mind because he was bringing replacement radio batteries to the OP and on the way up, he got hit by some shrapnel."

Z went on to announce with school boy enthusiasm that he'd also talked to Everett Allen and Everett had agreed to a sworn testimony concerning Höfen. Gradually our new ammo arrived. We received NBC's statement of December 27 proclaiming George as the artillery observer at OP 6 on December 18th of 1944.

Though prognosticated by so many wise and foolish alike, the sky did not come crashing down with the new millennium and on January 19, 2000, Everett Allen formally answered questions in Memphis asked by a notary public. Nothing new, the heart of his testimony proclaiming that he and Lt. Looney were ordered to replace Lt. Starter at the OP; ever the stickler for honesty, Everett refused to state under oath the OP number or the exact date because he could not remember. He did remember the destruction of the American bomb on the three story building,

George and Sinkler Scholze enjoy luxury accommodations.

adding that Lt. Looney, by radio, ordered it stopped immediately. An important event to acknowledge since records showed this took place on December 18.

We also received new testimonies from Sinkler Scholze and George Himmelman, the officers who dined with George in New York the night before their ship sailed for England. Neither man had, to my knowledge, communicated with the other in many years but startling similarities linked the two letters.

Highlights from Sinkler Scholze's January 20th letter:

I just do not remember Höfen or OP 6 I barely remember last week. I am 81 years old. I can verify only this. If George Looney said it happened that way, I would believe it, for I can only say George never told me a lie. Allen and Williams (the jeep driver) stayed with him always. Whatever they said yo, can depend on. They were together for a long time and performed efficiently at all times. If Allen seems unhappy, I'm sure he had good reasons for he was a good man. (Sounds like Everett's blood was boiling again) *Quiet, sincere, effective and very devoted to George. If anyone deserved a medal, it was George Looney. Your Dad was a fine person, soldier and friend. He served night and day, never complained, never asked to be relieved. Just did a great job on every assignment.*

Himmelman's letter of February 15th:

George and George Himmelman. One of George's notes say they're in England, another Germany. Not much meat left on either of their bones so I'd say this is in Germany at the end. Himmelman continued in the military, ultimately receiving the rank of Lt. Colonel.

I have a copy of the picture of us—Scholze, Looney and me at the Diamond Horseshoe in New York. I do know that Corporal Allen, radio operator, and Frank Williams, Looney's driver, were always with Looney. If they say they were there, Looney was there. If Lt. Starter was directing all the firing, he would have had his own radio operator. Looney and I were just like brothers. I still miss him very much and think of him real often.

In a sobering reminder of the aging process, a note accompanied Himmelman's letter from his wife, stating she had written the letter from her husband's halting, but accurate dictation. *Nothing wrong with his memory,* she added, *but he has still not completely recovered from a stroke and is having trouble with his speech.*

In direct contrast to his resolve, Z's patience bordered on the extinct; as if painfully aware of his own mortality. By February, Z reloaded again, firing off the newly arrived paper artillery in support of our quest.

Z submitted a cover letter with his new package. While reading one section, I felt the tremble from the passion of his words.

After having led ten badly wounded American infantrymen through a sniper infested forest to safety, probably saving their lives, the one he carried for sure. What must Lt. Looney have done at O. P. #6 in Höfen, Germany for him to consider it his "brightest star?" It must have really been something.

A few days later an emotional letter arrived from Z. He'd just learned of a Vietnam veteran receiving the Medal of Honor— only thirty-four years late!

This has given me renewed strength, commitment and determination to keep working on this matter until I am successful...or dead.

More than ever, the word purpose seemed more suited as a function found in a medical journal. Purpose—serves as a direct artery to the human heart; shortages may result in pulmonary damage.

Z, unwilling or unable to wait one day longer, wrote the Army's Board for Corrections of Military Records in May.

Every day (except Sunday) I eagerly await the arrival of the mail carrier, with the hope that I will receive some correspondence from the Board regarding the matter of the award of a medal to Lieutenant George W. Looney. So far, I have been disappointed!

With patriotic splendor, the Board responded on July 3rd— one last letter before breaking for the holiday.

Your case has been carefully analyzed by the Board to determine whether you have submitted any new evidence. While you have detailed your contentions once again, these do not amount to new matters. Accordingly, there is no basis for resubmitting your request to the Board.

I felt like somebody, probably an Army Board Member, had pounded my head between my shoulders with a baseball bat.

Chapter Twenty Two

We Can't Give Up

At the insistence of Thor Ronningen and Z, I immediately wrote my Congressman, Pete Sessions, informing him of our case and including our paper arsenal. One more time, we were "starting over." I soon received a letter from Z dated July 31, apologizing for his ineffectiveness in getting your father the recognition he so richly deserves thus exposing the first soft spot in his emotional armor.

Never fear; later in the letter, Z's fierce determination rebounded in the same manner Allied forces rebounded during The Bulge. A brief sampling of his words when referencing government officials contained all the vulnerability of Patton himself—*insensitive, cloistered bureaucrats and politicians.* Z closed with, *We can't give up!* I felt better already.

By August, I'd received word from Congressman Pete Sessions, serving the predictable gloomy notice that this process is usually a lengthy one and the longer the period of time that exists from the actual event, the more difficult it is to change the record. He forwarded a copy of a letter he'd already received from the military which was from a new department—the US Total Army Personnel Command. The Army's letter referenced a new array of forms; all, I felt sure would prove intimidating to complete.

I received a letter from Thor later that month, sensing not only his frustration with President Clinton, but also doubt concerning the outcome of our mission. *Medals worn by men who were in combat were earned. In many cases medals were earned but not awarded for a number of reasons. However, many medals were awarded to rear-echelon types that were not earned— particularly by high ranking rear-echeloners that awarded medals of valor to themselves and their buddies.*

Those three fellows captured in Kosovo were each awarded 6 medals which included the Purple Heart. (One of them suffered a few superficial bruises) *and the Soldier's Medal. Clinton recently upgraded 22 DSCs to Congressional Medals which, in my opinion, really demonstrates his contempt for military tradition. Captain George Looney was a good soldier. I think he rests easy with that, more easily than those with the phony awards.*

Along with a copy of his August 28 letter to Congressman Sessions, I received a letter from Z the first week of September; its mood, was both purposeful and optimistic, further proof that Z's recovery from our recent setback was total and complete. After expressing his belief that because of Sessions' influence, our ever expanding submission package would hopefully be forwarded from the Review Board to the Military Awards Branch, he closed with, *At the very least we* (the package) *should*

have enough to get an audience with Congressman Sessions. It hit with the force of a mortar attack—to win this battle, Z would travel to Dallas and face Congressman Sessions quicker than Lt. Looney stopped the American bombs at OP 6.

Z's letter to Sessions pulsated with the kinetic energy of an infantryman hell bent on advancing through heavy enemy fire. With his frustration approaching anger, Z expressed dissatisfaction with not only the Review Board's decision, but also its refusal of his request to send all the material used to deny our petition. *The materials should be available under the Freedom of Information Act,* he wrote. *As a combat veteran and perpetual taxpayer, I am unhappy with the cavalier, uncooperative attitude exhibited by this servant of the people!*

Z rehashed old news to all concerned but Sessions—he'd already provided proof on two occasions that Lt. Looney hastily replaced Lt. Starter on December 16 1944, and Lt. Looney deserved proper recognition. But I sensed Z's stance hardening with respect to Lt. Starter; for the first time, he made the crisp pronouncement that Lt. Starter's medal was a mistake. Z's claim hinted the heretofore unmentionable possibility that Lt. Starter wrote a false report. A different stance from one of Z's earlier letters to the Review Board, when he wrote, *we are not challenging Lt. Starter's right to a medal.* The gloves were coming off as sure as war tanks sink in water—a scene all too familiar at Omaha Beach on D-Day.

Z's subsequent reference to Kosovo not only gave me a welcome belly laugh but, once again placed him on common ground with Thor Ronningen. *If the President can give six medals to three enlisted men who got lost and strayed into "unfriendly" territory and got pistol whipped by some goons, surely there is an appropriate medal for Lt. Looney!*

I booked my trip to Wisconsin right on the spot.

With German machine-gun fire spraying the water around them, U.S. Army engineers ferry a vehicle on a pontoon across the Seine River at Montereau.

Frostbite!

During the Battle of the Bulge, more than 15,000 American soldiers were disabled by frostbitten feet or trench foot. The afflictions were quite similar: cold—accompanied by moisture in the case of trench foot—slowed circulation in the foot and killed tissue. Sometimes gangrene set in and the foot had to be amputated.

The U.S. Army had developed preventive footgear—insulated shoepacs (below) that would have helped had they been available in time. And the GIs had been taught to change to dry socks often and to massage their feet whenever possible to keep up circulation. But such measures were often impossible in combat.

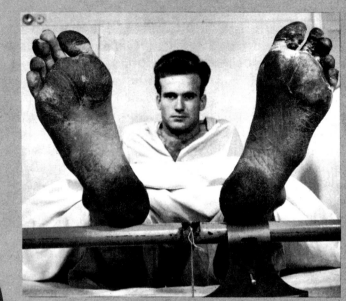

Under treatment for trench foot, a victim raises and exposes his feet.

A GI dons his shoepacs—rubber-bound boots with leather tops and felt insoles. Shoepac shipments did not begin arriving until late January

Chapter Twenty Three

Z In Person

With my CPA, and dear college friend Ron Salmon, as a traveling companion, we flew into Green Bay, Wisconsin toward the end of September. We left the sweltering heat of Dallas and landed with temperatures already dipping into the fourties. A foreshadow of past winter frost such as the infamous Ice Bowl, the miserable 1967 NFL championship game in Green Bay between the Packers and Cowboys, with temperatures well below zero.

Growing up in Chicago prepared Z for his stint in the bitter cold of Korea, I decided. Z was to meet us at the airport. We'd exchanged no pictures nor had we mentioned any descriptive traits that would allow one to identify the other. Z retired to Sturgeon Bay, Wisconsin.

How would I identify him? Better yet, how could I miss him? Near the baggage claim area, I spotted Z with the difficulty of spotting Eisenhower or Elvis or Ali or John Wayne which is to say, none at all. With a sharp nose and a face as lean as the rest of him, he wore the look of a combat veteran as effortlessly as he wore his 196th FA Battalion military ball cap. From underneath the cap's bill peered steely eyes. Our looks locked on the other like radar and he glided toward me with the long purposeful stride of Clint Eastwood in all those cop movies.

While extending his firm grip, he offered a sly grin laced with mischief. His voice, both high in pitch and affable in tone, betrayed his military demeanor. "Thought we'd take in the Packer Hall of Fame first," he declared, offering an unlikely tourist attraction for visitors from Cowboy country.

Z wasn't kidding; we drove directly to the Packer Hall of Fame. During the drive, I noticed that the town of Green Bay reminded me of a drive in movie with an overdose of the wrong colors. Everywhere you looked were Packer green and gold—storefronts, billboards, and even a tractor.

At the Hall of Fame, we watched the horrific site of Bart Starr, amid a sea of human smoke clouds, sneak across the goal line one more time for the winning touchdown in the Ice Bowl. Z, obviously a man capable of inflicting great torture, next drove to Lambeau Field, the home of the Packers. Deathly quiet on this chilly day, the giant bowl reminded me of a green and gold version of another deserted stadium—the Roman Coliseum. Beneath an overcast sky, I inhaled the enticing smoky aroma of stadium grub and felt the crowd's roar tickle my eardrums. I wondered if Z or my Father or any combat veteran could ever hear the eruption of a sports crowd, without remembering the roar of combat.

During lunch comprised of homestyle cooking at a modest,

but tasty Green Bay café, I showed Z a mesmerizing power point presentation of George's war pictures on a laptop computer. Prepared from many of the original negatives by my middle brother, Phil, some of the pictures looked to be taken yesterday. The Normandy Coast and bunkers, the French countryside, the allied advance into Paris and the celebration that followed, the French shaving the heads of Nazi sympathizers, the bitter cold and snow of winter and eventually pictures of Germany such as the city of Leipzig. No pictures of Höfen until George returned almost 50 years later. Too much hot action at the time for souvenir photographs, I'm sure.

With slightly stooped shoulders, Z scrutinized every picture with laser intensity; all the while, his look could only be described as wistful. "Now that was an army," he said softly as the presentation concluded. "This gives me a reason to keep going," he added, his decibel level managing to lower a notch. He referred to, I believe, his life more than the medal quest itself.

As if uncomfortable with hearing an internal replay of his own words, he suddenly sat erect, the width returning to his shoulders. "I'm buying lunch," he said, his voice back to full strength.

At about the time Namath guaranteed the Jets to win the Super Bowl, or maybe it was when Neil Armstrong stepped foot on the moon, or possibly it was during the period the Big E became really big, but about this time in history, a singer named Jonathan Edwards sang with great vigor: "In love and war, all is fair and he's got cards he ain't showin." Unknown to me at the time, like the song said, Z, a man loaded with vigor, had cards he wasn't "showin."

Later that day, after Z returned us to the airport, Ron and I said our heartfelt goodbyes. "The most passionate man I've ever known," said Ron as we watched Z drive away. Unlike my goodbye to Marie and Everett, I knew my path would cross with Z again.

In the interim, Thor Ronningen continued his own due diligence to unravel the mystery of OP 6. In this letter to me on September 30, 2000, he wrote:

I am sorry that all of this (research) reinforces Lt. Starter's claim to sainthood. I have no doubt whatsoever your Dad was THE MAN, but cannot find a written record to support it. The period from 16 – 20 Dec 1944 was really chaotic and a lot of records and reports were put aside until the worst was over. Each unit concentrated on their own people and since

Starter's name was on the records, no one saw fit to dig any deeper.

Thor wrote again on November 12.

I feel as though I am at a dead end in seeking data to support your Father's claim to a medal. Charles Biggio is a very active member of our 99th Div. Assn. He was in the artillery and has amassed very complete information on all the artillery that was active in The Battle of The Bulge. He could find nothing in his records to support your Dad's claim. Starter's citation for the DSC refers to his actions on 18 Dec 1944 and would be very hard to refute.

For the next six months, I felt as if I'd reached my own dead end and with no way out. I not only continued to receive a flurry of rejection letters for my novel of "Heroes Are Hard To Find," but we received no word from Congressman Pete Sessions or the military.

On May 29, 2001, Z, who by now bordered on the verge of an internal combustion, wrote to Pete Sessions. *For several years I have been engaged in an effort to obtain an appropriate medal for Lt. George W. Looney. I have written all I can. Accordingly, I hereby request that a meeting be set up with you and me and Mike at a time and place convenient to you to discuss the matter. Could I please have your response within a four week period?*

Congressman Sessions responded in a letter dated July 18, acknowledging receipt of Z's request, also enclosing a letter from the military outlining additional needed documentation. We'd already provided most of what the military requested so Z privately decided now was the time to play his trump card—the card, until now, he wasn't "showin."

Exhausted foot soldiers of the 80th Division wolf down a lunch of cold rations and lukewarm coffee. They were among the lucky minority who had galoshes. U.S. Army Signal Corp

As fellow members of a First Artillery team congregate around a morning campfire, two men boldly strip to the waist in order to wash and shave. U.S. Army Signal Corp

Chapter Twenty Four

Z's Final Letter

In the summer of 2001, Z fired his last and loudest round to the military with his letter to the Board for Correction of Military Records. As if a grenade exploded in the adjacent foxhole, the initial reading of Z's narrative left my ears ringing and a burning vacuum in my midsection.

Here it is:

As I mentioned previously, out of respect for Lt. Starter, no challenge was raised regarding his alleged participation in the defense of OP 6 at Höfen, Germany on 18 December 1944. Unfortunately, it appears as though proving that Lt. Looney was the FO at OP 6 before during and after the determined but, unsuccessful assault on that position on 18 December 1944 is not sufficient to award him the medal he deserves.

Evidence presented here will show that Lt. Starter sought to deflect attention from the fact that he was unable to perform his duty by fabricating a story about his role in the defense of OP 6. The most damning piece of evidence is "EXCERPT FROM REPORT OF LT. Starter ON THE ACTION OF THE FORWARD OBSERVATION PARTY.

Before I analyze this report I need to discuss my military background. Like James Everett Allen I was a radio operator in the 196th FABN in the Korean War. I also served on and near OPs. I achieved the rank of Staff Sergeant and completed my tour of duty as the Battalion Communications Chief.

When I read Lt. Starter's report I immediately became aware that it was fatally flawed. I also noted that Lt. Starter took the unprecedented step of presenting his report to an infantry officer. All such reports I have seen involving artillery operations were endorsed by artillery officers—not officers from other branches.

Lt. Starter mentioned that his OP party consisted of himself and 5 other enlisted men. In all my experience in being in and providing personnel for OP parties there were NEVER more than three men assigned at one time. The OP party consisted of one officer, one radioman and one wireman. In mobile or hotly contested areas such as Höfen, the wireman was eliminated from the OP partly because land lines could not be established or maintained. Another reason OP parties were small was because the men had critical specialties (MOSS) and

would be very difficult to replace should they become casualties or be captured.

Lt. Starter went into considerable detail about having Cpl. Webber and others crawl across the floor to shout commands to the radio operator who was stationed in the basement. That scenario is absolutely ludicrous! I have never heard of or experienced an O. operation where the FO and the radio operator weren't in close proximity to each other and the radio at all times, particularly during fire missions. It would have been impossible for the radioman to hear commands being shouted to him from the attic even if there wasn't a battle going on around the building.

Another problem with Lt. Starter's scenario involves the extraordinary amount of time that would be necessary to get the commands relayed to the radio operator from the FO even if they could hear one another. The targets, unless they were fixed objects such as buildings, would be in totally different positions once the firing batteries got the coordinates.

The limits of radio technology is yet another factor which mitigates against the believability of Lt. Starter's report. The radio in use at OP 6 was the standard army "walkie-talkie" SCR 610. The SCR 610 was a battery operated, crystal controlled FM radio. The set was rugged and reliable, but being FM meant it had a limited range with "line of sight" transmissions. It was equipped with a fixed length mounted antenna. In his report Lt. Starter stated the terrain was hilly and the radio was located in the basement of a stone and stucco building. These factors-hilly terrain and thick foundation walls present two insurmountable obstacles for the SCR 610. There is no way that that set could send or receive traffic from that location.

In order to cover up his failure to do his duty Lt. Starter avoided presenting his report to artillery officers, who would have known that he had been replaced at OP 6 before the incident he was supposedly describing took place. Artillery officers would also have realized that the method of "relaying commands" utilized by Lt. Starter would have been impossible! By doing this and co-opting several enlisted men, who no doubt received medals, Lt. Starter created a paper trail that succeeded beyond his wildest imagination.

The problem is that Lt. Starter's award which is based upon false and misleading testimony is a matter of record and has been the major factor in denying the award to the officer who actually earned it.

It is long past time for the government to set the record straight. The government should also consider the fact that Tec. 5 James Everett Allen was always with Lt. Looney when he was serving as a forward observer.

Holy mortar attack! I instantly detected a civil war brewing in my mind. One side believing my Dad would not only disapprove, but shun the considerable ruckus generated by Z's narrative. My other side remembering all too well the resignation, even desperation, in my Father's final written words.

For the first time during this journey, doubt tugged my conscious to the dark side, leading me to question the wisdom in continuing our mission. Doubt breeds more doubt. Previously buried in a remote section of my stretched and torn brain, a troubling letter from June of 1997 charged to front and center. An officer of the 196th, who will remain nameless, had answered my written inquiry for any information about Höfen; not only his words, but the letter's tone was like shrapnel buried into my chest.

It is difficult for me to understand why you are interested in downgrading Starter. I know nothing of his "cracking up." As a matter of fact, at the direction of Headquarters, I put in for him to receive the Silver Medal for bravery. After the army investigated, Starter was awarded the Silver Star. (Some confusion here as to whether Lt. Starter received the Distinguished Service Cross or the Silver Star.)

Still, I had neither the heart nor the guts to ask Z to retreat much less surrender. To ask him to stop our mission—even at the age of 70—was to tell an old soldier not to fight. Our country would soon endure the horror of 2001 as surely as Z and my family would endure the inevitable wait from the Board for Correction of Military Records. In a welcome breath of fresh air, I received an uplifting letter from the unsinkable Norm B. Cohen (NBC) only five days after the World Trade Center fell.

I'm just twenty blocks north of the World Trade Center and have been the recipient of a lot of dust in my apartment. From my windows, I saw the whole thing. I heard the first plane come over my building. I must confess my GI training caused a knee jerk reaction and I limbered up my personal armory, 357 mag, 38 snub nose, 30 cal. Winchester.

Random ranting from an old dog. Had a checkup at the VA hospital and found out I'm no longer 6 foot tall, shrunk to 5'8". Nurse wanted to know why I was laughing. I said, I'm not crying at 83. I'm still walking, seeing good, and enjoying the God given pleasures of the flesh (sans Viagra.) It's true, don't laugh.

But of course I laughed, and a good laugh at that.

Bundled up in blankets, two disabled soldiers arrive at a field station in Belgium on an "M29 Studebaker Weasel." U.S. Army Signal Corp

A battle casualty, sledded in on skies, is transferred to a jeep that has been rigged for carrying stretchers. U.S. Army Signal Corp

Chapter Twenty Five

Surprise

At precisely the time winter once again surrendered to spring, I received Congressman Pete Sessions' letter of March 19, 2002, which included the February 28 response from the U. S. Total Army Personal Command in Alexandria, Virginia. *We are processing this recommendation* (for George's Medal) *in accordance with Section 1130, Title 10, United States Code,* the Army wrote. At least, the words processing and recommendation allowed more hope than "no" and "regretfully," two words sprinkled throughout the endless stream of rejection letters still pouring in from publishers and agents for my novel. The Army concluded with; *we will inform you of the final decision as soon as it is determined.*

While Sessions' own letter fell short of suggesting victory, its mood threw off a ray of optimism with such comments as *my inquiry is receiving attention and I will continue to work on your behalf.* No word from the front for the next several months.

It came with as much foreshadow as the German attack at the German/Belgium Border on December 16, 1944. Congressman Sessions's office simply forwarded a copy of the Army's letter of May 14, 2002. The first paragraph ushered in that familiar feeling of disappointment, something I'd come to anticipate whenever reading letters from the military.

The purpose of this letter is to provide you further information concerning an award recommendation for the Silver Star to (then) *First Lieutenant George W. Looney. The award recommendation was forwarded to the Army Decorations Board for consideration. On May 6, 2002, the Board determined that the degree of action and service rendered did not meet the strict criteria for the proposed award.*

But just as I had resigned myself to the final and absolute failure of our near five year campaign, the results of Z's efforts finally kicked in.

Therefore, the Commanding General, United States Total Army Personnel Command, on behalf of the Secretary of the Army, has approved the award of the Bronze Star Medal. We are enclosing permanent orders announcing the award, Bronze Star Medal Certificate, and an engraved medal set.

The enclosed DD form 215 (Correction to Report of Separation) amends Mr. Looney's War Department AGO form 53-98 (Report of Separation) to reflect his entitlement to the Bronze Star Medal with "V" device (second Oak Leaf Cluster). The "V" device is for Valor and denotes a previous award of the Bronze Star Medal for heroism. We have also forwarded this information to the National Personnel Records Center so that his Official Military Personnel File can be updated. Consistent with tradition and Army regulation, awards and decorations should be presented with an appropriate degree of formality in a fitting ceremony.

It is an honor to issue the Bronze Star Medal in recognition of the late Mr. Looney's faithful and dedicated service to our Nation during a time of great need.

"I knew we should have asked for the Distinguished Service Cross. Then we would have gotten the Silver Star," Z said over the phone, the pride and satisfaction in his voice easily smothering the disappointment of his words.

"It's enough Z." I said through a crack in my own voice. "The Military has acknowledged he was there."

We both agreed to request a similar medal for Everett Allen. I soon sent Everett a copy of the good news and told him of our plans on his behalf. The reply arrived from Everett's daughter with a date of June 24, 2002. It must have been a dark gloomy day.

Congratulations on the Bronze Star "V" for your Father. However, my Dad, Everett Allen, passed away March 29, 02 from a recurring bout with pneumonia. Thank you for your desire to pursue the same award for him, but this was not his wish. I have all his medals proudly displayed in my home alongside the American Flag and a service photo.
Thanks again.
Joanne A. McKnight

Same song from Jonathan Edwards, but different verse. "Sunshine go away today, I don't feel much like dancing." As sure as the culinary habits of Everett's neighbors would suffer, the radio operator from Tennessee and the 196th Field Artillery Battalion would finally meet up with his Lieutenant again.

Combat engineers use mine detectors to clear a road of German mines, enabling 4th Armored vehicles to advance closer to Bastogne. U.S. Army Signal Corp

An excellent photo of a towed 155mm Howitzer and it's M5 towing tractor and gun crew. The gunner makes his breakfast in a foxhole near the gun's firing position. Note the end of the trail embedded fully in the ground for recoil. Photo taken after an all night battle near Bigonville. U.S. Army Signal Corp

Chapter Twenty Six

The Ceremony

The office of Congressman Sessions notified our family he would present the award to my Mother at the downtown Rotary Club in Dallas on August the 14th. A perfect setting considering George had joined the Dallas Rotary when Eisenhower occupied the White House, Mantle, Mays and Snider roamed the outfields of New York and a skinny kid from Tupelo Mississippi was altering the course of popular music forever. Further appropriate since the same Rotary Club awarded George the Paul Harris Award, its highest honor, a few years before his passing.

Quicker than I could spell Zinngrabe, Z had booked a bus ride from Sturgeon Bay Wisconsin to Dallas—a twelve hour ride and at his own expense! One phone call to American Airlines and an explanation of the event resulted in a deeply discounted roundtrip ticket. As reluctantly as Z would back down from a challenge, he accepted my gift and a refund of his bus ticket.

Z was to arrive in Dallas, in the early evening of August 13th, but due to bad weather, Z's connecting flight in Chicago stayed on the runway for six hours! His plane landed at DFW airport in the early morning of the 14th. The trip took over twelve hours, an exhausting day for anyone, but especially a seventy year old man.

His expression combat ready, Z once again came lumbering toward me in an airport terminal with a purposeful stride. Despite his fatigue, Z radiated the bright glow of a man buzzed on purpose. "Is there any place in this town a man can get an early morning breakfast?" he practically growled, a warm smile creeping across his travel weary face.

Though Z survived the plane trip, I feared the sweltering heat of Texas summer might melt him like butter to the pavement.

Z and my wife, Sandra, reflect on the moment prior to the Awards Ceremony at the Dallas Downtown Rotary.

Z telling it like it was at the Awards Ceremony.

Attendance had suffered at the downtown Rotary the last few years, I was told. More losses beside my Dad. Younger Rotary members often joined clubs in the suburbs. Probably only about fifty people would show.

The Looney clan included myself, wife, Sandra, daughters, Sloan, Kate and CeCe, my Mother, Mary, brothers Phil and Dean along with Dean's wife Kelly and, of course, Z. As we entered the Union Station meeting room in downtown Dallas, my eyes grew with delight at the sight of several long time friends in attendance. I also felt pride at the sight of the SRO crowd of over 100 people. People remembered George Washington Looney.

Congressman Sessions, a silver-haired dignified man of about fifty, made a poised presentation of the Bronze Star to my Mother, who understandably resembled a deer in headlights while accepting the medal. Though my voice cracked a couple of times, I managed to explain to the reverent audience the sequence of events leading to the ceremony. Time for the headliner; I introduced Z who took the stage with the aroma of anticipation overriding the scent of banquet food. The muted hum of conversation or occasional rattle of silverware or soft clink of glass against glass totally vanished.

As soon as Z took the podium, his left hand covered his eyes which pointed to the floor. The silence quickly grew louder. Preparing to speak, Z took a breath so deep his chest swelled and he lowered his hand, but then tugged on his nose before once again covering his face. Tears were on the verge of an attack yet Z stood his ground.

 Congressman Pete Sessions
with Mary Looney
Presentation of the Bronze Star to
George Looney Posthumously
August 14, 2002

Congressman Pete Sessions with Mary Looney. Presentation of the Bronze Star to George Looney posthumously on August 14, 2002 at the Downtown Rotary Club of Dallas. GWL was a member of Rotary for almost 50 years.

"You know," Z said, finally breaking the silence while rubbing his hands together nervously, his glance now alternating between the crowd and the podium. "When you get old, it's hard to speak. But we are going to do this anyway for George."

He was massaging his hands harder now, trying to rub away his nervousness. His eyes locked on the podium, as if searching for his notes but there were no notes.

"Sam Houston…I'm sure you know him," Z continued, his face briefly brightening at the mention of a Texas hero to a Texas audience. "In 1861, Sam said: 'those damn Yankees, once they get something in their head, they'll never give up no matter how long it takes.'"

Z's eyes reverted back to his imaginary notes and his head shook a bit. "So that's what I did," he said, his voice suddenly shivering like a radio operator stranded in a Korean blizzard. "I never knew George and uh, I wish I did, but," he paused, his hand darting to his forehead. His eyes now traveled to a far away place that only he knew.

The crowd was now visibly nervous for him, but Z now played another trump card—his sense of humor. "I think my two minutes are up," he said grinning. The crowd's laughter released the air out of the tension balloon.

Z's hands started tugging on his face and nose again but he suddenly blurted out, "I understand you people from Texas are interested in the game of football. I understand you have a professional football team nearby." More laughter; Z visibly relaxed, his shoulders becoming less rigid, his eyes on the crowd.

Z clasped his hands together. "Now, hear me out on this.

Congressman Pete Sessions
with Looney Family
Presentation of the Bronze Star to
George Looney Posthumously
August 14, 2002

My family at the awards ceremony. The men from left to right: Donald Zinngrabe, brothers Dean, Phil and yours truly along with Congressman Sessions. The females: daughter CeCe, my Mother Mary, daughter Sloan, daughter Kate and wife Sandra flanked by Congressman Sessions.

This is a story about a third string halfback." Z was talking with his hands now, occasionally holding them up the way a base coach holds up a runner at third.

"Anyway this kid was kinda mediocre. He was third team, the dummy squad," Z said, shaking his head in disappointment for the kid. "Before his last game, he went to the coach and he pleaded with him. 'Coach, I got to get in the game today. I got to get in the game today!'" said Z, his voice rising with emotion, his hand darting to his chin, then his nose.

"The coach decided to give it a shot so Billy went into the game and had a terrific game, scoring a couple of touchdowns. The coach can't believe what he's seeing and after the game, he grabbed the kid and he said, 'Billy what happened? You tore up the field!'"

Z abruptly stopped talking. As quickly as his right hand masked his face, he lowered it in an attempt to speak, but the words refused to come out so his hand returned to his face. After a brief silence and with both hands now in a death grip on each side of the podium, Z forged on, the words tumbling out fast. "The kid says, 'You know, my Dad has been blind for many years and he died at the beginning of the week, so this is the first time he ever had a chance to see me play.'"

A collective gasp settled over the crowd but somehow not in an unsettling way.

"I think that George . . .." said Z, his voice wavering.

Z hesitated, allowing the linebacker from Emotion U to tackle him from behind and I wondered if he would reach the goal line. During this hesitation, I saw in his face a man full with purpose. Suddenly, something too powerful for explanation invaded his body. A calm spread across his face; his posture became erect, his hands steady.

"I believe that George is as pleased as the boy's Father was." said Z, his voice as sure as the voice of a good radio operator in combat. Z was looking upward now, as if staring directly into the

Mary Looney at the awards ceremony with Donald Zinngrabe who worked 5 years to see that George Looney, a man he'd never met, was properly recognized for his efforts at Höfen.

smiling face of his fellow comrade from The 196th Field Artillery Battalion. "I think we should all look up and smile to let George know we are pleased also. Thank you."

And Z walked off the podium to a standing ovation, flashing a smile strong enough to drain the English Channel.

Z and the Looney clan relish the moment after the ceremony was over and everyone else had gone home. Sandra took the picture.

Chapter Twenty Seven

Oh Hell Yeah!

My Father never told me that he loved me, at least not after I was old enough to remember. I doubt my brothers heard anything different. No hugs after childhood either, but some of my first memories of life itself are his "whisker kisses"—a facial embrace that left your cheeks red from his heavy beard, but in a pleasing sort of way. We only shook hands once, an instant before I piled into Dee Owen's auto to leave home for college. With a handshake as firm as his look, he delivered a simple message: "You're a man now, so act like one." Probably similar to the words he once told teenage soldiers.

My brothers or I never needed spoken words or touches of affection from our Father to know his feelings. His eyes became dull brown headlights when we suffered or his face would explode into an ear to ear grin during our triumphs. On a really rambunctious moment, he would offer a chest swelling half-chuckle, half-laugh and an upbeat, "golly," his version of a hearty guffaw and bravado laced profanity.

The war had not totally rid our Father of his ability to inflict physical punishment. As a twelve year old, I learned this during a live drill—no instructional video for me. While suffering from a lack of oxygen to the brain induced by the complications brought on by pre-teenage adolescence, a few school chums and myself, broke into the grade school after hours. Or more accurately, we probably entered through an unlocked back door.

The mission: to test our metal slugs, the approximate size, weight and shape of a nickel, in the school Coke machine. Yes, this was the day of Davey Crockett on TV, black and white Converse tennis shoes and five-cent Cokes. After the slug repeatedly and wearily crashed to the coin return without delivering the goods, we stifled our disappointment by darting through the deserted halls, sliding down the stairway banisters like a waterslide and committing other random acts of boyish mischief. Our poor judgment escalated into a full scale brain cloud when we scaled the school's roof for a bit of rock throwing only to be spotted by nearby residents and reported to school authorities the next day.

Imagine the blood temperature of George, current superin-tendent of the Hutchins County Boys Home, a residence for juvenile delinquents, after receiving the call from the grade school principal concerning the juvenile delinquent activities of his own son. Failing to recognize the severity of the moment, I managed to call my Mother an "Old Fart" in front of my same pals the next day at school. To further darken a rapidly deteriorating situation,

my Mother had come to deliver me to my Father who'd just received the call concerning the "Break In." At that precise moment, to better welcome me home, George was converting a wooden baseball bat into a paddle at the Boy's Home Wood Shop. I still see that weapon as clear as I see the face of my Father: white ash, about thirty-two inches in length, three round holes drilled in the sweet spot of the surgically created flat surface.

To borrow words of wisdom from George's radio operator, Everett Allen: "I believed it then and I believe it now." It was the worst possible time to call my Mother an "Old Fart."

My only harsh paddling left an impression on me as deep as the whelps on my bottom. Shortly before his death at near age seventy-nine, I mentioned the incident, citing the long term benefits to his oldest son.

"I don't remember that," he said softly through a stare loaded with regret and possibly shame.

"No, Dad. It's okay. I had it coming," I assured him.

"I just don't remember," George repeated softer than before, practically shrugging the words; he suddenly looking tired, especially around the eyes.

As sure as the human memory bank can be conveniently accommodating, remembering what it wants to remember, the aging process will sleave some bitter and downright cranky while others mellow like fine wine. Years after the school incident, George reached a fork in life's pathway that required him to decide which route he'd choose. At age sixty-one, the former high school agriculture teacher, war hero, college Dean of Men, current Chief Probation Officer of the Dallas juvenile system and head of our family suffered a nervous breakdown induced by the loss of a political battle that forced him into unwanted early retirement. Once again, a lack of purpose in life demonstrated the strength to crack the emotional armor of a man durable as tank armor.

For several months, George became a walking zombie, on one occasion unable to determine if his family was celebrating Thanksgiving or Christmas. Understandably, this rocked the foundation of his loved ones, leaving us on ground shaky from life's sudden uncertainties.

Each day delivered a day darker than before. More and more time spent in bed. No progress from several shrink visits. "He's too worried about paying the bill to benefit from the session," complained the shrink. Talks of suicide. "Get the guns out of the house," oldest brother Andy advised. Concern for what would become of his family after he was gone. "I'm worried about your Mom and Dean," (a teenager at the time) George would say, his every word scaring the sceewad out of me.

A ray of sunlight arrived in the form of a visit to George's home from a minister, Don Anderson—no relation to the Dr. Anderson who performed my father's funeral service. George greeted Don in the den wearing a bath robe in the middle of the day, looking tired, defeated and older than dirt.

"Mr. Looney, are you aware you are in the midst of a nervous breakdown?" Don Anderson asked after taking one look at George.

"Yes," my father said softly.

"Has God ever failed to provide for your needs?" asked Don.

"No," George said barely above a whisper.

"Do you think he's going to let you down now?"

George offered a weak shrug; stared at his visitor through hollow sunken eyes.

The minister promptly gave George a series of Biblical based cassettes entitled "The Cure For Depression." With orders to listen to them immediately, George crawled back into his bed and listened to the tapes non-stop, as if the words contained his personal oxygen supply. After several days, he rose from his bed like Christ from the tomb and never had another bad day the rest of his life.

After my Dad's resurrection, never again saw him lose his temper or say a bad word about any man—though he struggled a bit with O. J. Simson. Never heard him use profanity. Hugged his grandkids every chance possible. Only saw him irritated once and that's when the yard man carelessly destroyed one of four tiny oak trees he'd planted in my front yard. The other three prosper today, the missing tree symbolic of the man who planted them.

And speaking of missing, as a kid, I sometimes wondered where were my Dad's pals? Someone to take in a ballgame with or drink a beer or two. The man worked, came home, and spent time with his family. Unlike kids hanging with school pals, maybe dads don't hang out with other dads, I reasoned. Hard to believe George's inner sanctum allowed no room for close friends since no man received more respect in our community than George Washington Looney.

"A prince of a man," my Mother-in-law, Marian Williams, would say.

In his retirement years, from time to time my Dad received invitations to various World War II Reunion Groups. He'd wordlessly study the announcements with distant down turned eyes, consider attending, but then stay home. He attended only The Battle of The Bulge trip in 1990.

With many of my high school and college friendships still intact, these questions of friendship for my dad troubled me from time to time. My answer came on June 1st of 2005, the night I visited Norm Bud Cohen or NBC, in Manhattan while in New York City on a business/pleasure trip.

Norm had informed me only a few months prior by letter that he had his pistol license and was doing security work at of all places...NBC! *My lady friend calls me a beast. Wants to know if I take Viagra. Hell no!* Norm had further declared. Bud, a native New Yorker, enthusiastically greeted me at his front door, his grip strong and sure.

"Come on in! I've been expecting you," he said, his cadence rapid, his tone, though coarse from age, was full throttle. His eyes, magnified by thick tear dropped shaped glasses, were as inviting as an ear to ear smile that divided his round jolly face. As one of his letters previously suggested, NBC was now a short man, reduced by eighty-six years of the earth's pull. He still moved with the youthful energy of a dancer or an athlete. A quick survey of his apartment living room cast a shadow over his youthful manner. Book shelves covered by a thin coat of dust; same for the hardwood floors. A dozen prescription bottles lined the coffee table. On the living room walls, black and white photos taken long ago of his now grown children, also of his wife. "Lost her twelve years ago to Alzheimer's," he said softly.

Oops! Current color pictures of an attractive black woman and two black children on the book shelves. NBC saw what I saw.

"That's my Dark Angel," he said through a boyish grin. "And that's my two little dark angels—eight and ten," he offered, pointing to the picture of two children.

"Your children?" I asked incredulously, the awe wiping the neutrality from my face.

"Oh, hell yeah!" he replied, but there was no need for NBC to answer. His grin, now ridiculously wide said this: a woman and children, for many men including NBC at age eighty-six, the twin fibers of purpose.

NBC volunteered that he "came into some money a few years ago" and gave it to the woman, a forty-five year old nurse from Jamaica. She lived and worked in Brooklyn and NBC would see his new family a couple of times a week. "The kids go to good schools," NBC said his chest swelling. "When she and I go to restaurants, I tell the maitre d she's a Jamaican Princess and we always get the best tables," he later revealed, his eyes twinkling with delight.

Reflecting on NBC's previous correspondence, none of this surprised me in the least. Okay, maybe a tad. After NBC tossed his NYPD hat on his shiny head, we walked across the street to a neighborhood bar.

"Been coming in here for thirty years," he said.

Nice quaint bar? Hardly. We entered to the sounds of loud music, Zeppelin maybe and the hip hop energy of youth.

"Bud!" Everyone seemed to yell simultaneously. No one else in the packed crowd was over thirty.

"Is this okay, Bud?" A young man asked, leading us to our seats, his voice laced with an equal mix of admiration and affection. I felt like I was with a former President of the United States, or at least Jack Nicholson.

NBC's big eyes traveled the room before landing on the bar area. "Got drunk in here every morning before I went to work," he said, referring to his days with the Manhattan Shirt Company. "Haven't had a drink in twenty years. Quit cold turkey. No AA—nothing."

While searching the past brought no recollection of Lt. Starter, the subject of Höfen practically brought NBC to his feet. "Oh hell yeah! I remember your Dad fighting in that building!" he said, his voice and possibly temperature escalating with the subject. "I delivered a battery and got hit by some shrapnel." he said, reiterating his earlier written testimony.

"Those Jerries were either doped up or the SS was behind them with guns aimed at their backside," he continued, shaking his head with disbelief. "We kept dropping grenades on them from the third floor and they kept on coming. It was a slaughter."

NBC's animation quickly dissolved into melancholy at the mention of James Everett Allen's passing. "Jimmy died, huh? One time I got beat up in a fight. Not real bad or anything, but Jimmy came and helped me. He was a good man," he declared, his voice lowering a few decibels, possibly contemplating the irony of a Tennessee Hillbilly rescuing a Yankee Jew.

NBC shared his thoughts on Iraq. "Dumfield and all of

George Senior's buddies got George Junior into this."

We both enjoyed a good laugh at the mention of the jeep driver, Frank Williams, turning over that "dern old trailer" in Paris and then later drinking an entire case of champagne—a gift to my Dad from the French and intended for an officer's party.

"Your Dad came to visit me once," NBC said, his tone crammed with pride. "He was a fine gentleman, I'll tell you that for sure."

The realization suddenly washed over me like the giant waves of Normandy. NBC and James Everett Allen and Frank Williams and Sinkler Scholz, George Himmelman and Vance Boren. These men and the rest of The 196th—my Dad's real buddies; men who drew strength from one another in the absence of anyone else.

"You think George is up there looking down at us?" NBC asked, his smile smoothing every wrinkle in his cherub face.

Before replying, time out for some melancholy wisdom from the Jayhawks, the world's greatest band that few ever heard.

"We were so close together
Yeah, you were like a brother to me
Thought we could live forever
But there's more to life than we'll ever know
I'd swim across the ocean for a sign
Though you're gone, you'll always be a friend of mine
Will I see you in heaven
Shine your lights from above
With your love, I am never alone
Won't you carry me
Won't you carry me…home"

Is George looking down on us? Oh, hell yeah, NBC. Oh hell yeah!

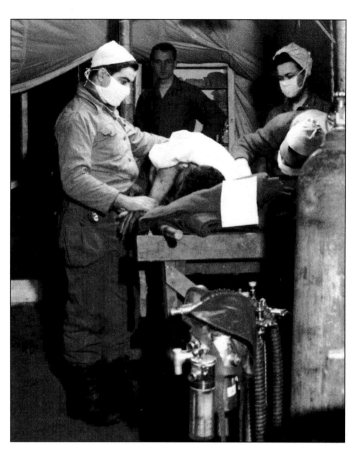

Inside a tent, surgeons perform a critical operation with the aid of a nurse. In one 63-hour period, this hospital in the Ardennes handled 1,000 casualties. U.S. Army Signal Corp

A medical service ambulance, hit by a German plane despite Red Cross markings, burns near a village in Luxembourg. The driver and patients perished. U.S. Army Signal Corp

American artillerymen defending the southern Ardennes in Luxembourg, pitch white tents that will help camouflage their campsite in a snowy field. U.S. Army Signal Corp

GIs stand guard behind a camouflaged, heavy water cooled 1919A4 Browning machine gun. U.S. Army Signal Corp

Crewmen of a U.S. armored battalion paint their M-4 tank white after a heavy snowfall. U.S. Army Signal Corp

Epilogue

Did George believe he was taking the story of Höfen to his grave? Or did he hope a family member would rifle through the rubble by his bed and uncover the heroics of a field artillery observer from Charleston, Arkansas and his radio operator from Memphis, Tennessee?

According to James Bradley in his stirring World War II book, "Flags Of Our Fathers," his Dad, who was one of six flag raisers at the horrific battle of Iwo Jima, achieved peace by willing the past into a cave of silence. Conversely, the sting of my Father's only return trip to Europe after the war, stirred a hornet's nest in his mind, leaving an interior wound for the rest of his days. No way, the trail of words he left behind was a ploy to receive recognition or accolades posthumously, but more of an effort for him to understand the importance and purpose of his life—to define his brightest star.

Am I disappointed by the lofty status George accords Höfen in his lifetime achievement rankings?—possibly a higher slot than his role of parent. As NBC might say: "Oh hell no!" No one could ask for a more loving or caring father, enough said.

Since I've started this journey, we've lost Buddy Wagner, George Himmelman and, of course, the beloved Everett Allen. No further word on fellow officer Sinkler Schloze or the fun loving jeep driver, Frank Williams. Adhering to Frank's request in 1997, I never contacted him again about the war, but thought of him and the pony horseshoe many times.

During the compilation of this manuscript, I finally mustered the courage to write Marie Herman in Belgium, delving fully into the controversy of Höfen and the conflicting stories of two lieutenants she so obviously cared a great deal. Marie, more than any person I've ever met, possessed a photographic memory, a historian without equal; and her attention to detail concerning events over half a century ago was nothing short of extraordinary. I asked hard questions: since Lt. Starter stayed with the Hermans before Lt. Looney, did he appear shaken when he originally arrived? Did Starter disclose anything about Höfen when he stayed with Marie's family or when he visited her years later?

Marie never replied. Maybe a painful subject matter or even her passing was the reason for her silence. Regardless, I decided against disrupting this quiet with a trans-Atlantic phone call, allowing the story of Höfen to rest in peace.

Norm B. Cohen continues to tiptoe through life with all the timidity of a Bradley tank, alternating nights between the tavern across the street from his New York flat and dining with his "Dark Angel."

"Do you two still get the best tables at the restaurant?" I asked long distance in the fall of 06.

"Oh, hell yeah!" he snapped, his voice instantly charged at the subject matter. "The other night, we were walking to our table and I told her to give me a kiss since everyone was looking at us." With a short white man, approaching the age of 90, walking hand in hand with a tall attractive black woman half a century younger, the sight must have pulsated with contrast to the other diners. "She did too," NBC added, cackling with joy.

Our conversation concluded with NBC inviting me to stay at

Thor and his wife Ruby at a 99th reunion about 4 years ago. Thor took the picture of GWL in front of OP 6 in 1990.

127

his place my next visit to the Big Apple. "No need you spending two dimes a night, course that's as long as you stay away from my woman," he warned, his hearty laughter soothing my ear.

Thor Ronningen and I still exchange Christmas cards and letters, though I've detected a wistful strain in his correspondence, probably due to the relentless passing of so many of his comrades; an excerpt from Thor's letter of August 27, 2007: *I can recall very vividly that at about 0545 on 16 December 1944 (the opening of The Bulge) I "knew" I would be dead in a very short time and, as I recall it, I was not terribly concerned, as it was inevitable. I know that my death grows closer everyday, but I feel it is still some time from now. However, I know now, as I knew then, that the outcome is inevitable and, so far at least, I feel the same way now as I did then. The world will not end at my death any more that it began at my birth. I have had a full and happy life and hope that I have carried my end of the load and added something to the lives of others.*

At the age 83, Thor remains the "Brightest Star" for the American Military.

In February of 2004, only eighteen months after his trip to Dallas, Z was diagnosed with colon cancer. "I kept passing so much gas, MiMi (his wife) made me go to the doctor," he joked, his crusty sense of humor providing a protective shield against death. "Only thing I can eat is cottage cheese and I don't like cottage cheese," Z growled. Predictably, Z remained upbeat. "At least I know what will eventually kill me," he said, his throaty raspy voice somehow still assuming a tenor's pitch. "I'm just not going any time soon."

Fearing the worst, on September 2, 2005, I traveled to Sturgeon Bay, Wisconsin, a slice of green paradise lined with tall trees and lakes, to visit Z—the same weekend Hurricane Katrina also visited Louisiana and Mississippi under unpleasant circumstances. Looking more exhausted than defeated and less gaunt than I had expected, Z was sitting on his front steps when the rental car containing myself and two pals, Eric Johnson and John Jackson, cruised to a halt in front of Z's residence.

Green everywhere. A lush green front yard and flower bed, both immaculately maintained. Towering trees of the north, loaded with green, practically swallowed Z's tasteful two story brick home. No wonder the Packers favored the color green.

Moving with the dexterity of Grandpa, Z's first halting steps exposed the advanced stage of his illness. He offered a weak smile, but his handshake remained strong as his inner self. A closer inspection revealed a face with an abundance of red. His white eyebrows sprouted forth at wild angles, as if taking a direct hit of chemotherapy.

We moved to the cedar deck, built by Z, located in his spacious and wooded back yard. Flower beds, containing an explosion of colors, flanked us on all sides, standing erect and in perfect formation as if saluting its master.

Z put up a brave front during our afternoon visit, fighting fatigue with a war hero's determination. His tired voice would raise two octaves and pick up steam when discussing our victory in Dallas on August the 14th, 2002.

"That was a good day," he said, nodding his head approvingly, his voice overflowing with pride.

With daylight bleeding into dusk, we returned to the front yard to say our goodbyes. Z clutched the first draft of this manuscript that I had delivered in one hand and waved with the other as our car pulled away. A feeling kin to sadness invaded my sprit—a feeling recognizable from when I was leaving the home of Marie Herman or Everett Allen. I knew I'd never see Z again.

My friends and I spent the night in Appleton, a two hour or so drive, enduring a heavy rainstorm, all the while oblivious to the perfect storm approaching the Gulf Coast with the force and speed of artillery fire. Fittingly, Appleton was the home of Doc Bradley, the central figure in the previously mentioned war book, "Flags Of Our Fathers."

In the early part of 2006, Z called, his voice surprisingly bright and happy and full strength. "There's too much about me in the book," he complained. "You need less about me and more of your Father."

Z also wanted comments George made concerning "deflection and range" during the battle at Höfen included in the book—comments providing further proof of George's presence at the battle site. Due to my limited understanding of "deflection and range," and yielding to Z's experience as a radio operator, we agreed he would write this portion of the book, borrowing on George's notes.

Several months passed; no word from Z. I knew the reason why, but procrastinated on making the call.

Z's wife, Mimi, called the afternoon of June the 26th. "He's too weak to talk, but he still tried to reach up and plant one on me," said Mimi, battling her tears, once again proving humor evolves from tragedy.

As surprising as say, US retaliation for Pearl Harbor or 9-11, I learned Z had battled the final stages of his own private war with the same mad dog intensity that he once battled for justice for a man he'd never met. Donald Zinngrabe, a builder of four homes and countless theater sets with his own hands, educator, artist, author, son, husband, father, grandfather and finally righter of wrongs, joined his buddies of The 196th Field Artillery Battalion on June the 27th, 2006.

Thor while recently speaking to a group of veterans in his home town of Wilmington, North Carolina.

128

Acknowledgements

To my wife, Sandra and our three daughters-Sloan, Kate and Cece for continued love and support. To my brothers, Phil and Dean, who, after a decade of nostalgic reminiscing of GWL, anxiously await the release of "The Battle of The Bulge: The Untold Story of Höfen," and a special thanks to brother, Phil, for having the foresight years ago to scan and archive many of our fathers' war pictures that were in his private vault from the past. Thanks to a friend from childhood, Charlie Taylor, for providing the pictures in the proper format for Victory Publishing. With deep gratitude for my assistant of the past 25 years, Adrienne Perutelli, for typing every word of this manuscript.

Readers will find the influence on certain passages from Flags of Our Fathers, the stirring account of Iwo Jima by James Bradley and Ron Powers. Also, consideration to Geoffrey C. Ward and Ken Burns' book, "The War," which served as a reference point for several facts and figures in this work.

Certainly, this book is a tribute to not only my father, but the 196th Field Artillery Battalion, including Donald Zinngrabe, Thor Ronningen, Everett Allen, Frank Williams, George Himmelman, Sinkler Schoize, Norm B. Cohen, Vance Boren (who was unfortunately already gone by the time I decided to write this book) and to all the men and women who served the Allied cause in World War II. You are truly the best of us.

Finally. this book is dedicated to my mother, Mary Looney, who after battling back from brain surgery on October 11, 2005 with all of the courage of any GI, lost her life to a wheelchair accident on September 30, 2008.

"Greater love hath no man than this, that a man lay down his life for his friends."

"Höfen, Germany. My brightest star. I helped save the day."

Pretty strong stuff coming from a man drenched with humility. These words, written secretly by George Washington Looney, referred to his role as a field artillery observer with the 196th Field Artillery Battalion in a battle at Höfen, Germany in World War II during what became known as "The Battle of The Bulge." It was the largest battle in American History. Over a half-million Germans attacked 600,000 GIs and the Bulge eventually involved some two million troops on both sides who fought over a 2,500 square mile region called the Ardennes forest during Europe's coldest winter in twenty-five years. The Americans suffered over 76,000 casualties, the Germans 100,000, and the outcome changed the world. Lt. Looney played a vital part in altering history, but kept it to himself. Amazingly, his family knew nothing of his role until his passing. More amazing, someone else possibly took the credit. This is that story—a story told not only by eyewitness accounts of Lt. Looney's fellow soldiers, but also by journal entries, letters and pictures spanning six decades.

Reviews!

"A great book of a WW II hero as related by very talented son. Even though my own WW II experience was as pilot in China-Burma-India my greatest admiration has always been for those, who fought the Nazis on the ground in the European theatre. The Battle of the Bulge was one of our toughest military challenges but was also one of our greatest but necessary victories thanks to troops like George Washington Looney. I have enjoyed these never before seen photographs."

John Paul Hammerschmidt—
U.S. Congressman '67-'93 (3rd District-Arkansas)
Pilot of 217 Combat Missions during W. W. II

****

From the European combat to the business, to the family, George W. Looney distinguished himself as a great American who understood how to operate from a position of strength. I am honored to have delivered his military Silver Star medal — a fitting symbol of a great man's lasting legacy. Now through Mike Looney's book in moving tribute to his father's life, more Americans will know the inspiration, strength of character, and principled responsibility which encompasses George W. Looney's journey as a member of America's Greatest Generation."

Photo by Jenice Johnson as printed in the Nov. 6, 2009 edition of The Dallas Morning News Neighborsgo section.

Pete Sessions—U.S. Congressman
Texas

****

Mike Looney crafts a thoughtful, compelling story about a father's sense of duty and honor and a son's quest to complete his father's legacy. It's filled with insight into two men who take seriously their vows to their country and to each other.

It was a great read - nice job!

Rick Wamre; Publisher,
Dallas Advocate Magazines

"A father who was an authentic war hero. A son who has mastered the art of words and willing to do the hard work of research to tell his father's story. Put the father and son together and you have what I consider one of the great true stories of George Washington Looney's life in WWll as only his son can tell it. A must read!"

Steve Binder Ph.D
Emmy and Ace winning Producer/Director and
Golden Globe nominee
The Caucus 2008 Director of the Year

****

The book is superb!

"Our current fighting men and women at war help make Mike Looney's "The Battle of The Bulge—The Untold Story of Höfen" a much needed sharp reminder of the lives of American's Fighting Men in the European Theatre of WWII.

George Washington Looney's tale is told in the a matter of fact style so common from those of "Our Greatest Generation" The never before seen photographs will bring you into the foxholes, fights and front porches of the era at the warfront and the home front! You will not put it down!"

Mike Schikman-
WSVA AM 550 Radio,
Harrisonburg, VA

****

The stories of war are often couched in numbers and words that render the impact on history almost business like, as if the author thought the reader ill-equipped to deal with the horrific human reality. Mike Looney gives us a personal tale instead: He walks in his father's boots. The image that emerges is larger than life.

Kevin Sherrington
Award Winning Sportswriter
Dallas Morning News

Braced for a German counterattack that never came, the crewmen of a half-buried 7th Armored Division tank keep a sharp lookout for panzers along a road near Manhay on December 27. When time permitted, a U.S. armored unit to prepare for a defensive battle, bulldozers gouged out pits, so that the tanks presented a minimal target to enemy gunners. U.S. Army Signal Corp

Patrols of the American First and Third Armies meet near Houffalize, Belgium, on January 16, completing the pincer movement that cut off the Bulge at its waist. For both patrols, the trek to Houffalize had been an agonizing struggle against frigid weather and diehard German resistance. The First Army troops had spent nearly two weeks fighting 15 miles south from Grandménil and Manhay, and the GIs of the Third Army took a week to cover the seven miles from Bastogne. The bulk of the German forces were able to escape before the pincers snapped shut. U.S. Army Signal Corp

Appendix A

History of the 196th Field Artillery's Campaign during W.W.II in Europe.
1944-1945

The following History of the 196th Field Artillery Battalion manual was presented to members of the 196th in Czechoslovakia during 1945, soon after the war's end.

GWL added his inscriptions throughout the manual, practically speaking in his familiar voice, thus allowing us to follow his journey of World War II thru the conduit of his own words.

Somewhat legible and sometimes haunting, I've included these notes providing readers not only a peek of what I saw, but a chance to feel some of what I felt.

DEDICATED

TO

LIEUTENANT COLONEL B. G. CROSS

under whose inspiring leadership

we received our training and who led us through

nine months of combat

AND TO

1st Lt George W. Looney

who, as a member of our unit, helped in no small way
to achieve our goal.

FORWARD

After considerable research, and digging into years of dust and memories, the undersigned finally gathered together material to compile a history of this battalion. Before we go further, let it be known to all who are about to ponder over the accomplishments of this unit, that all that follows is semi-official. It has been compiled and written by one who was not a National Guard product, but one of the Army's first "Selectees".

There are many stories, incidents and various actions that the individual can recall that took place during the period covered by this history. Due to limited amount of time and space allowed, it is impossible to record all of them. It is hoped that what is recorded here will help those incidents and personal memories to always live in the mind and heart of the individual.

This history is supported by memories, worries, horrors, official journals, and a few more items that seemed helpful in summarizing the accomplishments of the battalion. Acknowledgment is made to our Executive Officer, Major A. J. Tothacer, and our Personal Adjutant, Mr. Switzer, for their valuable assistance in getting the material for this history; and to all the other officers and men of this unit who helped to make this book a reality.

MEYER H. WEISS, M/Sgt.
Sergeant Major - Editor.

CHAPTER I
ORGANIZATION

When history is written and the accomplishments of men are praised and talked about, there always seems to be some that are left out. This is very understandable due to the fact that small men and small organizations are always a part of the big things and as the big people and big things are recorded for all time to remember, it isn't necessary for the individual comprising the smaller world to be remembered. But those individuals are a world in themselves. It is because of their accomplishments that the world goes on and is able to read the deeds and glories of our armies.

As others see our battalion, it is one of many such organizations that comprise this great army of ours. To the man on top of it all, we may be noticed when he happens to skim through a book that may contain the various organizations that make up our army. But we, the members of the 196th F. A. Battalion, have seen our accomplishments and have that self-satisfaction in knowing that even though we are one among a thousand, we did our share and have contributed much.

The history of this organization has been built of many things: personalities, achievements, memories of jobs well done, places and circumstances of action, and a lot more. It comes from a long line of history making organizations and now stands out as the finished specimen of years of experience and toil.

The First Tennessee Infantry Regiment was a great outfit and fought gloriously at Eagle Pass, Texas on the Mexican border. It moved to the Mexican border in July 1916 to help other US Forces put down the acts of violence of the then famous Pancho Villa. It fought there and on through the Mexican campaign, returning to Camp Sevier, N.C. in September 1917. The First Tennessee Infantry was redesignated as the 115th Field Artillery at that camp on September 8, 1917. Embarking for France soon after that, the regiment fought in many of the campaigns of World War I. Among them were the campaigns of St. Mihiel, the Argonne, and Chateau Thiery. They were armed with Schneider 155 mm howitzer. The 115th F. A. Regiment returned to the United States and was demobilized at Fort Oglethorpe, Georgia on April 15, 1919. The organization then went into five years of inactivity.

The 2nd battalion, 115th F. A. Regiment came into being again in the form of a National Guard organization activated and federally recognized on August 4, 1924 in the town of Andrews, South Carolina. From then until 1937, the 2nd Bn, 115th F. A. (75 mm Horse Drawn) functioned as a training organization, a part of the S. C. National Guard. In 1937 the name of the 2nd Bn 115th F. A. was transferred from the state of South Carolina to the State of Tennessee and was organized as a functioning National Guard organization among the towns in Eastern Tennessee. A few years later, in 1940, the 2nd Battalion, 115th F. A. (75 mm Howitzer, Truck Drawn) was transferred from the towns in Eastern Tennessee to the city of Memphis, Tennessee.

On March 1, 1940, the 2nd Battalion, 115th Field Artillery Regiment was accorded federal recognition at it's home station in Memphis, Tennessee, as a 75 mm Gun, truck drawn outfit, and a part of the Tennessee National Guard. Most of the officer personnel of the battalion were drawn from 115th F. A. Regimental units that were also stationed in Memphis. A selected cadre of enlisted men was drawn in the same way. The staff of the battalion on March 1, 1940, was made up of Major E. G. Cross, battalion commander; Captain Fisher, executive officer; 1st Lt. J. O. Frerichs, S 3, 2d Lt. A. J. Tothacer, S 2. Battalion Headquarters Battery, and Batteries D, E, and F were activated the same date as the battalion headquarters. From March through July 1940, the battalion was principally engaged in recruiting new members to bring the organization up to authorized strength, drawing new equipment and clothing, and in training the battalion and schooling the personnel in basic artillery subjects. For twenty one days in August, 1940 the battalion participated in the 1940 Louisiana Maneuvers.

CHAPTER II
ACTIVE SERVICE

On September 16, 1940 the 115th Field Artillery, then a part of the 30th Infantry Division, was ordered into active Federal Service by authority of President Franklin D. Roosevelt, under Public

Resolution No. 96, made and approved by the 76th Congress
August 17, 1940. Upon receipt of the call into Federal Service, activities were speeded up within the battalion. Physical examinations and detailed administrative work was accomplished. After recruiting to the new VO strength, the 115th F. A. Regiment moved to Fort Jackson, S.C., as a permanent change of Station, arriving there on September 28, 1940.

After arrival at Fort Jackson, S.C., the battalion went through a very intensive training program and a complete maneuver exercise June 1941. In that month the battalion participated in the Second Army maneuvers in Tennessee that were held under the direction of Lt. General Ben Lear. During the maneuvers Cpl. W. R. Houston and Pfc. W. Taylor of Hq Btry, 2nd Bn, 115th F. A. were awarded the Soldier's Medal for their actions in extinguishing the flames from the clothing of another soldier, Pvt. Henry G. O'Daniel.

Prior to participation in the Tennessee Maneuvers of 1941, new blood entered the organization on January 11, 1941, in the form of the first Selective Service Trainees to be inducted into service. These men came from the battalion home state, Tennessee. They received their basic training at Fort Jackson's famous "Dust Bowl" and were instructed by officers and enlisted men of the battalion. After 1941 maneuvers in Tennessee, the battalion returned to Fort Jackson to again set up headquarters and resume training. They remained there until the start of the First Army maneuvers held during the months of September, October, November and December 1941. The battalion again left their camp and participated in these maneuvers held in North and South Carolina under the direction of Lt. General Hugh Drum. After the maneuvers the battalion returned to Fort Jackson. The second group of Selective Service Trainees came to the organization in early December 1941, after having received their basic training at Fort Bragg, N.C. The battalion was continuing its training program as a part of the 30th Infantry Division when the United States declared war against Japan and Germany on December 8, 1941.

On February 16, 1942. the battalion was redesignated as 1st Battalion, 196th F. A. Regiment. The 196th F. A. Regiment was composed of a regimental headquarters battery, medical detachment and band drawn from the 113th F. A. Regiment, the 2nd Bn, 115th F. A. Regiment, and the 2nd Bn, 113th F. A. Regiment. The 196th F. A. Regiment was organized as a 240 mm Howitzer organization, and later changed to a 105 mm Howitzer, truck drawn, organization. The organization was a result of making a triangular organization of the 30th Infantry division. A separate organization, the 196th F. A. Regiment was assigned as GHQ Reserve Troops.

After the redesignation of the battalion, the organization moved to newer and betters quarters on the Post at Fort Jackson. Here again a change in the type of guns used by the battalion took place. For a while the battalion was equipped with 155 mm Howitzers, but after a few months the organization was again equipped with it's present basic weapon 105 mm Howitzer. The battalion continued training and taking AGF tests at Fort Jackson until August 23, 1942, when it was transferred to Fort Sill, Oklahoma, as a permanent change of station, to be employed as school troops.

CHAPTER III
FORT SILL, OKLAHOMA

At Fort Sill, Oklahoma, the battalion as a part of the 196th F. A. Regiment was employed almost entirely on Field Artillery School assignments, doing a great deal of firing with 105 mm and 75 mm howitzers, including demonstration work on the massing of fires for the students of the school and the Officer Candidate Classes. Demonstrations were also conducted in the art of massing fires through efficient fire direction control, survey problems, and communications and motor problems.

In March 1943 the regiment was redesignated as the 196th F. A. Group. The two battalions were made separate battalions. The 1st Battalion, 196th F. A. Regiment was redesignated 196th F. A. Battalion. The 2nd Battalion, 196th F. A. Regiment was redesignated the 690th F. A. Battalion. The 196th F. A. Battalion was then attached to the 196th F. A. Group for administrative and tactical control.

During the last few months at Fort Sill, the battalion had achieved a high degree of perfection in firing and coordination. It was rated by the instructors and Commandant of the Field Artillery School as one of the best F. A. battalions ever to fire for the school. Firing over the heads of troops on exercises and demonstrations was habitual and frequent.

On June 18, 1943, the battalion was transferred to Camp Gordon, Georgia on a permanent change of station.
(I was assigned here, Fort Sill, as 2nd lt. just out of OCS. Lt. George Looney GWL).

CHAPTER IV
RECOGNITION FOR WELL
PERFORMED TASKS

Upon arrival at Camp Gordon, Georgia, an intense physical arid tactical training program was undertaken. The battalion was engaged in taking the Army Ground Forces tests during the period from August 11 to 15, 1943. Concerning the performance of the 196th F. A. Group (to which this battalion was attached) during the AGF tests, the endorsement from the Commanding General, III Corps, in forwarding the reports of the tests, to the Commanding General, Army Ground Forces on August 17, 1943, included the following:

"The 196th F. A. Group made the best grades of all comparable units tested by this headquarters in the past eighteen months. Such mistakes as were made were of the type usually noted when units are under tension of a formal test. There were no mistakes in fundamental

principles and procedure. This entire Group is well trained and can be made ready for combat in a very short time."

The battalion continued training at Camp Gordon, Georgia, until November 8, 1943 when it left to participate in the Second Army Maneuvers in Tennessee that were being held under the direction of Lt. General Fredendall. During this maneuvers, the 196th F. A. Group was attached to various divisions, one of which forwarded the following commendation:

"To Colonel Roberts. 196th F. A. Group:
    I desire to express my full appreciation for the efficient cooperation and splendid performance of your headquarters and all of your battalions. It was a real pleasure to have your units attached to us and I feel that they are all deserving of commendation for the excellent performance of duty under grueling maneuver conditions. I would appreciate your passing my feelings to all of the units under your command.

Signed: FUTCH
    CG Div Arty"

The battalion was called back from the maneuver area on December 17, 1943, and returned to Camp Cordon, Georgia under an alert for overseas movement. From December 20, 1943, date of arrival at Camp Gordon, until the battalion readiness date of January 25, 1944, all time was spent in completing the equipping of the battalion, completing furloughs and leaves, and carrying out preparation for overseas movement instructions.

At 1315 hours on February 2, 1944, the battalion entrained and departed from Camp Gordon, arriving at the staging area, Camp Kilmer, N. J. at 1535 hours, February 2, 1944. Upon arrival at Camp Kilmer, a staging area for the New York Port of Embarkation, the battalion started a rapid program of finishing all administrative work, getting last items of clothing and equipment, and complying with other requirements of the port authorities. Passes to New York City were enjoyed while at Camp Kilmer. At 1725 hours on February 10, 1944, the battalion departed from Camp Kilmer, N.J. via rail to Jersey City, N.J. then by ferry to the Staten Island Terminal. From Pier 22, at 2000 hours 10 February 1944, the battalion boarded the new army transport ship, USS Marine Raven enroute for overseas duty.

CHAPTER V
ENGLAND

Marine Raven was a new transport on her maiden trans ocean voyage, having come down the ways in a shipyard at Boston, Mass just three weeks prior to our boarding her. She was a very modern ship but had a frequent roll and toss that didn't make anyone on board too happy during the trip. The ship

traveled as a part of a large convoy which was made up mainly of ships carrying troops. Three aircraft carriers, the battleship Nevada, and 26 destroyers of the U. S. Navy formed the escort. After a trip with no unusual occurrences, **(Not quite. We were in large convoy. About half way over it blew out one engine. We fell out of convoy for one day. The next night we caught up with the convoy. GWL)** the convoy arrived in the Firth of Clyde, Scotland, on February 22, 1944. The battalion debarked at Gourock, Scotland, at 1800 hours on February 26, 1944 and proceeded by lighter and train to its destination in the Midlands of England.

At 1000 hours, February 27, 1944, in a blinding snowstorm, the battalion arrived at Albrighton Shropshire, England, proceeding from there to the billets arranged for them by an advance detachment. Headquarters Battery and the Medical Detachment were quartered at The Grange, an estate in Aibrighton; Battery A at Bishton Hall, about two miles from Albringhton; Battery B at Cayton Hall, about three miles from Albrighton. Battery C and Service Battery were quartered at Stanton Stables, about four miles from Albrighton, and about a mile distant from the town of Shifnal.

The following is a list of the battalion staff officers and the battery commanders of the battalion upon arrival in England:

Bn Comdr: Lt. Col E. G. CROSS
Executive: Major A. J. TOTHACER
S 2: Capt. G. C. LANGSTON
Asst S 2: Lt. G. POEHLMANN
S 3: Major J. B. FARLEY
Asst S 3: Capt. C. H. MOORE
4 Sv Btry Comdr: Capt. A. M. HEILMAN
Asst S 4: CWO W. H. ROWLET
Bn Surgeon: Capt. F. P. SCHRAFFA
Pers Adjutant: Mr. W. L. SWITZER
Btry Comdr, Btry A: Capt. G. W. WATKINS
Btry Comdr, Btry B: Capt. S. E. SCHOLZE
Btry Comdr, Btry C: Capt. J. P. MORGAN
Liaison Officer: Capt. N. E. WATTS
Liaison Pilots: Lt. J. W. KILKENNY
Liaison Pilots: Lt. K. G. THORPE
Battalion Motor Officer: Lt. R. W. CUMMINGS.

A complete training schedule for the battalion was started as soon as it reached its destination in the vicinity of Albrighton, England. Supplies and the full T/E allotment of equipment were drawn from all corners of England. Alert orders for the battalion were received on April 14, 1944, from the Commanding General, First U. S. Army. The battalion went into final phases of combat training and awaited further orders. On June 12, 1944 a movement warning was received from ETOUSA directing the battalion to be ready for movement any time on or after 20 June 1944. The battalion received movement orders and left its quarters at Albrighton, England and vicinity, at 1400 hours on June 21, 1944, enroute to a concentration area at a camp near Witney and Oxford, England. Arriving there, waterproofing of vehicles was brought to a near completion and last supplies were drawn. The battalion moved to Camp Holmes, near the port of Southampton, England on July 3, 1944.

Camp Holmes was in the marshalling area where last minute preparations were made prior to the trip across the English

Channel. Waterproofing of vehicles was completed here. Personnel put on all battle equipment including the gas proof clothing, and on 6 July 1944, the battalion left for Southhampton, England, to board LST's for the trip to France. At 0830 hours July 7, 1944 Hq & Hq Battery, and Battery A left the port on U.S. Navy LST 379. Battery B and Battery C left port on LST 490 at 2230 hours the same date. Service Battery left the port at Southampton on LST 179 at 0115 hours July 8, 1944.

CHAPTER VI
FRANCE

The entire battalion landed on the Utah Beach in Normandy, France, on July 8, 1944, Hq Btry and Btry A debarking at 0415 hours; Battery B and Battery C at 0420 hours; Service Battery at 1520 hours. After landing, the battalion proceeded to its first bivouac area on the continent in the vicinity of ST. COM-DU-MONT in the Cherbourg peninsula. The Battalion Commander reported, *(Forward observer. Went with him. He told us it was an easy war on everybody except F.O. and infantry. Forward Observer me. GWL)* to First Army Headquarters on 8 July 1944. On 9 July 1944 the battalion was attached to VII Corps of the First U.S. Army and moved into its first firing position in the vicinity of MONTMARTIN en GRAIGNES, approximately three and one half miles south of CARENTAN. The battalion was further attached to the Ninth Infantry Division, *(9th Inf. Division first assignment from Beach until breakout at St. Lo. GWL)* and was assigned the mission of general support, reinforcing the fires of the 60th F. A. Battalion. Battery "C" under the command of Capt. J. P. Morgan fired the first round for the battalion in actual combat at 2215 hours on 9 July 1944. *(I called for it. GWL)*

The battalion moved forward on July 10th to new positions in the vicinity of GOUCHERIE. On the 11th of July air observers of the battalion were sent up in the battalion Cubs (L-4A) and missions were fired through the air OP. Captain C. H. Moore, then Asst S-3, registered the battalion for the first time in combat with a high burst registration. On 12 July 1944 the battalion went into position south of Goucherie and received considerable counter battery fire from German 88 mm guns. Forward observers with the 60th F. A. Bn credited Battery C with a direct hit on an enemy tank and battalion fire was responsible for neutralizing an 88 mm gun battery *(I spotted this unit from (cub plane) air and got credit for knocking it out. GWL)* at that time. The first air activity on the part of the enemy ever encountered by this battalion was during the night of 14 July 1944 when bombs were dropped in the vicinity of battery positions and around the battalion CP. However, no casualties were suffered.

Forward observers were sent out by the battalion for the first time on 16 July 1944. *(Me. GWL)*

During a battalion reconnaissance for forward battery positions near AMIGNY on 19 July 1944, the area was found to be heavily mined. The 1/4 ton vehicle in which the Asst S-2 and his driver were riding, hit a German teller mine. Both occupants were serious casualties. *(I was with lead troops on left side. As we moved up ditch by side of road, we had a tank coming up road with us. It was hit close to me. I could hear boy screaming and tank burst into flames. I don't think anybody got out. We moved on. GWL)* On the same reconnaissance the battery commander of Battery C died of a heart attack. On the night of 20 July 1944 the battalion moved into forward positions near Amigny after encountering considerable enemy air activity while in the process of moving forward. In this position, counter battery fire was received daily, and at night there was enemy air activity overhead. During a heavy shelling of battalion positions one enlisted man of Battery A was killed and seven other members of that battery became casualties.

The next few days found the battalion firing continuously, and receiving quite a bit of incoming heavy enemy gun fire, believed to have come from a large enemy railway gun. The battalion worked with the entire corps artillery in probing for the gun with the aid of F. A. Observation Battalions.

On the night of 23 July 1944 a false gas alarm was spread through the entire sector. All precautions were taken and the battalion made ready for the appearance of a gas attack on the part of the enemy. *(I remember this. A truck driver got too close to front line and smelled gun powder from shells and put out word of gas. GWL)*

On the morning of the 25th of July at 1000 hours the battalion assisted laying a red smoke line, *(I directed this from our positions. GWL)* on our front line positions to mark a bomb line for the coming bombing by our air forces. During the next hour and a half, fighter-bombers, mediums, and heavies bombed the entire area ahead of our positions. Bombs, which fell short of their target, landed all through the battalion area. *(General McNair and Major Aid came up to our position. General went out front looking around. Aid asked me if he should be out there. I told him no. He could get shot. He asked me to get him. I said it is your responsibility. He (McNair) did come back in. The next day he came back to our unit. Was killed by our bombs. GWL)* A stick of four 500 pound bombs fell in the Headquarters Battery position about one hundred yards from the CP and ten yards from the Aid Station and Radio Section area. Luckily, no casualties were received, although some of the troops were badly shaken up. That afternoon, following up the bombing attack, infantry troops from the First and Ninth Infantry Divisions pushed off to capture their objective and open a hole for the tanks of the newly arrived Third U.S. Army to go through and exploit the breakthrough. *(We ran back two or three hundred yards. Bombs dropped. Artillery started bombing smoke and near dusk killed many boys. Bombers dropped bombs in smoke. Several Soldiers were killed and the general. GWL)* The main objective was to take the ST. LO PIERRE LESAY Highway. *(I remember the S-curve on road. St. Lo-Pierre-LeSay. GWL)* The battalion continued to support the attack and fired continuously for the Ninth Division during the attack. As soon as the objective was taken, the battalion went into reserve awaiting further orders.

On 28 July 1944 the battalion was released from its operational attachment to the Ninth Infantry Division, and on the 29th of July was released from attachment to VII Corps. It was then attached to V Corps and further attached to the 2nd Infantry Division. On the 30th of July the battalion moved into the V Corps area, which was on the American left flank next to the British sector of the front. On 31 July 1944 the battalion went into firing positions in the vicinity of TORIGNI-SUR-VIRE with the mission of reinforcing the fires of the 15th F. A. Bn, an organic battalion of the 2nd Division.

Upon moving into this new position, the battalion CF was placed in an apple orchard, which at that time was 600 yards from the enemy front line on the left flank. The battalion by passed infantry mortar companies and cannon companies while moving into the position. The battalion remained in this position firing continuously for the Second Division until 3 August 1944 when the battalion crossed the VIRE River at 1520 hours and fired from new positions in support of the Second Division.

On 5 August 1944 the battalion was released from attachment to V Corps and from attachment to the Second Division. Reverting to control of First U.S. Army, the battalion was attached to the First U.S. Army Provisional Ranger Group, moving into an assembly area with the Provisional Ranger Group in the vicinity of SOULLES, and CANISY, south of ST. LO. This Ranger Group was made up of the 5th Ranger Battalion, the 99th Infantry Battalion (Norwegians naturalized as American citizens), the 18th F. A. Battalion, the 196th F. A. Battalion, and a light tank battalion. On 10 August 1944 the Ranger Group went into positions in the vicinity of the town of BUAIS and was given the mission of protecting the main roads in the vicinity of that town. On 14 August 1944 the battalion moved forward and went into positions in the vicinity of ST. GERMAIN de ANXURE, in support of the 5th Ranger Battalion, whose mission was to protect the Mayenne River crossings in that vicinity. This was at one end of the Falaise pocket that was being protected in case of an attempted German breakout. On 16 August the unit moved to new positions in the vicinity of MAYENNE and supported the units defending the river crossings at that town.

Orders were received on the afternoon of 18 August relieving the battalion from Attachment to the Provisional Ranger Group and placing the battalion with V Corps. Moving to an assembly area in the vicinity of SEES, north of ALENCON, the battalion received further orders on 19 August 1944 attaching the unit to Combat Command L, of the Second French Armored Division, and moving the battalion to a firing position in the vicinity of EXMES with the mission of reinforcing the fires of that command's organic artillery. The battalion did a great deal of firing in this position and helped to reduce the size of the enemy pocket that was holding out in the Falaise Gap. On the night of 20 August 1944 enemy patrols were reported in front of the battalion position. All batteries were alerted and heavy security patrols were sent out to the front and flanks of the battalion. Prisoners were taken the next day by these patrols.

On the afternoon of the 22nd of August, the battalion was withdrawn with CC "L" of the 2nd French Armored Division and was sent to an assembly area for a rest in the vicinity of ST. CHRISTOPHE le JAJOLET, *(I pitched tent and made down good bed, but did not get to sleep in it, but a few hours. GWL)* but was alerted for forward movement the

next morning. Moving with Combat Command "L," in the general direction of PARIS, the battalion on the 23rd and 24th of August occupied positions in the vicinity of CHEVREUSE and CHATEAUFORT. At this last position, one thousand rounds were fired inside of a two hour period on area targets designated by the Combat Command Commander. *(Me with him. GWL)* That same afternoon (24 August 1944) five prisoners were taken from a SMALL-WOODS in vicinity of the Battery "A" firing position. Enemy artillery fire was falling at the crossroads near where the battalion was in position and in the field nearby.

At about 1830 hours 24 August 1944, the battalion received orders to resume the march on PARIS. The route of march was via TOUSSUS le NOBLE, and through VILLACOUBLAY where the battalion was held up for over two hours because the road was being subjected to enemy time fire. *(I directed some of this fire. GWL)* After the enemy guns were destroyed, the battalion continued on its march. All along the route crowds of French people swamped the vehicles of the unit with flowers, wines and fruit to show their joy at liberation. *(I was up front with lead French unit. GWL)* In places the crowds were so dense that vehicles had to halt to keep from hitting someone. The march continued through VANVES, on through CLAREMONT and into the town of ISSY les MOULINEAUX. The march to Issy les Moulineaux was made by way of the above mentioned towns and over side roads and across the fields. This was necessary because road intersections along the route were being subjected to both time and percussion fire by the enemy. Upon arriving at Issy les Moulineau on the night of 24th August 1945 the vehicles were parked double on a side street and the battalion halted for the night. Security guards were put out and a general plan for the future operations and the march on Paris was made.

CHAPTER VII
PARIS AND THEN
A RAT RACE

On the morning of 25 August 1944 the battalion was alerted for movement directly into the city of PARIS with CC "L" of the Second French Armored Division. *(I was with lead troops for artillery when needed-French that is. GWL)* Leaving Issy les Moulineaux at 1240 hours, the battalion proceeded through the town of SEVRES and across the SEINE RIVER at the Porte de St. Cloud, *(I remember the sign on street bridge. GWL)* the head of the column entering Paris at 1300 hours on 25 August 1944. After crossing the Seine and coming into the city, the battalion was halted for three hours along the streets at Boulogne Bilancourt while all efforts possible were made to obtain information as to the route, destination and mission of the battalion within the city. Information was finally received and with the help and assistance of markers placed at important street intersections by Captain C. H. Moore, the battalion proceeded toward the ARC DE TRIOMPHE. The road markers stayed at the posts despite enemy sniper fire, and the masses of people getting their first view of their liberators.

During the move along the streets of Paris the column was forced to move slowly because of the huge masses of people who thronged the streets, cheering and throwing flowers on each vehicle as it passed by. Along the route too, the entire column was subjected to quite a bit of sniper fire from Germans who were still hidden in many of the buildings. *(I was up front with leading French troops. We got to Arc-de-Triomphe about noon 25th. I was standing by a command core with French officer. Sniper fired bullet. Passed by my head on right and bounced off my left. Good miss. GWL)* Several casualties were suffered by the battalion from sniper fire. Among them was one enlisted man who later died in a hospital in Paris. The battalion arrived at the Arc de Triomphe and stopped there in the midst of heavy machine gun fire, light artillery and anti aircraft fire. *(French officer was pulling on my arm, hollering for me to not be afraid. Of course he meant be afraid and get down which I did. GWL)* When the resistance ended, the battalion proceeded to an assembly area a block north of the Arc along the street in the vicinity of 72 AVENUE DE LA GRAND ARMEE closing there at 1820 hours.

Prior to the entry of the battalion into the city, vehicles of the battalion maintenance sections and the Service Battery became separated from the battalion on the 24 August 1944 when the column was broken up by enemy artillery fire. These vehicles entered the city of Paris on the morning of 25 August 1944 in two elements. One element, led by Capt. A. M. Heilman entered the city at 0830 hours. The second element led by Lt. Armel J. Couture entered the city at 1100 hours. 1st Lt. Ray searched the city for the scattered elements, and by 1000 hours 26 August 1944 all scattered vehicles had rejoined the main body of the battalion.

During the morning of 25 August at about 1000 hours, a part of a German garrison on the outskirts of the city opened fire with small arms about 100 yards from the rear of the Battery C column. Several men went to investigate and were fired upon by small arms fire and an anti-tank gun. Several of the men were injured and were evacuated by the battalion medical section. The enemy garrison and the anti-tank gun were destroyed by a tank from Combat Command L of the Second French Armored Division.

The two liaison planes of the 196th F. A. Battalion were the first American planes to land on the streets of Paris after the liberation of the city. The planes were piloted by Lts. Thorpe and Kilkenny and Lt. W. R. Coyne was riding as aerial observer when the planes were brought to a landing on the Avenue de la Grand Armee at 1840 hours, 25 August 1944. *(Our plane flew 1st news release out late in afternoon.GWL)*

The battalion put out security guards and bedded down on the streets of Paris for the first night. The next day the battalion was instrumental in rounding up and disposing of many German snipers and soldiers that still remained in the vicinity of the battalion assembly area. During the night of 26 August 1944 the city received two very heavy enemy air raids. No bombs were dropped near the battalion area. On the morning of the 27th of August, the battalion marched to the Northern outskirts of Paris and there along the road to ST. DENIS stopped to check materiel and give all personnel a chance to get cleaned up.

At about 1315 hours that same afternoon orders were received releasing the battalion from the French Division and directing the battalion to withdraw to an assembly area. The battalion moved once again through the city of Paris and into an assembly area in the vicinity of CHEVREUSE where the battalion CP was established and the personnel of the battalion settled down to await further operational orders.

As the weary never get any rest, the battalion received orders at noon on 28 August 1944 that reattached the unit to the Second French Armored Division. The battalion started moving toward new firing positions northeast of the city of Paris on the outskirts of a town named PIEREFITTE sur SEINE. There the battalion set up in fields while the battalion CP was set up in an old iron foundry. All that night and the next day the battalion fired continuously on targets designated by the French Armored Division, and by the Battalion observers. *(Me. GWL)*

Again orders came, relieving the unit from attachment to the French, and attaching the battalion to Combat Command "R", 5th Armored Division on 31 August 1944. The battalion moved to an assembly area with the 5th Armored Division in the vicinity of BARON. From there a move was made to HULEAUX. Late in the afternoon of 31 August the battalion once more moved to firing positions in the vicinity of NERY. The unit was acting in direct support of CC "R"'s armored infantry. In the mission, the battalion had a platoon of tank destroyers, and a battery of anti aircraft artillery attached. The TD's were put out to cover all roads leading to the battalion position and the anti-aircraft was spread out over the battalion area. This position was about three thousand yards from the edge of the COMPIEGNE FOREST. The battalion fired continuously from that position in support of the armored infantry of the division. In one instance, after placing 180 rounds of battalion fire on a large target on the edge of the Compiegne Forest, an observer who was adjusting the fire for the battalion from a tank, credited the battalion with knocking out three tanks, two 76 mm cannon, a number of vehicles, and some machine guns, together with enemy personnel. *(Not me. GWL)*

Moving from positions in the vicinity of Nery at 1213 hours 1 September 1944, the battalion went into position in the Compiegne Forest in the vicinity of LIES CLAVIERES. This position was occupied until 2015 hours that same night when the battalion started on a long race, trying to keep up with the armored column running through the night at a rate of sometimes 40 miles per hour. Combat Command "R" was with the American advance through Northern France in pursuit of the enemy that only was stopping now and then to give fight and hold up the column for a while so that their troops could withdraw. After the battalion pulled out of positions inside the Compiegne Forest, the city of Compiegne was entered. In this city the battalion made a river crossing via a pontoon bridge in complete blackout and then started on another race with the armor through the night. Along this route the first V-1 (Buzz bombs) Bombs ever seen by members of this battalion were observed flying through the night.

One firing battery, Battery "A", went forward with the leading elements of the combat command at this time as an advance guard and to support the fires of the tanks when they encountered any opposition. The rest of the battalion followed the main column of CCR.

The column traveled at a fast pace all that night and most of the next day, stopping only a few times to destroy roadblocks, take prisoners, and refuel the vehicles. At about 2345 hours on the night of 2 September 1944, the column stopped with the CC "R" in an assembly area in the vicinity of ST. HILAIRE.

Just prior to the arrival in this area, a part of the battalion column was ambushed by the enemy. The column was fired upon by antitank and heavy machine guns, and a few Panzerfaust as well. Because of quick thinking and clear minds there was no panic among the men. Major Tothacer, the executive officer, whose car was near the head of the column turned around and started the column back, turned them on another road and directed them to the assembly area. Two casualties were sustained by the battalion in this ambush. One, a member of the Headquarters Battery, was killed by machine gun fire. Another, a member of Battery "B", was slightly wounded. Loss of equipment was small. The battalion lost one trailer, and a half-track vehicle with multiple 50 cal. machine guns belonging to an attached anti-aircraft platoon.

Having arrived at the assembly area with the CC "R" of the 5th Armored Division, the battalion settled down for the night for some much needed rest and maintenance of the vehicles. Security guards were put out and personnel got their first rest in days.

Early the next morning the battalion moved again with the armored column and closed into bivouac in the vicinity of HASPRES near the Belgian border at 1645 hours 3 September 1944. Orders were received from higher headquarters and CC "R" with the battalion still in support, made a forced march to CHARLEVILLE. There the unit went into firing positions at 1730 hours on the 4th of September. The battalion fired constantly in support of the infantry trying to make a crossing of the MEUSE RIVER at that time. *(I directed fire from top of house on cliff overlooking Meuse River. I adjusted fire on a bunker across river. Finally got a round into cave. They came out with hands up. Alonzo Pierce (from his hometown) heard me on radio that night. GWL)* On 6 September 1944, the battalion crossed the Meuse River via pontoon bridge, occupying positions first at ST. ALBERT, and then at LES PRESS ST. REMY, firing from each position in support of the armored elements. On the night of 6 September 1944 the battalion went into positions in large grain fields in the vicinity of ILLY, near the strategic town of SEDAN. The battalion mission was to prevent the enemy from breaking out of a pincer that was being drawn around Sedan by the armor and the 28th Infantry Division. Infantry elements of the 28th Division, *(I was out on line all night here. No action. GWL)* were dug in behind the battalion positions and if the enemy had made a breakout, our battalion was the element they would have encountered. Much firing was done that night and heavy enemy fire was received in forward battery positions. The battalion held fast and the armor succeeded in surrounding Sedan while all types of fire was placed on the town. After a stiff fight in stormy, cold, rainy weather, the enemy gave up and armor and infantry troops moved into Sedan.

On 7 September 1944 orders were received releasing the battalion from attachment to the 5th Armored Division, and from its attachment to V Corps. Reverting to First U.S. Army control, the unit moved into bivouac in the vicinity of ST. MIHIEL. The battalion was then attached to the 32nd F. A. Brigade and on 8 September moved into bivouac in HIRSON, France, near the Belgian border. *(Near Aachen, Germany. GWL)*

After the battalion was released, the following commendation was received from the Commanding Officer of Combat Command "R", 5th Armored Division:

SUBJECT: *Commendation*
TO: *Commanding Officer, 196th F. A. Bn, APO 230, U.S. Army*

1. I wish to express my appreciation to you and your unit for the valuable and effective support, and wholehearted cooperation received from you in the FORET de COMPIEGNE during the campaign there in September 1944.

2. In addition, I wish to commend you for the very high state of training and discipline manifested by all of your personnel. You went into position rapidly and delivered prompt and accurate fire upon designated targets.

3. The high standard of your performance was noticed not only be me, but also by subordinate commanders. We all consider it a privilege and a pleasure to have had you with us.

GLENN H. ANDERSON
Colonel, Infantry
Commanding, CC "R"
5th Armd Division.

CHAPTER VIII
RED BALLING IT

After arriving at the new area in HIRSON the battalion settled down to getting organized on a new mission to which it was assigned. Vehicles and drivers were drawn from the battalion to form companies in the First Army Provisional Truck Battalion, both light and heavy vehicles being used. This truck battalion was used for the purpose of aiding in the moving of necessary supplies from rear to forward supply depots. On 17 September 1944 the battalion moved to ANOR, France. In addition to the truck companies that were formed from the battalion, the battalion air section was busy performing ferry service for the Army Quartermaster. Other men were furnished to form a Provisional Signal Company that was used to reclaim wire laid along the roads in France, for the Signal Corps. At times personnel were also used to load and unload ammunition at various rail heads.

The battalion moved from Anor to the vicinity of MONTZEN, Belgium on the 4th day of October 1944 and from there continued on their mission as outlined above.

On the 13th day of October 1944, Battery A along with additional personnel from the other batteries of the battalion, was relieved from control of the battalion and attached to V Corps and the 4th Infantry Division for a special counter-mortar mission. Captain C. H. Moore was in charge of this mission as Counter-mortar Officer. The battery remained on this mission until 23 October 1944 at which time it returned to control of this battalion.

On 31 October 1944 the truck companies that were furnished by the battalion including personnel and the battalion air section returned to control of the battalion to await further orders as to the future mission of the organization.

During this period the battalion received commendations from the Chief Signal Officer and the Artillery Officer of the 1st Army complimenting the organization for the part the Provisional Signal Company played in the recovery of wire left behind by troops in the rapid advance across France.

A commendation was received from the commanding officer of the 42,2 F. A. Group, which read as follows:

SUBJECT: *Commendation.*
TO: *Commanding Officer,*
196th F. A. Bn.,
APO 230,
US Army.

1. *The Commanding Officer, Provisional Heavy Truck Battalion indicates that the Provisional Truck Platoon furnished by the 196th FA Ba hauled* **(Took ammo down to Bulge area including Bastogne. GWL)** *forward 2,372 Tons of urgently needed ammunition and covered a distance of 4,059 miles during the period 17 September — 31 October 1944.* **(I directed our 20 truck unit all over area with ammo and engineering supplies. GWL)**

2. *The members of the 196th FA Bn Provisional Truck Platoon are commended for the highly successful accomplishment of the difficult mission entrusted to them. This mission required aggressive and untiring action and the solution of many unforeseen route difficulties. It involved working for extended periods with inadequate rest. The fine spirit with which, under adverse conditions, they adapted themselves to the job at hand indicates initiative, discipline and morale of high standard.*

WM. CLARKE
Colonel, F. A.
Commanding.
422 F. A. Group.

CHAPTER IX
HÜRTGEN FOREST

During late October 1944 the battalion received orders to store their 105 MM Howitzers and temporarily use a new weapon, the 75 MM Howitzer. From 1 November through 7

November 1944 the battalion was engaged in familiarizing the firing battery personnel with the 75 MM Pack Howitzer material that the battalion was issued. The training consisted of gun drill and service of the piece. On 6 November the battalion was attached to VII Corps and awaited orders for movement to operations area. The 7th of November, after having been located at Montzen, Belgium, more than a month, found the battalion moving again. **(Stopped convoy outside Leige Belgium one night. I let boys sleep because Germans bombing city. And had no lights or signs to follow. Moved on early next morning to ammo dump near Bastogne. GWL)** Leaving the assembly area in the vicinity of ROTT, Germany, arriving there at 1300 hours the same day, after having crossed the Belgium-German border at 1215 hours, 7 November 1944. On 10th November 1944 the battalion received further orders from VII Corps attaching it to the 4th Infantry Division and further attaching the unit to the 42nd F. A. Battalion of that division with the mission of reinforcing the fires of that battalion. At 1200 hours on 10 November the battalion moved into firing positions in the Hürtgen Forest in the vicinity of HÜRTGEN. **(Joe Ostrowski killed here. GWL)**

(The battalion fired a total of 387 missions' during the time it was in this position, expending 15,841 rounds.)

Counter battery fire was received all day and night in this position, and heavy enemy shelling could be expected almost every minute of the day. The bad weather, with the cold, rain, snow, and ever present mud made life not too pleasant for the personnel of the battalion. The battalion fired preparations for many attacks in this position including one on the morning of 16 November that preceded a heavy air attack on the enemy front lines by our planes. Battery C moved to new position in the Hürtgen Forest on November 20th after having received more than 100 rounds of counter battery fire in their old firing position. While in this position three men of headquarters battery wire section were wounded while laying and servicing wire along the road in front of the battalion positions (Purple Heart Alley). During this time headquarters battery personnel took ten enemy soldiers who surrendered to them in front of the battery position. **(I took 3 of these (German prisoners) up there myself. GWL)**

At 1415 on 27 November 1944, the battalion displaced to new firing positions in the vicinity of ZWEIFALL (still in the Hürtgen Forest area) in order to render better support to forward troops. In this position the battalion fired a total of 8,740 rounds in 236 fire missions in support of the 42nd F A. Battalion of the Fourth Infantry Division. **(I got cut off with infantry here and they moved off and left me. When I got out 3 days later I found jeep driver. Went to HQ and found out where my unit was. Found them next day at Kalterherberg. GWL)**

CHAPTER X
BATTLE OF THE BULGE

At 1200 hours on 3 December 1944 the battalion was relieved from attachment to VII Corps and the Fourth Infantry Division and was attached to V Corps. The battalion moved that same afternoon into a bivouac area in the vicinity of MONTZEN, Belgium. Along the route from the firing position to the new bivouac area, the battalion column was subjected to strafing by enemy planes. No casualties or materiel damage resulted.

Next two days at Montzen was spent in storing the 75mm pack howitzers, which the battalion had been using during the Hürtgen Forest campaign, and getting the organic weapons of the battalion - 105mm Howitzers - out of storage and in proper firing condition. At 1100 hours on 6 December 1944, the battalion left Montzen and moved into firing positions in the vicinity of KALTERHERBERG, Germany. *(Here they were. GWL)* Effective at 1330 hours that same day the battalion was attached to the 99th Infantry Division and took over the fires of the 400th Armored. F. A. Bn., with the mission of direct support of the 3rd Battalion, 395th Infantry Regiment. Moving into position in the vicinity of Kalterherberg, the men of the battalion thought they would be settling down for the winter in a supposedly quiet sector. A thin screen of cavalry and reconnaissance troops were spread over the sector that ran from MONSCHAU to ELSENBORN, with a battalion of infantry spread out around HÖFEN. *(Remember the road covered with tarps to protect vehicles from direct fire. GWL)*

A forward switching central was established at HÖFEN, Germany, northeast of Kalterherberg and southeast of Monschau, Germany. There the battalion Liaison Officer, Captain N. E. Watts established his headquarters where he could be in constant contact with the battalion observers. These observers were located in four observation posts that were actually infantry outposts. The entire area of the 3rd Bn., 395th Infantry could be well observed from these OP's and fire missions were delayed to the Liaison Officer who passed them on to the battalion fire direction center. At the forward switching central, a complete crew of switchboard operators and wire linemen were on constant duty operating the switching central twenty four hours a day and constantly servicing the wire communications between the forward switch and the OP's. At each OP, was a battalion forward observer, a radio operator, *(Me and James Allen, Radio. GWL)* a wire telephone lineman and two or three enlisted men who acted as auxiliary observers. The distance between the battalion CP and the forward switch at Höfen was approximately four miles through hills and rough country. Three telephone lines were laid. These lines were laid between the battalion CP and the forward switch. These lines required constant servicing through all types of weather and operations. Much of the road over which the wire was laid was under constant enemy observations and shellfire. *(I traveled up to OP over this road. GWL)*

Also at the forward switching central were two radio operators with three different type radio sets, one to be used at a time and the other as alternates in case one set went out. Back at the battalion CP another radio was in constant operation to receive missions from the forward switch in case the primary communication wire went out, as it often did, due to the constant shelling of all roads leading up to Monschau and Höfen. In the operations that followed, through the breakthrough by the enemy, and after that, radio was the primary means of communication.

Without it, it is seriously doubted if this history would be written in the way it is. Instead, another story may have been told with a tragic conclusion. There is no one person that did more than anyone else in the operations that followed the opening of the German winter offensive. Without the initiative and sacrifices that were made by all personnel we could never have held out in our position while the line a little below ELSENBORN bent inward to form "BULGE". The fire direction personnel, communication men, gunners, cannoneers, ammunition trains, observer teams, officers and enlisted men alike in every battery did their share. There are so many little individual stories that could be told that don't seem small at all. At least they didn't seem small at that time when the fate of our operations were hanging in the balance. We feel that by holding out at Höfen as we did, supporting the 3rd Battalion, 395th Infantry, helping to form "the shoulder at Monschau", the battalion helped materially in disrupting the well planned advance of the enemy. Had the Germans broken through at Höfen and advanced through Monschau and Kalterberg, opening the way down highway N-31 toward EUPEN, LIEGE, and AACHEN, the world would be writing another story and it is seriously doubted if any of us would be here at present to read it, or want to. This all very unofficial some may say, but you who were there during those nights and days know differently.

On 12 December 1944 the battalion was relieved from attachment to the 99th Infantry Division and was attached to the Second Infantry Division, however, its mission of direct support to the 395th Infantry's 3rd Battalion remained unchanged. *(Was supposed to attack Heartbreak crossroad. They beat us to the punch. GWL)*

(On the 15th (Dec) I watched Germans come out of pillboxes in line and go to rear. Could not call for artillery because 2nd division was to move up that day. Could only use mortar. This only made them duck. Did not reach far enough. GWL)

At 0530, 16 December 1944, after a very heavy artillery, rocket and mortar shelling, the enemy launched a vicious attack on the front held by the 3rd Battalion, 395th Infantry in the town of Höfen. Germany. *(I was there. GWL)* This attack was broken up and repulsed at 0730 hours. Four battalion observers in the town of Höfen were in position to observe this attack and they directed the battalion fires on enemy tanks and infantry. These fires were major factor in breaking up and repulsing the attack. Prisoners of war taken during this action stated their orders were to take the town of Höfen at all costs, *(My observation post. Not over my position. GWL)* but the curtain of steel laid down by the battalion prevented that. The enemy again launched a very heavy attack at this position at 0430 hours, 18 December 1944 and succeeded in penetrating the front line elements in three places, gaining entry into the town of Höfen itself. Again the battalion observers and the Liaison Officer were active in observers and directing the fires of the battalion on the enemy. In one instance, 1st Lt. Starter, *(I relieved him as FA observer that day the 17th, at around 8 am. Was up there 5 days and nights because he was to shook up to return. This was me. GWL)* one of the observers, was for a time surrounded and called for fire on his own OP. *(I relieved him after first attack. I helped stop 2nd attack. I was observer in Höfen during this time. GWL)* This fire killed or dispersed all the enemy elements but no casualties were suffered. *(Not? GWL)* The battalion fired almost continuously until this attack was dispersed at 1130 hours. At one time, during a night attack. the fire direction personnel handled fifty-eight fire mission in fifty minutes. (This included receiving the fire mission via the radio, computing necessary data, passing it on down to the firing batteries, and the actual firing of the mission.) *(Starter went up on 15th and out on 16th after first attack. GWL)*

The battalion air section, boated in the vicinity of BULLINGEN Belgium, was forced to abandon their air field in the face of enemy tank and infantry forces on 17 December 1944. Our corps artillery laid down several concentrations on this airstrip after evacuation was completed in order to destroy the planes and abandoned equipment *(These were the planes I observed from Normandy. GWL)* The two-battalion liaison planes along with some other equipment were destroyed.

During all this time the battalion was the only artillery battalion that was firing in support of the Höfen front. Occasionally support was received from corps artillery units in additional fire. *(Yes, I called for it several times. GWL)* For a few days this battalion was the only unit that was in position in the vicinity of Kalterherberg. The rest either moved south to support units that were trying to stem the Nazi drive into Belgium, or withdrew to the rear.

Reports were coming in from all over the sector that enemy tanks were around our forward positions, and coming in on our flanks. Extra precautions were taken in respect to security around battalion positions. Bazooka personnel were put out to man the rocket launchers; machine guns were put out to guard against enemy infiltration and paratroopers that were being dropped by the enemy all over the sector to disrupt communications and hinder our defense of the area. An infantry mortar company went into position next to the battalion CP. Tank destroyers were put into position along the roads in front of the CF along with some anti-tank guns, one of which was set up at the battalion CPs front door. All of this didn't improve the morale of the personnel of the battalion, but great confidence in ourselves, our weapons, and our battalion did the trick in the respect that everyone worked that much harder and stuck to the task before them.

At 1645 hours on 18 December 1944, the battalion was released from attachment to the Second Infantry Division and attached to the 47th Combat Team of the Ninth Infantry Division. The battalion retained the same mission, that of direct support of the 3rd Battalion, 395th Infantry Regiment. *(Second moved backward instead of forward. GWL)*

On 21 December 1944, in the midst of a heavy enemy mortar shelling, the battalion moved by battery to positions west of Kalterberg and from there on the 22nd of December, while being shelled by enemy guns. the battalion displaced to positions near MUTZENICH Belgium. *(They could not tell me they had moved guns so I could not adjust on target for almost a day because range became deflection. GWL)* From these positions the battalion kept firing in support of the infantry at Höfen, Germany. Enemy counter battery fire raked the battery positions on an average of three to four times daily. The battalion spent Christmas 1944 in these positions in the midst of the coldest weather yet experienced in the war. A blanket of deep snow covered the entire countryside. New Years Eve 1944 —

1945 will be remembered by all that were with the battalion in those positions along the EUPEN ROAD in the vicinity of Mutzenich. Around 2200 hours that night a heavy enemy shelling covered the entire battalion area. This lasted about fifteen minutes and resulted in five casualties in Battery A and one casualty in Battery B. From the start of operations in Kalterherberg on December 6th until midnight 31 December 1944, the battalion fired over 1304 fire missions in support of the infantry at Höfen, Germans with a total of 25,680 rounds of 105 mm howitzer ammunition expended. *(Much at my request. GWL)*

The battalion fired in support of the infantry with their organic weapon, the 105 mm howitzers, until 11 January 1945 when each firing battery received one British 25 pounder gun. British NCO's and gunners were then attached to the battalion to familiarize the firing battery personnel in servicing the 25-pounder. The battalion continued training on these guns while firing missions with 105's until 22 January 1945 at which time the full quota of four 25-pounders per firing battery was received and the organic howitzers were turned in.

At this time a commendation was received from the Commanding Officer, 3rd Battalion, 395th Infantry Regiment, 99th Infantry Division, for the battalion's supporting fires rendered during December 1944 during the German attacks at Hofen. It read as follows:

SUBJECT: *Commendation*
TO: *Commanding Officer, 196th F. A. Battalion, APO 230 (Thru channels)*

On the 6th of December 1944, the 195th FA Bn was placed in direct support of my unit, 3rd Bn, 395th Inf. This unit's supporting fires were immediately felt by the members of the 3rd Bn and even prior to the time the Germans made an attack on Hofen, Germany, numerous company commanders remarked to me how well the FA unit was giving us support and the cooperative spirit they had. On the 16th of December 1944, the Germans launched an attack against my position. (Me for? GWL) This attack was preceded by an intense rocket, artillery and mortar barrage at 0525 in the morning. By 0550 the barrage had ceased and the Germans were attacking the front line with infantry. Although the attack of the Germans was an infantry regiment, the position was not penetrated and the attack was repulsed. One of the major factors that contributed toward repelling the enemy was the artillery fire that the 196th FA Bn gave us when called for. In addition to this, the 196th FA Bn was also largely responsible for the capturing of 14 prisoners, as the five laid down by the artillery in front of our front lines not only killed or drove back any enemy that might be in that position but also prevented the enemy in front of the artillery barrage from retreating and the Germans had their choice of either staying in front of our lines and being killed or surrendering. On the morning of 18 December 44, time 0430, the enemy again attacked the positions in Hofen, Germany. This attack although not preceded by a heavy barrage of rocket, artillery or mortar, was increased in strength to include two new regiments of infantry plus the remnants of the regiment left after the previous attack, and 10 tanks. (Me. GWL) Here again the 196th FA Bn was a major factor in repelling the enemy, driving them from our positions and holding this town. The fighting in this vicinity became intense and it was necessary for me to request six different concentrations of 5 minute duration on my front lines by the artillery to prevent the enemy from over running my front lines. The 196th FA Bn demonstrated that it was an efficient, well-trained and fighting outfit. They placed the fire where requested, when requested, and in the intensity requested when needed. To demonstrate my point, at two different times, this FA Bn Fired 58 missions in 50 minutes in support of my unit. In addition to this they fired on this particular day in a 9 1/2 hour period, more than 3,600 rounds.

When it is taken into consideration that the German mission was to take Hofen Germany, *(I stayed here **six days and nights without relief, as FA observer** GWL)* at all costs regardless of price and that to the south the enemy had been successful in making some penetration of the Allied lines, this unit (196th FA Bn) disregarding reports that came in and the confusion that existed around them, fired efficiently and accurately when and where they were requested and in a volume that is a credit to any outfit if not a record. I believe that they deserve a commendation for their noble efforts and efficient work

MCCLERNAND BUTLER
Lt. Col. Infantry
Comdg., 3rd. Bn. 395 Infantory.

The battalion continued firing the 25 pounders throughout that month and remained in the same defensive position. While in those positions during the month of January 1945, the battalion fired 309 fire missions expending a total of 5,634 rounds of 105 mm howitzer ammunition, and fired 362 fire missions expending a total of 7,601 rounds of 25-pounder (British) ammunition.

On 2 February 1945 the battalion displaced to new firing positions in the vicinity of KALTERHERBERG, Germany. Another displacement further into Germany was made on 5 February 1945 to positions in the vicinity of DREIBORN. On the 7th and 8th of February, the battalion, displacing by battery echelon, moved into new forward firing positions east of Dreiborn, and fired in these positions until 0600 12 February 1945. At this time the battalion was relieved from attachment to the Ninth Infantry Division and was attached to the 3rd Tank Destroyer Group. The battalion moved out of the line and into a bivouac in JALHAY, Belgium.

CHAPTER XI
A NEW JOB

At Jalhay, Belgium, the battalion was reformed to function as Military Government Security Guards in the V Corps area and to displace along with V Corps in the advance across Germany. The period of 13 February through 17 February 1945 was devoted to turning in equipment not essential to the new mission of the battalion, and planning for the reorganization of the battalion into a headquarters and eight letter detachments. In this reorganization under the supervision the 3rd TD Group, the battalion transferred six officers and ninety five enlisted men to other units, and received six officers and seventy-two enlisted men as replacements. The men transferred into the battalion had considerable previous MGSG experience. From 17 February to 26 February 1945 the battalion went through an intensive period of instruction on MGSG work. While at Jalhay, the battalion air section was placed on detached service with V Corps Artillery. On 26 February 1945, Detachments "C" and "D" left the battalion bivouac area and took up their duties in the towns of AMBLEVE and WAIMES, Belgium, respectively. On 27 February 1945, Detachments "E" and "F" arrived in their areas in the town of MONSCHAU, Germany. On 28 February 1945, Detachments "G" and "H" displaced to new areas, Detachment "G" to WEYWERTZ and Detachment "H" to ROBERTVILLE, Belgium. On 1 March 1945, Detachment "A" and "B" displaced to new areas, Detachment "A" to SOURBRODT and Detachment "B" to EUPEN, Belgium. HQ and HQ Detachment moved into Elsenborn, Belgium. *(I had command of B Detachment. **Two officers and 50 soldiers.** GWL)*

The battalion from that time on displaced with V Corps, and worked at its new mission as the Military Government Security Guard Force in the V Corps area. Having been released from attachment to the 3rd TD Group, the battalion was detailed as V Corps Military Government Security Guard, and as such worked directly under the Corps A C of S, G-5. During the month of March 1945, the mission of the battalion was to control civilian population within the V Corps area. Insofar as possible the entire corps area was controlled by suballotment of area to the various detachments of the battalion. Because of the rapid advance of V Corps it was impossible for the detachments to completely cover their allotted areas because of frequent displacements.

Check points and patrols were set up and maintained twenty four hours a day in the whole area. Civilians and military personnel alike were checked. Investigations were initiated on civilians suspected of having connections with the Nazi Party and of being high party officials. Many were apprehended and disposed of through regular PW channels. The detachments working closely with CIC detachments, rendered valuable assistance in apprehending certain characters, questioning them and generally maintaining the security of the V Corps area.

All of the detachment commanders and certain members of the battalion staff were appointed Military Government Summary Court Officers, to be able to try any civilian cases that came before them in the line of MGSG work. In many instances the detachments operated as Military Government Detachments in addition to their security guard duties when they were located in an area in which there was no Military Government detachment.

Because of the rapidity of the American advances, large numbers of displaced persons and allied PW's were overrun and were a problem to deal with on the highways. Numerous enemy soldiers changed into civilian clothes and either remained in hiding or attempted to infiltrate through our lines. The constant attention of all MGSG men was required in weeding out these enemy PW's and getting the displaced persons settled in DP camps where they could be housed and fed until the time for their repatriation came about.

Allied PW's that were overrun in our fast advance were evacuated through PW channels. Just prior to crossing the Rhine, a Displaced Persons Detachment was set up. This detachment consisted of five enlisted men; four interpreters and one medical aid man. This DP Detachment also moved along with the Corps and set up DP camps where they could congregate the displaced persons and make them ready for ultimate shipment to their home lands.

Elements of the battalion crossed the RHINE RIVER along with leading elements of V Corps and proceeded to establish order and maintain security in the forward areas. The remainder of the battalion had crossed the Rhine by 28 March 1945 and followed the advance of V Corps deep into Germany, much of the time coming along with the leading elements. At many locations, MGSG detachments entered towns to set up even before the town was cleared of enemy personnel and before resistance had ceased. *(I did one. Bad. GWL)*

Throughout the month of April 1945 the mission remained the same, with the detachments functioning throughout the V Corps area controlling the civilian populace and enforcing the laws and ordinances of the Supreme Allied Commander. Searches were made of towns and villages for weapons and enemy soldiers. Many were apprehended in this manner.

On 19 April 1945, before the city was completely taken, the battalion headquarters and Detachments "A", "B", "E", and "G" moved into the city of LEIPZIG, *(Have my picture made on corner in Leipzig. Probably could find exact spot. GWL)* with a mission of patrolling the city and enforcing the laws and ordnances posted under the supervision of the Military Commander of Leipzig acting on all calls for riots and disorders, as well as operating with the CIC in raiding houses and building where information indicated stores of arms were being kept or German soldiers or Party members were hiding. The city was zoned into four areas, for better control. Each detachment was placed in an area and was responsible to the Military Commander of that particular zone. Battalion headquarters and all four of the detachments remained in Leipzig until 30 April when at that time the entire battalion displaced south into BAVARIA near the border of CZECHOSLOVAKIA.

On 7 May 1945, the first elements of the battalion moved into the city of PILSEN, in Czechoslovakia with V Corps Headquarters. Also at this time the battalion was released from First U. S. Army and assigned to the Third U. S. Army. V-E Day, 9 May 1945, found the battalion continuing MGSG duties in the Corps area.

This history of the 196th F. A. Battalion, which started from way back in other days, ends here in Czechoslovakia on V-E Day. What the future holds for the battalion and the personnel of this grand organization, only time will tell. But, we know that no matter what mission we are called upon to perform, it shall be done, with the same high standard of efficiency that has made the 196th Field Artillery Battalion the organization it is. *(My unit moved to Swehoff Czechoslovakia and remained until disbanded and reassigned to armored Div. for movement back to states. GWL)*

. . . Finis . . .

STATISTICS ON ARTILLEY ACCOMPLISHMENTS DURING THE WAR IN EUROPE

From 9 July 1944 through 12 February 1945, the 196th F. A. Battalion fired a total of 87,496 rounds of ammunition in a total of 13,346 fire missions as follows:

47,574 rounds of 105 mm howitzer ammunition—12,075 missions.
23,581 rounds of 75 mm howitzer ammunition—723 missions.
16,341 rounds of British 25 pounder ammunition—548 missions.

STATISTICS ON MILITARY GOVERNMENT SECURITY GUARD ACCOMPLISHMENTS

Following are a few of the accomplishments of the battalion from 1 March 1945 through 9 May 1945 while engaged in MGSG duties.

13,385 German prisoners of war apprehended and turned over to PW cages.
653 high Nazi Party officials apprehended.
76 Gestapo agents apprehended.
12 war criminals apprehended.
90,288 civilians checked for security purposes.
3,910 civilians apprehended for investigation by CIC and MG.
2,385 foot and motor patrols manned for a 24 hour period.
1,400 check points manned for a 24 hour period.
412,000 displaced persons transported to various DP camps.
9,821 allied PW's sent to allied re-location camps.
Four million dollars transfered from Leipzig to Frankfurt-on-Main, Germany for SHAEF.

COMMAND POST LOCATIONS OF THE 196th F.A. BATTALON IN THE WAR AGAINST GERMANY

Camp 189, Witney	England	21 June 1944
Camp Holmes	England	3 July 1944
Southhampton	England	6 July 1944
LST 379	English Channel	7 July 1944
Ravenoville	France	8 July 1944
St. Com du Mont	France	8 July 1944

St. Jean de Daye	France	9 July 1944
Goucherie	France	10 July 1944
Les Landes	France	12 July 1944
Amigny	France	19 July 1944
St. Pierre le Semilly	France	30 July 1944
St. Jean des Baisants	France	31 July 1944
Torigni - Vreux Calais	France	31 July 1944
Banville	France	2 August 1944
Campeaux	France	3 August 1944
Souelles	France	7 August 1944
St. Symphorien	France	11 August 1944
St. Germam de Anxure	France	14 August 1944
Mayenne	France	15 August 1944
Exmes	France	19 August 1944
St. Christophe le Jajolet	France	22 August 1944
Chevreuse	France	23 August 1944
Longny	France	23 August 1944
Chateaufort	France	24 August 1944
Issy Les Moulmeaux	France	24 August 1944
72 Avenue de Ia Grand Armee, Paris	France	25 August 1944
Chevreuse	France	27 August 1944
Pierrefitte sur Seine	France	28 August 1944
Huleux	France	31 August 1944
Nery	France	31 August 1944
Les Clavieres (Compiegne Forest)	France	1 September 1944
St. Hilaire	France	2 September 1944
Cambrai	France	3 September 1944
Monchaux sur Ecaillon	France	3 September 1944
Charleville	France	4 September 1944
Mezieres	France	5 September 1944
Sur Vivian au Court	France	6 September 1944
St. Albert	France	6 Sepiember 1944
Les Pres St. Remy	France	6 September 1944
Illy (Sedan)	France	6 September 1944
St. Michiel	France	7 September 1944
Hirson	France	8 September 1944
Anor	France	20 September 1944
Montzen	Belgium	4 October 1944
Rott	Germany	7 November 1944
Hürtgen Forest	Germany	10 November 1944
Zweifall (Hürtgen Forest)	Germany	27 November 1944
Montzen	Belgium	3 December 1944
Kalterherberg	Germany	6 December 1944
Kalterherberg (west)	Germany	21 December 1944
Mutzenich	Belgium	22 December 1944
Kalterherberg	Germany	2 February 1945
Dreiborn	Germany	5 February 1945
Dreiborn (east)	Germany	8 February 1945
Jalhay	Belgium	12 February 1945
Elsenborn	Belgium	2 March 1945
Elsenborn (east)	Belgium	5 March 1945
Mechernich	Germany	23 March 1945
Ahrweiler	Germany	23 March 1945
Neuweid (East of Rhine River)	Germany	28 March 1945
Weilberg	Germany	29 March 1945
Neustadt	Germany	31 March 1945
Balhorn	Germany	6 April 1945
Kassel	Germany	7 April 1945
Weissensee	Germany	12 April 1945
Naumberg	Germany	15 April 1945
Leipzig	Germany	19 April 1945
Bayreuth (Bavaria)	Germany	30 April 1945

"MAY GOD KEEP THEM CLOSE FOR ETERNITY."

✝

LEST WE FORGET

"THE BRAVEST SOULS WHO GAVE ALL THEIR TOMORROWS, FOR OUR FREEDOM."

Captain JAMES P. MORGAN, 19 July 1944, North Carolina

Tec 4 WILLIAM C. TERRELL, 22 July 1944, Virginia

Corporal FRANCIS WILSON, 25 August 1944, Ohio

Tec 4 JEWEL J. HARRIS, 3 September 1944, Mississipi

* Corporal JOE G. OSTROWSKI, 11 November 1944, Tennessee

Pfc. ALBERT V. MULESKY, 24 December 1944, New York

Pvt. ASA H. HARVEY, Jr., 31 December 1944, Montana

** Tec. 5 WINFRED E. MILLER, 16 April 1945, South Carolina

"NEVER FORGET US . . . . WE WILL MEET AGAIN."

* (It was late at night. We moved on road trying to get guns up and in position. Very deep mud and ice.
I went back down line and told all personnel to come up and help with 1st gun. And by all means, get off crossroad. A few minutes later, they shelled crossroad. Joe had not left. A piece of shrapnel went thru front of helmet into brain. GWL)
**(In my unit, very good soldiers. GWL)

The passing of old soldiers

By LEWIS GRIZZARD

It's happened to me before, running into men who served with my late father in World War II.

This time I was in Greensboro. NC, at a bookstore. I was signing copies of one of mine.

I noticed the old man during the first of the hour. He stood at the entrance of the store, looking at me.

After the hour, the signing was over. Meekly, the man walked to where I was sitting.

He had one of those faces that said, here's somebody's beloved

Paratroopers of the 141st Airborne Division share a bottle of wine with a private of the 4th Armored Division (center) in an impromptu celebration following the linkup that finally broke the siege of Bastogne. U.S. Army Signal Corp

grandfather. There was a lot of knowledge and caring in it.

Without another word, he said. 'your daddy was my first sergeant in World War II."

I've studied my father's record as a soldier closely and I know he was in France, then in Germany, and I know he later was sent to Korea.

"He saved my life in Germany," the man continued. "He saved a lot of lives, and they gave him a battlefield commission."

According to a copy of the citation I have, the colonel had been killed and the unit was under heavy German fire. Sergeant Grizzard reorganized the company, running in the open where the bullets flew and saved himself and his men from certain annihilation.

"If it weren't for your daddy." the man said, "I wouldn't be here today."

How do you respond to something like that? I certainly was proud of my father at that moment to think that this man, for half a century, had carried the memories of what my father did that day. And to think he would come to me after all this time. It was like he was trying to thank me for something my father did 50 years ago.

I think I managed a "bless you," or a "thanks for looking me up."

We shook hands and the old man walked away. My eyes teared as he did.

My parents' generation, I sincerely believe, had more to bear than any other in this country's history. Their lives were affected and some were ruined by the Great Depression, World War II, Korea, and Vietnam, where some lost sons and daughters. And, now, the last of them are fading into the shadows cast by the young they brought into this world.

A national magazine, noting the passing of the Bush presidency, offered a spread titled, "Goodbye Old Soldier."

George Bush was the youngest fighter pilot in the Navy during World War II.

Now, he has gone to his retirement having been replaced by one with no military experience whatsoever, one whose dealings with the draft system still leave a number of unanswered questions.

The Old Soldiers have moved out, and the Baby Boomers have moved in.

That is unsettling to me. The country's leadership, save a few veteran members of Congress, is in the hands of those never tested by fire.

Few of my generation really know the meaning of sacrifice. What did we ever want for and couldn't have? When have we ever been hungry? When did most of us ever have to run through a hail of bullets in a foreign land in order to save comrades? I never have and neither has Bill Clinton.

After the man in Greensboro had walked away, I realized I had made a mistake by not sitting with him and asking him in tell me what happened that day in Germany. I would have liked to have known about it from a survivor, not from some document.

But you know how it is. We're all in a hurry. We just don't know where it is we're hurrying to.

Goodbye, Old Soldiers, and thank you.

You are the very best of us.

Appendix B

Artillery the 196th was trained on and used during combat in WWII.

Medics set up a battalion aid station under the cover of a thicket. To stay near the shifting front line, aid stations for the infantry sometimes moved daily; stations for armored units often moved almost hourly. . U.S. Army Signal Corp

MORTAR, 81-MM, M1; MOUNT, MORTAR, 81-MM, M1 AND M4

MORTAR M1 ON MOUNT M1

MORTAR M1 ON MOUNT M4

RELATED SIGHTING AND FIRE CONTROL MATERIEL
(ADDITIONAL MATERIEL LISTED ON FOLLOWING PAGE)

SIGHT, M6

RA PD 107959B

152

GENERAL

The 81-mm mortar M1 is a smooth bore, muzzle-loading, high angle of fire weapon. The mortar consists of a mortar tube with a base cap containing a firing pin. The mount consists of a base plate with a bipod assembly provided with elevating, traversing, and shock absorbing mechanisms. The traversing mechanism of the mount M1 consists of a horizontal screw, operating in a yoke, and actuated by a traversing handwheel.

The traversing mechanism of the mount M4 telescopes; this telescoping action is accomplished by the traversing tube and the traversing nut which houses the traversing screw. All mounts M1 are being converted to mounts M4.

MORTAR

Weight	44 lb 8 oz
Length	3 ft 9½ in.

Muzzle velocity:

HE, light	700 fps
HE, heavy, w/fuze M52A1	583 fps
w/fuze M53A1 or M77	544 fps
ILLUM	580 fps
SMOKE, w/fuze M52A1	544 fps

Range (max):

HE, light	3,290 yd
HE, heavy, w/fuze M52A1	2,560 yd
w/fuze M53A1	2,596 yd
w/fuze M77	2,431 yd
ILLUM	2,200 yd
SMOKE, w/fuze M52A1	2,431 yd

Rate of fire:

Normal	18 rounds per min
Maximum	30 to 35 rounds per min

MOUNTS M1 AND M4

Weight of mortar and mount	136 lb
Weight of bipod	46 lb 8 oz
Weight of base plate	45 lb
Elevation (approx)	40° to 85°
Traverse, right or left, approximate	90 mils

AMMUNITION

Types .... HE; SMOKE; ILLUM

Weights:

Complete round	7.28 lb HE light
	10.97 lb HE heavy w/fuze M52A1
	11.48 lb HE heavy w/fuze M53A1
	11.90 lb HE heavy w/fuze M77
	11.83 lb SMOKE (WP) w/fuze M52A1
	12.76 lb SMOKE (WP) w/fuze M77
	12.33 lb SMOKE (FS) w/fuze M52A1
	13.26 lb SMOKE (FS) w/fuze M77
	10.69 lb ILLUM
Powder charge	0.10 lb HE light
	0.12 lb HE heavy, SMOKE, ILLUM

SHIPPING DATA

Mortar M1 only

Number per box	2
Length	4 ft 5¾ in.
Width	11¾ in.
Height	7 in.
Volume	2.5 cu ft
Gross weight	125 lb
Ship tons	0.06

Mortar M1 w/mount M1 or M4 (KD) in two packages

Pkg No. 1/2-mortar and mount w/equipment:

Length	4 ft 5¼ in.
Width	1 ft 5¾ in.
Height	1 ft ¾ in.
Volume	7.0 cu ft
Gross weight	225 lb
Ship tons	0.18

Pkg No. 2/2-aiming post and cleaning staff:

Length	6 ft 9⅜ in.
Width	4¼ in.
Height	4¼ in.
Volume	0.8 cu ft
Gross weight	27 lb
Ship tons	0.02

REFERENCES

FM 23–90; TM 9–1260; SNL A–33

NOTES

Mortar M1 w/bipod and different baseplate is also installed in 81-mm mortar half-track carriers M4, M4A1, and M21.

RELATED SIGHTING AND FIRE CONTROL MATÉRIEL NOT ILLUSTRATED ON OPPOSITE PAGE

Binocular, 6 x 30 or 7 x 50 type
Board, plotting, M10
Circle, aiming, M1
Finder, range, M7 or M9A1 w/infantry equipment
Light, aiming post, M41 (green filter)
Light, instrument, M37
Post, aiming, M10 or M4, M6, M7, M8, M9
Setter, fuze, M14, M22, M25, or M27
Sight, M4 or M4B1
Table, firing, 81–B–3, 4; 81–C–2, 3; 81–F–2; 81–H–2; 81–I–1; 81–S–1; 81–T–1; 81–V–1

TRAINING

HIGH EXPLOSIVE (*LIGHT*)

PRACTICE

HIGH EXPLOSIVE (*HEAVY*)

SMOKE

ILLUMINATING

RA PD 103503

Color Identification of Mortar Shell

154

Chest deep in a pit dug laboriously with shovels, members of an 81mm mortar team fire on German positions near Saint-Vith. The Americans, advancing or retreating with the tide of battle, spent much of their time digging new positions. U.S. Army Signal Corp

HOWITZER, PACK, 75-MM, M1A1; CARRIAGE, HOWITZER (PACK), 75-MM, M8

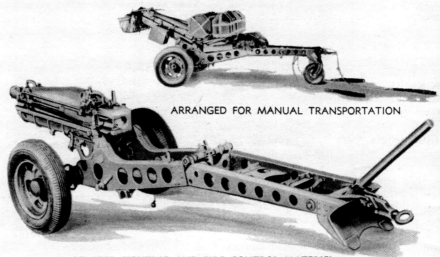

ARRANGED FOR MANUAL TRANSPORTATION

RELATED SIGHTING AND FIRE CONTROL MATERIEL
(ADDITIONAL MATERIEL LISTED ON FOLLOWING PAGE)

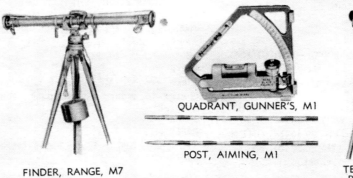

QUADRANT, GUNNER'S, M1

POST, AIMING, M1

FINDER, RANGE, M7

TELESCOPE, B.C., M65

SETTER, FUZE, M22

CIRCLE, AIMING, M1

SIGHTUNIT, M28A1
RA PD 114757

GENERAL

This howitzer is arranged for quick disassembly into nine loads for paracrate packing for parachute delivery or for pack loads for transport by pack animals over difficult terrain. It can also be transported as a unit in either an airplane or glider. It is a standard weapon for animal-packed and airborne field artillery. The caster wheel is used when the weapon is transported manually by the gun crew after parachute delivery. Otherwise the caster wheel and drawbar are removed from the weapon.

The carriage M8 is provided with steel disks and rims and pneumatic tires and towing drawbar. Other distinguishing features of this carriage are its spring equilibrators set within the front trail and the fact that its trail can be disassembled into two parts, a front and rear trail.

156

HOWITZER

Caliber 75-mm
Length ....4 ft 11 in.
Muzzle velocity:
    HE, SMOKE (chg 4) ....1,250 fps
    HE, AT–T ....1,000 fps
Range (max):
    HE, SMOKE ....9,610 yd
    HE, AT–T ....7,000 yd
Firing mechanism ....Continuous pull
Rate of fire:
    First ½ min ....8 rounds
    First 4 min ....24 rounds
    First 10 min ....48 rounds
    Prolonged fire......150 rounds per hour
Type of breechblock . Horizontal sliding wedge
Weight (tube and breech
    mechanism) ....342 lb

AMMUNITION

Types:
    Semifixed ....HE; SMOKE
    Fixed ....HE, AT–T
Weights:
    Complete round .....16.28 lb HE, AT–T
                      18.34 lb HE
                      18.89 lb SMOKE (WP)
                      19.05 lb SMOKE (FS)
    Projectile ....13.29 lb HE, AT–T
                      14.70 lb HE
                      15.25 lb SMOKE (WP)
                      15.41 lb SMOKE (FS)
    Powder charge ......1.06 lb HE, SMOKE
                      0.41 lb HE, AT–T

CARRIAGE

Modified box trail, high-speed pneumatic tires, drawbar, no firing segments, no brakes, axle traverse. Dependent sighting system for direct or indirect laying.
Maximum elevation ....45°
Maximum depression ....—5°
Traverse ....3° R or L
Tire size and type.......6.00 x 16 standard
Tire pressure ....20 lb

RECOIL MECHANISM

Type and model... Hydropneumatic (constant
               w/floating piston); M1A6
Maximum recoil ....32 in.
Normal recoil ....25 to 31 in.
Initial pressure at 70° F...........1,250 psi
Capacity ....3 pt

EQUILIBRATOR

Spring-type

OVER-ALL DIMENSIONS (firing position)

Length ....12 ft 1 in.
Height ....3 ft 1 in.
Width ....4 ft
Road clearance ....10 in.
Weight, complete ....1,440 lb
Center of gravity ....7 in. aft of axle

STEEL PARACRATE LOADS

Paracrate load M1

Front trail assembly ....230 lb
Paracrate M1 58
Drawbar 20
Lifting bar 9

_____
                            317 lb

Paracrate load M2

Rear trail .... 95 lb
Axle and traversing mechanism....... 65
Trail handspike 7
Bore brush staff 6
Spare parts and tool box 40
Caster wheel 40
Paracrate M2 38

_____
                            291 lb

Paracrate load M3A2

Bottom sleigh and recoil
    mechanism M1A4 ....217 lb
Aiming circle w/case 20
Lifting bar 9
Paracrate M3A2 123

_____
                            369 lb

Paracrate load M4A2

Cradle ....105 lb
Top sleigh 108
Lifting bar 9
Paracrate M4A2 124

_____
                            346 lb

Paracrate load M5A2

Tube ....221 lb
Lifting bar 9
Paracrate M5A2 120

_____
                            350 lb

Paracrate load M6A1

Breech assembly ....121 lb
Telescope w/mount 11
Paracrate M6A1 146

_____
                            278 lb

Paracrate load M7A1

Wheels (2) ....180 lb
Paracrate M7A1 22

_____
                            202 lb

Parachest load M8A1

Ammunition, 10 rounds in
    individual fiber containers ....223 lb
Parachest M8A1 114

_____
                            337 lb

Paracaisson load M9A2

Ammunition, 8 rounds in individual
    fiber containers ....178 lb
Paracaisson M9A2 134

_____
                            312 lb

Weight of (9) parachutes ....207 lb
Total weight paracrate loads and
    parachutes ....3,000 lb

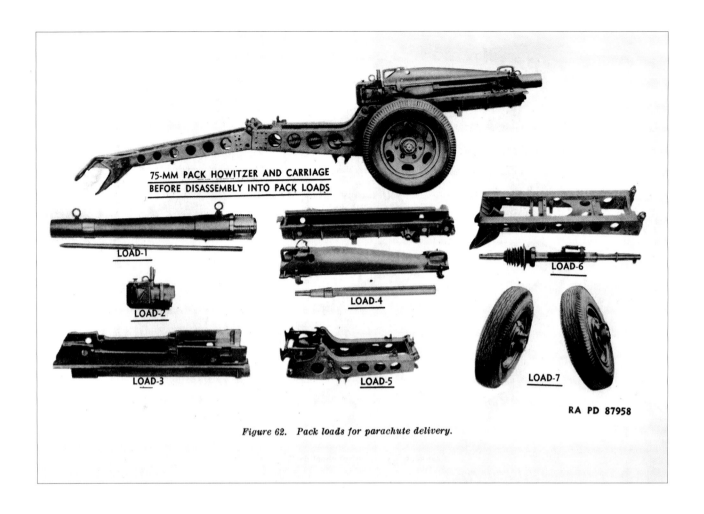

75-MM PACK HOWITZER AND CARRIAGE
BEFORE DISASSEMBLY INTO PACK LOADS

LOAD-1

LOAD-2

LOAD-3

LOAD-4

LOAD-5

LOAD-6

LOAD-7

RA PD 87958

Figure 62. Pack loads for parachute delivery.

A 75 mm pack howitzer is being wrestled from a landing craft to the beach as part of the training for D-day.

HOWITZER TUBE ON PACK

BOTTOM SLEIGH ON PACK

CRADLE AND TOP SLEIGH ON PACK

FRONT TRAIL ON PACK

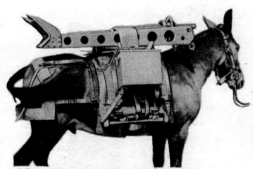

REAR TRAIL AND AXLE ON PACK

BREECH AND WHEELS ON PACK

RA PD 108104

Figure 63. Pack loads for animal transport.

HOWITZER, 105-MM, M2A1; CARRIAGE, HOWITZER, 105-MM, M2A1 AND M2A2

RELATED SIGHTING AND FIRE CONTROL MATERIEL
(ADDITIONAL MATERIEL LISTED ON FOLLOWING PAGE)

FINDER, RANGE, M7

QUADRANT, GUNNER'S, M1

CIRCLE, AIMING, M1

TELESCOPE, PANORAMIC, M12A2

SETTER, FUZE, M22

MOUNT, TELESCOPE, M21A1

QUADRANT, RANGE, M4A1

MOUNT, TELESCOPE, M23

RA PD 114756

GENERAL

This is a mobile, general purpose, light field artillery piece used for direct and indirect fire. The howitzer is manually operated, single-loaded, and air-cooled. It can be towed at speeds up to 35 miles per hour on good roads. Sleds M3 are provided for use on snow, ice, and swampy terrain.

HOWITZER

Caliber 105-mm
Length ....8 ft 5⁵⁄₁₆ in.

160

Muzzle velocity:
HE, AT–T ....1,250 fps
HE, SMOKE (BE), CHEM....1,550 fps
Range (max):
HE, AT–T ....8,590 yd
HE ....12,205 yd
SMOKE (BE), CHEM ....12,150 yd
Rate of fire:
First ½ min ....4 rounds
First 4 min ....16 rounds
First 10 min ....30 rounds
Prolonged fire ......100 rounds per hour
Type of breechblock. Horizontal sliding wedge
Firing mechanism ....Continuous pull
Weight (tube and breech
mechanism) ....1,064 lb

AMMUNITION
Types—Semifixed—HE; HE, AT–T; SMOKE
(BE); CHEM
Weights:
Complete round ......37.06 lb HE, AT–T
Complete round (dualgran)..42.84 lb HE
(HC) 42.72 lb
(Yellow) 40.15 lb
(Red) 40.55 lb   } SMOKE (BE)
(Violet or green)
40.35 lb
(WP) 44.20 lb
(FS) 44.71 lb   } CHEM
(H) 43.27 lb
Projectile ..33 lb HE, 29.29 lb HE, AT–T
(HC) 32.87 lb
(Yellow) 30.28 lb
(Red) 30.68 lb   } SMOKE (BE)
(Violet or green)
30.48 lb
(FS) 34.86 lb
(WP) 34.35 lb   } CHEMICAL
(H) 33.42 lb   } ILLUMINATING
33.60 lb
Powder charge (charge 7).1.54 lb HE, AT–T
3.04 lb, all, except HE, AT–T
3.66 lb, dualgran, all, except HE, AT–T
Flash reducer M4 is used with the propelling charge to reduce muzzle flash when firing at night.

RECOIL MECHANISM
Type and model...Hydropneumatic (constant
recoil with floating piston); M2A1
Normal recoil ....42 in.
Maximum recoil ....44 in.
Initial gas pressure at 70° F.......1,100 psi

Capacity ....1 gal 1 qt
Reserve capacity ....4 oz

EQUILIBRATOR
Spring type

CARRIAGE
Two-wheel, split trail, single axle, pintle traverse with equalizer
Maximum elevation ....66° 13'
Maximum depression ....—4.45'
Traverse ....23° R or L
Tire size and type ....9:00 x 20, combat
Tire pressure ....40 lb
Type of brakes ....Hand parking

DIFFERENCES BETWEEN MODELS
The M2A2 has larger shields, counterrecoil buffer, and an enclosed screw-type traverse.

OVER-ALL DIMENSIONS (traveling position)

	Carr. M2A1	Carr. M2A2
Length	19 ft 8 in.	19 ft 8 in.
Height	5 ft	5 ft 2 in.
Width	7 ft ½ in.	7 ft ½ in.
Road clearance	1 ft 3½ in.	1 ft 2 in.
Weight, complete	4,475 lb	4,980 lb

SHIPPING DATA
Howitzer only
Number per box (double-end style)........1
Length ....8 ft 11⅜ in.
Width ....1 ft 5⅛ in.
Height ....1 ft 8⅞ in.
Volume ....22.4 cu ft
Gross weight ....1,200 lb
Ship tons 0.56
*Howitzer M2A1 w/Carriage M2A1 or M2A2
(KD) w/equipment*
Number per crate (fully sheathed
skid-type crate) 1
Length ....11 ft 11 in.
Width ....6 ft 1½ in.
Height ....4 ft 1½ in.
Volume ....301.8 cu ft
Gross weight ....6,425 lb
Ship tons 7.55

PRIME MOVER
2½-ton, 6 x 6, cargo truck or 13-ton high-speed tractor M5

TIME TO EMPLACE
3 min

SUBCALIBER EQUIPMENT
Gun, subcal., 37-mm, M13

REFERENCES
TM 9–325, TM 9–1325; SNL C–21

RELATED SIGHTING AND FIRE CONTROL MATÉRIEL NOT ILLUSTRATED ON OPPOSITE PAGE

Binocular, 6 x 30 or 7 x 50 type
Chest, lighting equipment, M21
Compass, M2 or compass, prismatic, M1918
Finder, range, M7 or M9A1 (M7 illustrated)
Light, aiming post, M14, w/equipment
Post, aiming, M1 w/equipment
Quadrant, gunner's, M1 or M1918
(M1 illustrated)
Quadrant, range, M4 or M4A1
(M4A1 illustrated)

Setter, fuze, M14, M22, M23, M26, or M27
(M22 illustrated)
Table, firing, 105–H–3
Table, graphical firing, M23 or M39
Telescope, B.C., M65 or M1915 series
Telescope, elbow, M16 or M16A1D
Telescope, observation, M48 or M49 or
instrument, observation, M3
Thermometer, powder temperature, M1
Watch, pocket
Watch, wrist

RA PD 131184

105-mm howitzer and recoil mechanism in carriage M2A2 — left side view.

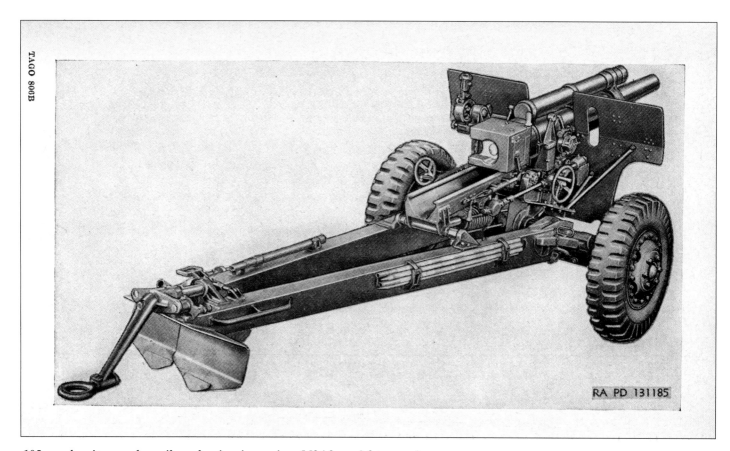

RA PD 131185

105-mm howitzer and recoil mechanism in carriage M2A2 — right rear view.

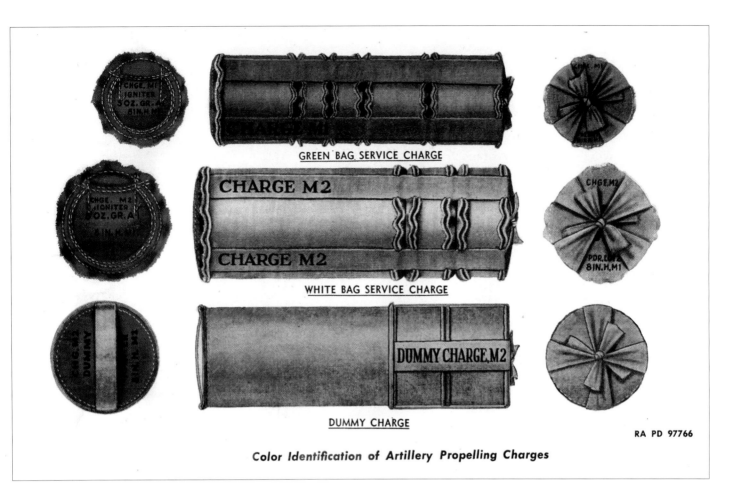

GREEN BAG SERVICE CHARGE

CHARGE M2

CHARGE M2

WHITE BAG SERVICE CHARGE

DUMMY CHARGE, M2

DUMMY CHARGE

RA PD 97766

Color Identification of Artillery Propelling Charges

An excellent photo of Marines using the same 105mm howitzer as George's 196th Field Artillery used in Europe in WWII. I was a forward observer, and we used the same gun in the early 1970's in the National Guard. Tom Berndt.

6. Tabulated Data

a. 105-mm Howitzer M2A1.

Caliber of howitzer	105-mm (4.134 in)
Weight of howitzer (tube and breech mechanism, aprx)	1,064 lb
Weight of tube (aprx)	706 lb
Weight of tube and breech ring (aprx)	973 lb
Weight of tipping parts (howitzer, recoil mechanism, cradle, sight mount, ring quadrant, aprx).	2,028 lb
Length of howitzer (muzzle to rear face of breech ring)	101.35 in
Length of tube	93.05 in
Length of bore	22.5 cal.
Rifling:	
Length	78.02 in
Number of grooves	36
Twist	uniform, RH, one turn in 20 cal.
Type of breechblock	horizontal sliding wedge
Weight of breechblock	74 lb
Type of firing mechanism	continuous pull
Estimated accuracy life of tube (equivalent full charge rounds).	20,000 rounds

b. 105-mm Howitzer Carriages.

	Model M2A1	Model M2A2
Weights:		
Howitzer and carriage (complete with accessories, traveling position, aprx).	4,475 lb	4,980 lb.
Wheel with combat tire, 9.00 x 20 (aprx).	287 lb	287 lb.
Wheel with combat tire and hub (aprx).	345 lb	345 lb.
At lunette (aprx)	235 lb	235 lb.
Dimensions in traveling position overall:		
Length (aprx)	19⅔ ft	19⅔ ft.
Width (over hub caps, aprx)	84½ in	84½ in.
Height (aprx)	60 in	62 in.
Road clearance (aprx)	15½ in	14 in.
Turning radius (aprx)	11 ft	11 ft.
Towed by prime mover:		
2½ ton	6 x 6 cargo truck	6 x 6 cargo truck.
13 ton	high speed tractor M5.	high speed tractor M5.
Limits of elevation:		
Maximum elevation	(66 deg.) 1,180 mils	(66 deg.) 1,180 mils.
Maximum depression	(−5 deg.) −89 mils	(−5 deg.) −89 mils.
Elevation per turn of handwheel	10 mils	10 mils.
Limits of traverse:		
Right	(23 deg.) 409 mils	(23 deg.) 409 mils.
Left	(23 deg.) 409 mils	(23 deg.) 409 mils.

	Model	
	M2A1	M2A2
Traverse per turn of handwheel (screw type mechanism).	19 mils	19 mils.
Traverse per turn of handwheel (worm and rack-type mechanism).	21 mils	21 mils.
Recoil mechanism	M2A1, M2A2, and M2A3.	M2A1, M2A2, and M2A3.
Model howitzer	M2A1	M2A1.
Normal length of recoil	39 to 42 in	39 to 42 in.
Maximum allowable recoil	44 in	44 in.
Elevation at which maximum recoil occurs (maximum elevation).	1,180 mils	1,180 mils.
Type	hydropneumatic	hydropneumatic.
Recoil oil:		
Type	(see LO 9–325)	(see LO 9–325).
Reserve in recuperator (fills of oil screw (filler) gun).	1½	1½.
Weight (complete with sleigh and filled, aprx).	463 lb	463 lb.
Initial gas pressure at 70° F., without reserve oil.	1,100 psi	1,100 psi.
Type of equilibrator	spring	spring.
Tires:		
Size and type	9.00 x 20 combat or 8 ply NDCC.	9.00 x 20 combat or 8 ply NDCC.
Pressure (combat or standard)	40 psi	40 psi.
Brakes	hand parking	hand parking.

c. 105-mm Howitzer Mounts.

	Model	
	M4	M4A1
Length of howitzer and mount	12 ft. 1 in	12 ft. 1 in.
Length of mount	9 ft	9 ft. 4 in.
Width	3 ft. 8 in	3 ft. 8 in.
Height	3 ft. 1 in	3 ft. 5 in.
Equilibrator type	spring	spring.
Limit of elevation:		
Maximum elevation	(35 deg.) 622 mils	(35 deg.) 622 mils.
Maximum depression	(− 5 deg.) − 89 mils.	(− 5 deg.) − 89 mils.
Elevations per turn of handwheel	10 mils	10 mils.
Limits of traverse:		
Right	(30 deg.) 534 mils	(30 deg.) 534 mils.
Left	(15 deg.) 267 mils	(15 deg.) 267 mils.
Traverse per turn of handwheel	21 mils	21 mils.

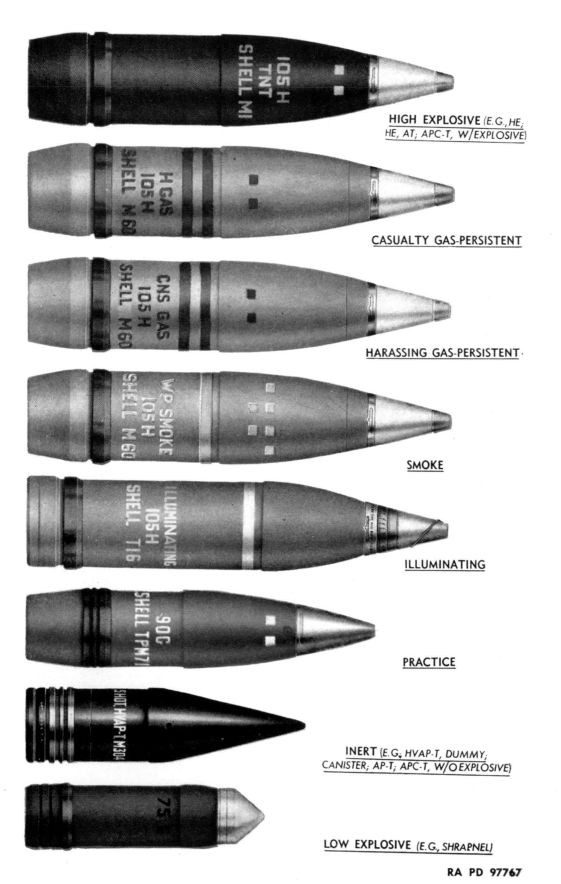

HIGH EXPLOSIVE *(E.G., HE; HE, AT; APC-T, W/EXPLOSIVE)*

CASUALTY GAS-PERSISTENT

HARASSING GAS-PERSISTENT

SMOKE

ILLUMINATING

PRACTICE

INERT *(E.G., HVAP-T, DUMMY; CANISTER; AP-T; APC-T, W/O EXPLOSIVE)*

LOW EXPLOSIVE *(E.G., SHRAPNEL)*

RA PD 97767

Color Identification of Artillery Projectiles

HE; APC-T.
W/HE   PRACTICE   CASUALTY
GAS   HARASSING
GAS   SMOKE   INERT
(DRILL: AP-T;
APC-T, W/O HE;
CANISTER)

INERT
(HVAP)   ILLUMINATING   LOW
EXPLOSIVE
(BLANK)   GREEN BAG
CHARGES   WHITE BAG
CHARGES

RA PD 97764

*Color Identification of Fiber Containers and
Cartridge Storage Cases*

167

HOWITZER, 240-MM, M1; CARRIAGE, HOWITZER, 240-MM, M1

FIRING POSITION - LEFT SIDE

FIRING POSITION - RIGHT SIDE

RA PD 107930

GENERAL

This howitzer fires the heaviest projectile of any United States Army field artillery weapon. It is broken down into loads for transport over roads, bridges, and favorable cross-country terrain, and for transportation by rail. It can be used as a coastal defense weapon.

The matériel is transported on two pneumatic-tired wagons; one carries the howitzer and cradle, the other the carriage. The weapon can be assembled for firing, or dis- assembled for transport, by either of two methods; using a mobile, truck-mounted crane, or by winching into position. It fires a 360-pound projectile at a range greater than 14 miles.

Separate loading ammunition is used in this piece, requiring insertion and ramming of the projectile by rammer and staff, followed by hand loading of the propelling charge. Firing is accomplished by use of a cartridge primer and firing mechanism attached to the breechblock.

HOWITZER

Caliber 240-mm
Length ....27 ft 7 in.
Muzzle velocity:
    Maximum charge ....2,300 fps
    Minimum charge ....1,500 fps
Range:
    Maximum ....25,255 yd
        (max chg at 823.4 mils elev)
    Maximum ....15,179 yd
        (min chg at 801.8 mils elev)
    Minimum ....8,450 yd
        (min chg at 267 mils elev)
Firing mechanism.......Percussion-Hammer
Rate of fire:
    First 4 min ....3 rds
    First 10 min ....6 rds
    Prolonged fire ....20 rounds per hour
Type of breechblock........Interrupted-screw
                step cut
Weight (tube and breech
    mechanism) ....25,100 lb

AMMUNITION

Types ....Separate-loading—HE
Type of charge—Base and 3 increments
Weights:
    Projectile ....360 lb
    Powder charge.......78.75 lb (max chg)
                (4 zones)

RECOIL MECHANISM

Type and model.......Hydropneumatic (con-
                stant); M8
Normal recoil w/max powder charge..60 in.
Initial gas pressure at 70° F......1,400 psi
Capacity ....22 gal 1 qt

EQUILIBRATOR

Type ....Hydropneumatic
Initial gas pressure at 70° F........640 psi
Oil capacity ....22 gal

CARRIAGE

Split-trail with pintle-type traverse. Carriage and cannon w/cradle carried in two loads on separate transport wagons.
Maximum elevation ....65°
Minimum elevation ....15°
Traverse ....22½° R or L
Weight, complete w/howitzer ......58,100 lb

OVER-ALL DIMENSIONS (traveling position)

	Carriage Transport Wagon M3A1	Cannon Transport Wagon M2A1
Weight, empty w/accessories	18,100 lb	22,620 lb
Weight, loaded, w/accessories	51,100 lb	47,720 lb
Wheel base	22 ft 10 in.	16 ft
Minimum turning radius	47 ft	34 ft
Height, over-all, loaded	10 ft 8¼ in.	7 ft
Width, over-all, loaded	9 ft 10 in.	9 ft 10 in.
Length, over-all, loaded	35 ft 9 in.	41 ft 9 in.
Minimum ground clearance (approx)	1 ft 3 in.	1 ft 3 in.
Tires	(6) 18:00 x 24 earthmover	(6) 18:00 x 24 earthmover
Tire pressure	25 lb	25 lb
Brakes	Air (four rear wheels). Hand parking brakes (two rear wheels)	Air (four rear wheels). Hand parking brakes (two rear wheels)

SHIPPING DATA

Howitzer M1 only
Number per crate (fully sheathed
    skid-type crate, breech end only)........1
Length ....27 ft 10¾ in. (over-all)
Width ....3 ft 2¾ in.
Height ....4 ft 3½ in.
Volume ....386.6 cu ft
Gross weight ....27,700 lb
Ship tons 9.67

PRIME MOVER

Tractor, high-speed, 38-ton, M6

TIME TO EMPLACE

Crane method ....1 hr
Winch method ....6 hr

NOTES

6–95; SNL D–31
The 240-mm howitzer carriage M1 is essentially the same as the 8-in. carriage M2.
    The transport wagons M2A1 and M3A1 are equipped with skids to facilitate assembly of the weapon.

REFERENCES

TM 9–341, TM 9–1341A, TM 9–1341B; FM 6–95; SNL D–31

RELATED SIGHTING AND FIRE CONTROL MATÉRIEL

    Sight, bore
    Table, firing, 240–C–1
    Table, graphical firing, M32 or M46
    Balance of equip. same as for the 8-in. gun
    M1; carriage M2.

CARRIAGE ON TRANSPORT WAGON

TUBE AND RECOIL MECHANISM ON CANNON TRANSPORT WAGON

TRUCK-MOUNTED CRANE, M2, AND CLAMSHELL TRAILER   RA PD 107949A

Section VIII

LOADING MECHANISMS

38. Loading Mechanisms

Loading mechanisms are provided to allow more rapid or convenient loading of weapons than would be possible manually. Some of these mechanisms consist of a folding or removable trough or ramp which

CHAMBER

LOADING RAMP

LOADING TROUGH

RA PD 10809 /

171

Medics unload an ambulance full of wounded GIs at a 5th Division clearing station in Luxembourg. En route to the rear, ambulances were frequently delayed by ice-covered roads, snowdrifts and enemy fire. U.S. Army Signal Corp

Soldiers suffering from minor wounds or frostbite wait their turn for treatment in a busy evacuation hospital in Huy, Belgium, during the Battle of the Bulge. U.S. Army Signal Corp

About The Author

Mike Looney

Mike Looney, Author

Mike Looney's first novel, "Heroes Are Hard to Find" was released in the summer of 2004. See Mike's website, **www.mikelooney.com** for much critical acclaim from the media and public alike.

For the past 35 years, Mike, a graduate of Texas Tech University, has served in his "day job" as an employee benefits consultant and insurance broker in Dallas, Texas. He and his wife, Sandra, are the proud parents of three daughters—Sloan, Kate, and CeCe and continue to live in Lakewood, a suburb of East Dallas. Look for the release of Mike's second fiction novel, "Tickle the Light," in the not too distant future.

Mike and family, wife Sandra, girls; CeCe, Sloan and Kate.

George Looney with Mike's brother, Phil and Dean.

The Dallas Morning News Review

Lakewood resident Mike Looney never fought in a war, but his father, George Washington Looney, did. In fact, the elder Looney played a key role in one of the biggest battles in World War II – something Mike didn't realize until many years after his dad died in 1996.

Lt. Looney served in the 196th Field Artillery Battalion in World War II. Throughout his life after battle, Mike's father only briefly touched on his experience as a war veteran. According to Mike, Lt. Looney only spoke of war stories with happy endings.

The story that went untold, though, was about the battle at Höfen, Germany, otherwise known as the Battle of the Bulge. Dec. 16, 1944, marked the beginning of the Höfen attacks, when the German army launched a massive counteroffensive against Allied forces. The battle was fought over several weeks across a 2,500 square-mile region of the Ardennes forest. The Americans suffered more than 80,000 casualties, including 19,000 deaths.

"Höfen, Germany. My brightest star. I helped save the day." These words were among many discovered by Mike in his childhood room after his father's death in well-preserved journal entries, notes, letters and pictures that had been hidden away for six decades.

Among them was a copy of the history of the 196th, and printed on the inside read, "Lt. George W. Looney, Reconnaissance Officer and Forward Officer. Discharged at Rank of Captain." In Lt. Looney's handwriting was this: "First night hell – several nights of torment in Höfen … my brightest star by me. I helped save the day. Lt. Starter (name has been changed) first night cracked up. Lt. George Looney – 2nd night, Peiper was ordered to run over us. He did not…I helped stop the Germans there on their second night trying to run over us. We had too much artillery. They could not get over us. Had done so, it would have opened up all Elsinborn Ridge to Germans and possible disaster for all. Fact by historians."

As an artillery observer, Lt. Looney was responsible for directing artillery fire from the highest point while he observed battle. Lt. Looney's orchestrated direction ultimately helped turn back German soldiers and get them off of Höfen.

"At times, American artillery rounds would land within a few feet of our positions, decimating the attacking enemy, but not touching us … George Looney was the forward observer directing these guns and assigning targets up and down our lines. He played it like a concert organist. I am here today because of his expertise … Men like him won World War II." – Thor Ronningen, an infantryman at the battle of Höfen.

Mike recalls immediately knowing the magnitude of his dad's accomplishment. Mike believes these comments were recorded later in Lt. Looney's life after he revisited the battle site in 1990 and realized the significance of the battle. Mike believes that his Dad never spoke of the battle because he didn't want to discredit another officer, and he knew that his family wouldn't have understood the battle's significance.

"We wouldn't have given the response it deserved because we were virgins to combat," Mike said. "We couldn't give it the respect it deserved." In addition to being a hero that

Photo by Jenice Johnson as printed in the Nov. 6, 2009 edition of The Dallas Morning News Neighborsgo section.

helped win the war, Lt. Looney was awarded one bronze star, two oak leaf clusters (all with a 'V' for valor) and five bronze service stars, meaning he served in five major campaigns including Normandy, Hürtgen and Ardennes.

According to Mike, in the battle of Hürtgen, the odds of surviving were almost non-existent. Lt. Looney not only survived, but rescued 10 other men along with him.

Mike, bringing light to Höfen caught the writing bug after the completion of his first book, "Heroes Are Hard To Find," put his second work on hold. He knew that the story of this pivotal battle needed to be told, especially for the few men who are still living that fought in World War II. "All these guys are dying, and they are gonna want to read this," Mike recalled.

He immediately started to research – he traveled back to Europe with a friend to follow in his Dad's trail. He used photos taken from his father and tracked down the very sights seen in the old images. He even visited the same home Lt. Looney rested in for several days after the Bulge ended.

After more than 10 years of research, The Battle of The Bulge: The Untold Story of Höfen is almost ready. Mike is shooting for a January 2010 publication date.

Throughout all the stories of heroism and sufferings of war that he uncovered, Mike also found that he had one regret. "It took my father dying to realize he was really my hero," Mike said. "He never put himself before his family." He added that the history recorded in the book can help teach today's youth about the sacrifices that previous generations made for this country.

"It's a history lesson for kids who don't understand," Mike said. "It gives a glimpse of the way the world was during that time." Throughout his long journey of following his father's footsteps, Mike's goal is simple: "To give my Dad his due, to record history accurately and to bring light to people who fought Höfen."

The Dallas Morning News Written by: Kendall Kirkham
© 2009 The Dallas Morning News, Inc., subsidiary of A.H. Belo Corp.

The Photos

I've poured over George's photographs from the war more times than his letters home reassure his family of his full tummy and swell living conditions; still, each viewing triggers a little mind shiver—but it's more than the visual adventure that provides passage to one of history's most riveting and toxic times. We are not seeing the war from a professional correspondent's polished viewpoint but through the wide eyes of either GWL or his comrades of the 196th. This rugged truth, inside the pictures, invites us to join the war up close and personal. Though without total success, I've attempted to present the images in some semblance of order—culminating with the day of one of our family's proudest moments.

Let there be peace in the valley. A tranquil moment as seen thru the eyes of George somewhere in England during a war that resulted in an estimated 55 million deaths.

German General Heinz Guderian stands in his communications vehicle during the Battle of the Bulge. Guderian was a great advocate in radio communications. Particularly between tank units, such as Pieper's 1st SS Panzer Division, that encountered George Looney's accurate and devastating American artillery barrages.

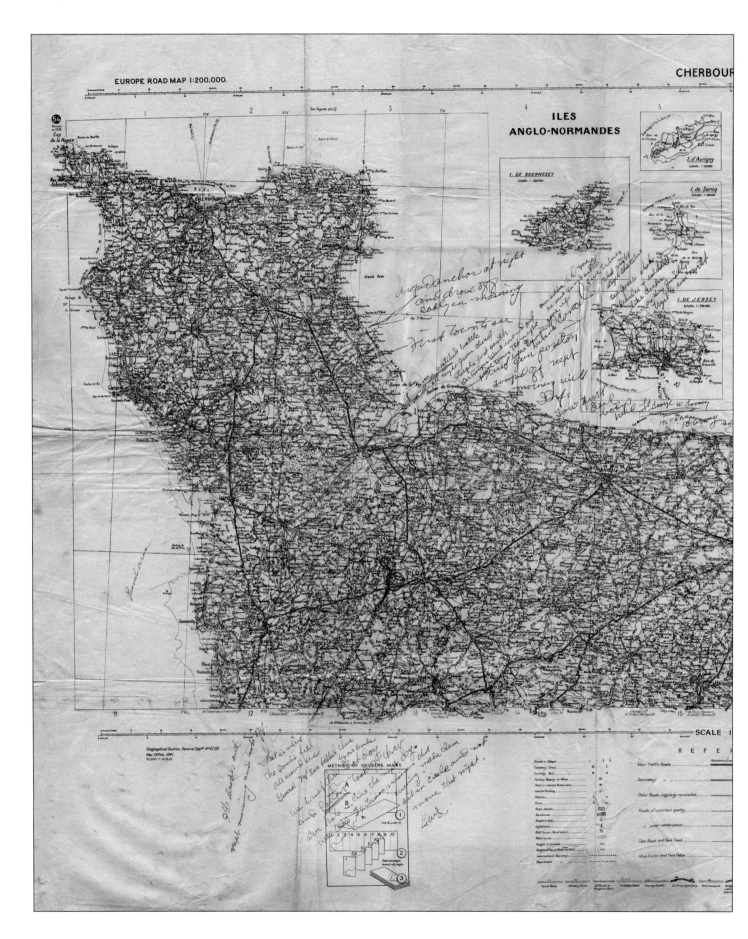

Complete with his own insceriptions, this image is of George's actual orginal map of the early European theater as his unit fought through it in 1944-45.

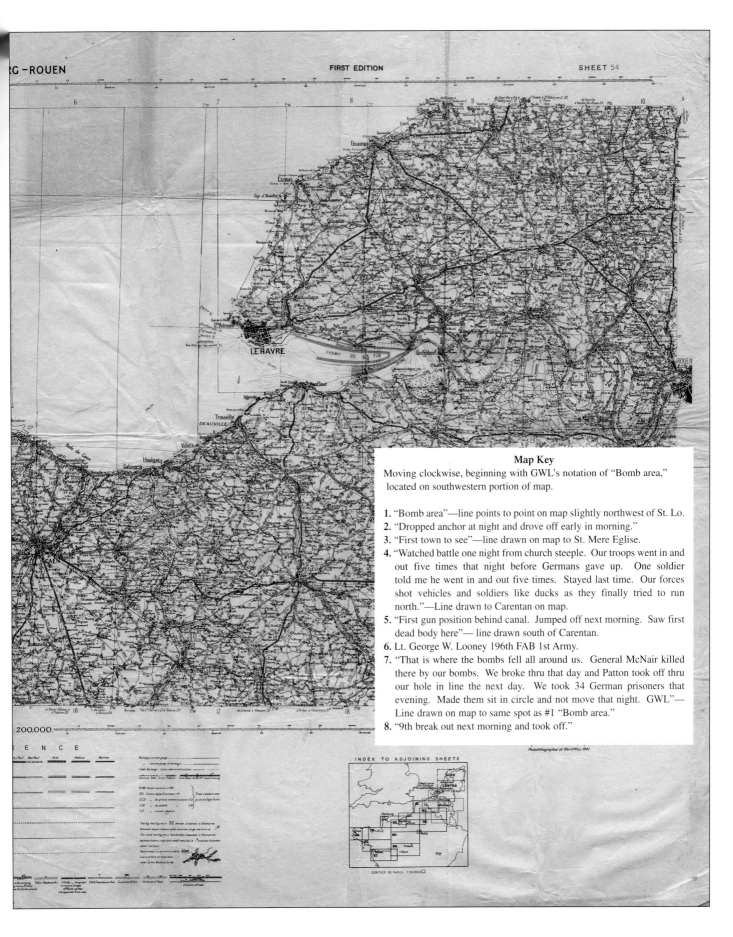

Map Key

Moving clockwise, beginning with GWL's notation of "Bomb area," located on southwestern portion of map.

1. "Bomb area"—line points to point on map slightly northwest of St. Lo.
2. "Dropped anchor at night and drove off early in morning."
3. "First town to see"—line drawn on map to St. Mere Eglise.
4. "Watched battle one night from church steeple. Our troops went in and out five times that night before Germans gave up. One soldier told me he went in and out five times. Stayed last time. Our forces shot vehicles and soldiers like ducks as they finally tried to run north."—Line drawn to Carentan on map.
5. "First gun position behind canal. Jumped off next morning. Saw first dead body here"— line drawn south of Carentan.
6. Lt. George W. Looney 196th FAB 1st Army.
7. "That is where the bombs fell all around us. General McNair killed there by our bombs. We broke thru that day and Patton took off thru our hole in line the next day. We took 34 German prisoners that evening. Made them sit in circle and not move that night. GWL"— Line drawn on map to same spot as #1 "Bomb area."
8. "9th break out next morning and took off."

The author, Mike Looney graciously had this photographed in its entirety for all of us to enjoy.